Basic Training Manual and Study Guide

Ministering healing and freedom to spiritual, mental, emotional, physical, relational, sexual and addictive problems

STEVE PIDD

Revised 2023 English Only Version
1st Edition

ABOUT US

Steve and his wife Em have spent the majority of their Christian life serving as Senior Pastors in a local Church environment.

They have been involved internationally in schools training and ministering in the areas of healing and freedom for over 20 years.

They have developed and conducted their 'School of Healing and Freedom' (SOHAF) in various locations in Australia and across the World during that time.

In more recent years their ministry abroad has mainly involved teaching and mentoring Pastors and leaders, as well as churches, to be equipped in the area of healing and freedom ministries.

Steve is the founder and International Director of Agape Orphanage Network Australia Inc. For information on how to help children in need please go to the website: www.aon.org.au

For information regarding 'School of Healing and Freedom' (SOHAF) go to the website: www.418centre.org The ministry name is based on Luke 4:18.

Copyright
Written and compiled by Steve Pidd
Revised September 2023

All enquiries can be directed in writing to:
Steve Pidd
Email: contact@418centre.org

All rights reserved. This book is copyright. Apart from any fair dealing for the purposes of private study, research, criticism or review, as permitted under the Copyright Act, no part may be reproduced in any form (including electronically) without written permission.

THE HOLY BIBLE, NEW INTERNATIONAL VERSION®, NIV®
Copyright © 1973, 1978, 1984 by Biblica, Inc, ™
Used by permission. All rights reserved worldwide

THE NEW KING JAMES VERSION (NKJV)
Copyright © 1975, 1982 Thomas Nelson Publishers
Used by permission. All rights reserved

HOLY BIBLE, NEW LIVING TRANSLATION®, NLT®
Scripture quotations marked (NLT) are taken from the Holy Bible, New Living Translation, copyright ©1996, 2004, 2015 by Tyndale House Foundation. Used by permission of Tyndale House Publishers, Inc., Carol Stream, Illinois 60188. All rights reserved.

CONTENTS

FORWARD		6
UNIT ONE	The Gospel of the Unders and Overs	8
UNIT TWO	The Church and the Holy Spirit	29
UNIT THREE	The Healing Streams of God	37
UNIT FOUR	Part 1: Truth Encounters: A Biblical Perspective	52
	Part 2: Ministering Truth Encounters	63
UNIT FIVE	Principles for understanding demons or evil spirits	82
UNIT SIX	Discernment	98
UNIT SEVEN	Dealing with Fear	107
UNIT EIGHT	Ungodly Control and Insecurity	115
UNIT NINE	Low self-image, Inferiority and Pride	121
UNIT TEN	Rebellion, anger and bitterness	124
UNIT ELEVEN	Sex 'Gods idea!'	133
UNIT TWELVE	Freedom from Pornography	150
Appendix One	Sample Sessions	163
Appendix Two	Popular Redemption Scriptures	167
Appendix Three	Other Resources from 418Centre	169

Forward

Having attended a great many conferences over the years my observation is that the modern church is largely concerned with matters such as leadership, growing the numbers in your congregations, or church planting.

There is no doubt at all that these are wonderful and necessary topics to facilitate the building of the Kingdom of God.

There is, however, very little focus on healing ministries and as a consequence the doctors are the first port of call for physical problems. For many churches, even large city congregations, if there are mental or emotional issues the people are sent to psychiatrists or Christian counselors trained in secular techniques.

In contrast if we look at the Jesus model, His focus was on healing the sick, freeing those with demonic bondages and healing the broken hearted.

Apparently, His disciples freely received this ministry from Christ themselves before they were commissioned to take the good news to the World.

> Mathew 10: 8 Heal the sick, raise the dead, cleanse those who have leprosy, drive out demons. *Freely you have received, freely give.* NIV (emphasis mine)

Perhaps we could look at it in this way. Imagine if you were putting together a football team and selecting your players. "Alright, I choose that man over there with one leg, the blind guy, that deaf fellow, the man with one eye, those chaps with the back braces on, and those cripples."

Then you launched them out onto the field, yelling with great enthusiasm and encouragement; "Go get them guys!" It doesn't make much sense to me, but many of us have been around churches where the focus is on trying to motivate broken people to live a victorious life of faith. We have all seen the fallout and problems from people with unresolved issues active in a church environment.

Remember the 'Vasa'

There is an old Swedish warship housed in a museum in Stockholm called by the name of 'Vasa.' She was commissioned to be built by the King of Sweden Gustavus Adolphus for use in the war with Poland-Lithuania and was constructed 1626-27. Upon completion she was considered to be one of the most powerful warships in the world at the time.

A tremendous amount of resource was put into her, and she presented with rich and ornate decorations. She was loaded with large and powerful guns. Unfortunately, all of the expense and efforts went into her appearance and equipment for war. Not enough time was spent on the design and what was done below the waterline out of sight.

The result was that she appeared to be a splendid, dangerous and formidable enemy, when in fact she was unstable in her foundation and not well ballasted. Sadly only 1400 meters into her maiden voyage she encountered a gust of wind which caused the ship to capsize and sink. The guns had just been fired as a grand salute to onlookers as the vessel left Stockholm.

Forward Cont.

The lesson for us appears to be that if we spend all of our time on presentation and how things look, and neglect dealing with the sub surface problems of the church we may not ever even get into battle.

If we train people in leadership, and develop or release gifts but don't deal with the unresolved issues in their lives, are we building on sand?

We have found that if we focus on the people being set free, the gifts and leadership come with motivation that God is pleased to bless.

At times I have ministered to leadership teams of larger churches and have been amazed at what is often going on in the background.

I thoroughly believe that healing the brokenhearted and setting the captives free was the main ministry of Jesus for a very good reason.

If we want to be the stable church that God is pleased to anoint, we may need to consider spending a little more time on working below the water line and sorting out the areas that are not always visible.

UNIT ONE

The Gospel of the Unders and Overs

Study 1: The Spiritual Realm and the Unseen World

UNSEEN SPIRITUAL BEINGS
It is evident that our World is influenced by the Spirit world. *John 3:8 Ephesians 6:12*

SPIRITUAL INSPIRATION

Luke 9:55 But He turned and rebuked them, and said, "You do not know what manner of spirit you are of. NKJV

Job 26:4 Who has helped you utter these words? And whose spirit spoke from your mouth? NIV

LESSON
Many times, we just assume that our thinking is simply OUR own thinking, when in fact it could be inspired by a spiritual entity.

Matthew 16: 23 But He turned and said to Peter, "Get behind Me, Satan! You are an offense to Me, for you are not mindful of the things of God, but the things of men." NKJV

LESSON
We can be used by either spiritual Kingdom and virtually everyone is at times working for the other side without realizing it. We need TRUTH from the Spirit of truth and to have developed discernment from the Word of God to be sure that we are cooperating with the right spirit.

LESSON
Jesus didn't say "come out" as the problem was not a demon inside Peter in this instance; it was a spirit working through him from the outside, and because of his beliefs he came UNDER and submitted to Satan working through him.

Principle: Anything that we SUBMIT to we come UNDER and give it authority OVER ourselves in that area. *(Note: the prefix sub means under. For example, a submarine = under the water) Romans 6:16, 2 Peter 2:19B*

JESUS AND SPIRITUAL INFLUENCES
Jesus himself lived under the constant inspiration of the seven spirits which constitute the sevenfold ministry of the Holy Spirit. *Isaiah 11:1-3*

Study 2: Spiritual Beings and human cooperation

ANGELS
Angels are mentioned more than 300 times throughout the scriptures.
Psalm 91: 11, Hebrews 1:14

Satan was formerly an Angel called lucifer. In the end his sin problem was PRIDE, which led to REBELLION. So, we could say that the root of his sin and wickedness was the distorted desire for SELF realization of his person, and living for SELF in that context. This led to SELF promotion, which caused him to seek to not be submitted to God. In the garden of Eden he managed to deceive mankind to come into agreement with him and be imprinted by his SELF seeking nature at the fall. *Isaiah 14:12-14*

LESSON
We could say then that 'SELF in pride' is the original basis for sin and rebellion against the knowledge of God. This is something that we should really pay attention to. Even Satan's wisdom became corrupted for the sake of his SELF realization and SELF promotion. *Ezekiel 28:17*

The scriptures warn us about the dangers of following a similar pathway. *Proverbs 26: 12*

In the case of Satan, the outcome of his rebellion was inevitable. He was evicted from heaven and cast down to the Earth. *Revelation 12:7-9*
If we are following the nature of Satan, we will be SELF willed or SELF seeking too.
By implication, if you are **led** by the Spirit you are not SELF willed or SELF seeking, you are Spirit seeking, and looking to His will and commands. *Galatians 5:16-22*

SONS OF GOD
In the Old Testament there are a number of references to the 'Sons of God.'
Genesis 6:2-4, Job 1:6 and 2:1

These appear to be spiritual beings that had access to God's presence.

In the New Testament, Holy Spirit led believers are referred to as 'Sons of God.'
Romans 8:13-14, Galatians 3:26

The evidence, or fruit, of being led by the Spirit is not living for SELF but mostly about caring about others. *Galatians 5:22-25*

Study 3: The fall of Satan and the arrival of man

The situation was that Satan and his angels were now on earth. It appears that Satan has not lost his cleverness or indeed his powers, but he evidently is now limited in his ability to use them. *Revelation 12:9*

WHAT HAVE SATAN AND HIS ANGELS LOST?

They formerly had responsibilities and authority to fulfill these responsibilities. So even though they apparently still have their gifts and abilities they now no longer have anywhere to exercise them. *Romans 11:29, 2 Peter 2:4, Jude 1:6*

MAN ENTERS THE SITUATION

Enter, man, who has delegated <u>authority over</u> the earth. He has been given a mandate and responsibility to rule over the earth and subdue it, or bring it <u>under</u> authority, and we also have Satan who is cast down to the Earth. He still has his gifts and capabilities but there is nowhere that he is now authorized to use them.

LESSON
A gift is not a guarantee of being right with God, it is a responsibility with the expectation of a fruitful outcome, as is well illustrated for us in the story of the talents. *Mathew 7:22-23, and 25:14-30*

LESSON
Authority is linked to responsibility. It is given so that we can fulfill our God given purposes, not so that we can have prestige or power. Authority is not for us to be above others, or Lord our position over any other person.

THE NATURE OF MAN

Man is created in the image of God a 'triune, tripartite or three part' being.
We would be surprised if it were any other way as God is Father, Son and Holy Spirit.
In the New Testament we know these three parts in man as Spirit, Soul and body.

THE HUMAN SOUL

The soul is considered to be the 'will' the 'mind' and the 'emotions.' We see this played out in life as; "I want," "I think" and "I feel".

The centre or middle of the will, mind and emotions, appears to be what the Bible calls the 'heart,' which has a deep influence on all of the activities of the soul.

FUNCTIONS

Perhaps we can illustrate here some biblical parallels for the spirit, soul and body concept.

	Spirit	Soul	Body
New Testament:	Spirit	Soul	Body
Old Testament:	Innermost place (God Conscious)	Inner parts (Self-Conscious)	Outer man (World Conscious)
O/T Temple Typology:	Holy of Holies	Holy Place	Outer courts

> Remember Jesus referred to both His body and our bodies as 'temples.' The physical picture of the temple building in the Bible always gives us functional pictures of the parts of our humanity. Perhaps we could add one more analogy to a practical understanding of how they work together.

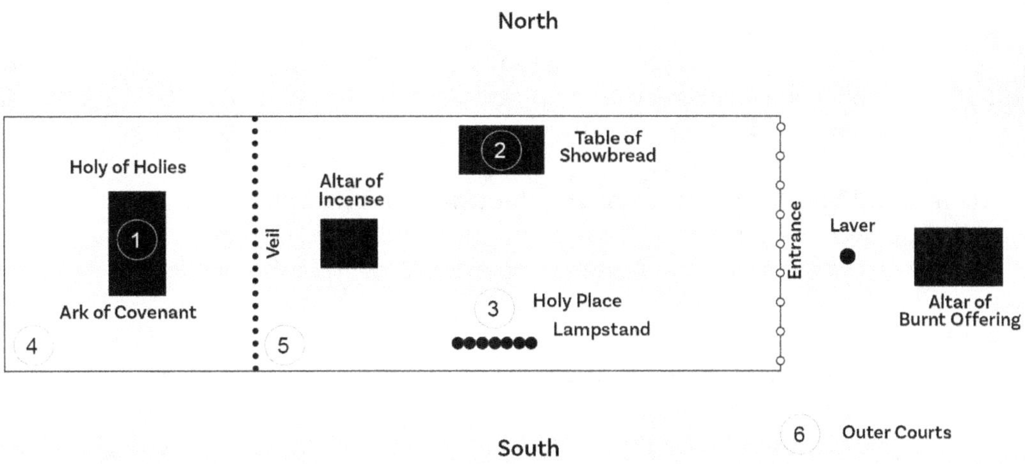

Tabernacle Diagram

North

Holy of Holies		Altar of Incense	Table of Showbread (2)		
Ark of Covenant (1)	Veil		Holy Place Lampstand (3)	Entrance	Laver • / Altar of Burnt Offering

(4) (5)

South   (6) Outer Courts

Legend:

1. The Ark of the Covenant containing Aaron's rod, the jar of manna, and the stone tablets with commandments on them

2. Table of showbread Representing Jesus, the bread of life

3. Menora - 7 candle lampstand symbolic of the 7 spirits or the 7-fold ministry of the Holy Spirit (Isaiah 11:2)

4. Most Holy Place or Holy of Holies represents the innermost parts (Hebrew) or the human spirit (Greek)

5. Holy place symbolic of the inner man (Hebrew) or the 'soul' (Greek)

6. Outer courts = the outer man (Hebrew) or the 'body' (Greek)

Pictured Above: Sanctuary tabernacle 3d rendering of the wilderness tent described in Exodus.

Study 4: The fall of man

We have established that man is created in Gods image and placed on the Earth to rule on Gods behalf. Satan has been thrown down to the Earth along with his angels. Now came the meeting of the fallen spiritual being with Adam and Eve.

Genesis 3: 1 Now the serpent was the shrewdest of all the creatures the LORD God had made. "Really?" he asked the woman. "Did God really say you must not eat any of the fruit in the garden?" NLT (emphasis mine)

What just happened?
1. The devil just created some areas of doubt.
   - Firstly, about the integrity of God's Word.
   - Secondly about whether or not God was withholding something good from them. Satan was implying that God was not good, loving or protective, and that in fact he was good and caring, and that God was bad and unfair.
2. Satan created a perception of God, which opened them to wrong belief. Wrong belief about someone's character leads to doubt and unbelief about their positive motives and intentions towards you.
3. Satan directly called God a liar when in *Genesis 3:4* he told the woman that if she ate from the tree that they wouldn't die. In believing Satan to be truthful they accepted that God was not. In so doing they made Satan the source of truth to be followed, evidently believing that he was the good provider and placed themselves under his deceptive instructions. This is the basic situation that unregenerate man lives under today, whether he is ignorant of it or not. Consequently, mankind still ascribes power to Satan in the Earth through submission and obedience.
Genesis 3:2-4

It is not surprising that the final covenant that we find ourselves under is one whereby everything comes to us by faith alone. *Romans 1:17*

That is, faith in what God has said, His Word. Faith in His character, nature, ability and good loving intentions for us. It is worth noting that when believing in, and accepting Gods perfect love was no longer the covering, deception came, and fear came as well! We could define fear as the expectation of negative things happening, and faith as expecting good outcomes. *1 John 4:18*

In considering Satan's counsel they were coming <u>under</u> another word……when this doubt and perception was created, it led to a misinterpretation, or misunderstanding of the situation………followed by a conclusion…. and this produced a decision…. which led to an action. The action was disobedience, transgression or rebellion…. the first SIN…. which resulted in a consequence!

> **Note:** None of us likes being misunderstood, and we are very imperfect…how much more offensive would it be for a perfect God?

We observe that 'sin' means 'an offense.' So, the first sin was doubting Gods character, love, goodness and protective intentions for us.

DEFINITION AND STATEMENT

Sin then, comes through being deceived into misinterpreting the TRUTH of a situation.... and what is actually good or best for us! We can say then that sin is most often OUR BAD SOLUTIONS to our 'PERCEIVED' or ACTUAL needs and circumstances.

The devil continues to work exactly this way today.... distorting the TRUTH and offering us his solutions to our situations.... deceiving us by causing us to misinterpret what is happening. He manipulates the whole World this way causing war, misery in relationships, and also in hurting and damaging individual lives.

For Adam and Eve this was causing them to submit to Satan, coming under him through doubt and unbelief. They were not 'seeing' what was going on. It is not surprising that the mission of the Apostle Paul involved helping those who were perishing to see the truth. *Acts 26:18*

Satan still deceives the World into thinking that what God has given is not enough....and that you need to be your own god and provision, to throw off the limits and get what you want for yourself. He subtly suggests that there will be no consequence for this self-seeking behavior. *Genesis 3:2-4*

LESSON
The power that Satan has over mankind comes through deception followed by submission.... whether or not people even believe that the devil exists is irrelevant.

LESSON
Basically, behind all sin choices is that which Satan was proposing about the forbidden tree in the garden. 'Good things are being kept from you...this is what you need, this will make you happy.' Perhaps we can add to this; 'don't trust God to have your best interests in His heart, get what you want/need for yourself.' *Genesis 3:6, 1 John 2: 16-17*

LESSON
The world system under the influence of the devil offers many things that supposedly will make you happy....this is generally the exact opposite of the truth.

> *1 Timothy 6:17b But their trust should be in the living God, who richly gives us all we need for our enjoyment. NLT*

SUMMARY OF THE FALL

1. So now we have God in heaven, the sovereign owner of the universe. Man, on Earth who had until now nothing between him and his creator. Up to this point mankind had authority and power over the World while they continued to remain UNDER God's authority through obedience to His instructions.

2. Satan had been cast down to the Earth still having abilities but with no authorization or place to use them. In doubting God man has accepted Satan's authority and integrity OVER that of God, and by doing so in obedience to him has come UNDER the power of Satan.

3. There is now another spiritual entity in between mankind and God. God will always be over all, so Satan, a created being remains UNDER God. Man, however is now UNDER Satan and is cut off from God spiritually. It is now that the 1st of the devils lies begins to come in to play. God is the source of power and life. The devil had stated that they would not die if they disobeyed. Being spiritually separated from God it was now inevitable that they must begin to die.

> **Principle:** All deception is rooted in moving you away from, and taking your eyes off what God has said. This includes adding to it or twisting it to suit your purposes. *Proverbs 3:1-2*

Study 5: Implication of the Fall for Humanity

Firstly, why do we call it the 'fall?' This term is mostly likely used because mankind fell from the high place of being in the likeness and image of God, and under God having dominion and authority over the Earth. In accepting and preferring the counsel of Satan, we chose to no longer follow Gods instructions, or to remain in His order under the protection of His wisdom and ways. We lost our position by disobedience and choosing to be led by Satan, thereby coming under his power and authority.

By submitting to his suggestions and following him in his rebellion, we were imitating his nature. Remember he was a fallen being himself, not wanting to submit to God and be under His authority, but rather raising himself up in pride and preferring his own way. What was the reason for his fall? Ezekiel 28:17

The Pride in his **heart** distorted his wisdom….. his own pride and desire for *self-realization and self-promotion* led him to fall from his privileged place. (Further studies on pride and its roots for mankind can be found in Unit 9)

THE INTRODUCTION OF ANOTHER NATURE

Earlier in this Unit we worked through a basic understanding of how we were created in God's image. Genesis 1:26-27 Our 'image,' or how we present, appear, and behave, is often a reflection of who we are most influenced by. That is, who we imitate, copy, or follow.

We need to make some very relevant and important notes here:
1. We were originally in God's image. In other words, we were in His likeness, or we could say, we were like Him. We were the result of being seeded by His nature. We were His children in this sense as the offspring of His influence and shaping. Prior to being exposed to Satan, as we understand it, mankind had only been in relationship with God, so He alone had been until that time the model for attitudes and behaviour.
2. Our identity then, came from His identity. We were His children. We were the product of His intentions for us. He who saw us before we were even formed. He already loved us. We had the identity that He intended for us, and we were content and accepting of who He had made us to be. This is vitally important in light of what we're going to propose.

For Adam and Eve, when they followed the suggestions of Satan that the forbidden tree was something that they should eat from, the issue was who they were submitting to….

who they were allowing to influence them, to imprint them. The important factor is whose <u>nature</u> they were following, co-operating with and now being shaped by. It was the original <u>introduction of another nature</u> for mankind, a nature that had already fallen from grace and relationship with God.

LESSON

The consequence and result of partaking with this <u>fallen nature</u> is the KEY to understanding the beginnings, or genesis, of every problem faced by mankind! Problems such as mental disorder, emotional and relational issues, along with disease are the result of a life out of God's perfect order. When we understand Gods loving, gracious, merciful nature, it makes sense that this is not something that God chose, wanted for us, or put on mankind. These troubles are the self-destructive result of choosing to follow the corrupted deceptive systems produced by Satan's ways.

Through joining in rebellion and disobedience against God's commands they were imprinted with the of <u>nature</u> of Satan who fell first. His fall was through pride which led to an attitude of...."*I don't want it to be all about God, I want it to be all about me!*" His pride and wanting to be <u>'above'</u> others, and like or equal with God produced rebellion, an attitude of; "*I will not submit...I want to be in control.*" These attitudes became entrenched in the <u>fallen nature</u> of mankind. In a sense we were converted to Satan's image, or how he appeared, acted, presented, and the attitudes that he held as a result of the internal thinking in his 'heart.' Isaiah 14:12-14

Note: Whether they believe in him or not, unredeemed, unregenerated mankind, are still looking to this fallen being that they chose to follow, to meet their needs through the provisions of the world system. They still accept his counsel in regards to what is perceived as best for them to have a successful, happy and meaningful life. His deceptive counsel about what to choose is still going on today, and rather than bringing wholeness, peace and joy, his ways still produce brokenness, separation, destruction and death.

THE FALLEN NATURE

What does the <u>old fallen nature</u> look like? It looks like <u>its</u> father, the devil. Jesus described some of the religious people of the time as 'children' of the devil. In other words, in spite of their religious activities their true motives for what they were doing were being done according to the leading of the <u>old fallen nature</u>. There is evidence in the scriptures that these religious leaders really didn't care about others, or Gods desire to help people, but rather they were seeking the praises of men. Jeremiah 8:11, Ezekiel 34:2-4

Their religion was SELF centred, all about self-promotion, self-importance, self-realization, and ungodly control of others. Wanting to have the 'upper hand' and be <u>over</u> or <u>above</u> others. Prioritizing worldly pleasures and wants to please SELF.

LESSON

The old fallen nature wants to control others in order to be in a place of ascendency or superiority. In other words, it lifts itself up, seeking to have others submit to you, come under you, and do your will. Jesus in contrast came as a servant to help mankind, and He instructed His followers to have the same attitude, walking again in His image and nature. Mark 9:35, Mark 10:43-45, Romans 15:8

> *John 8:44 "You are of **your father** the devil, and the desires of **your father** you want to do. He was a murderer from the beginning, and does not stand in <u>the truth</u>, because there is <u>no truth</u> in him. NKJV (Emphasis mine)*

The Bible describes this fallen nature in the original Greek language as; 'Sarx.' It is usually translated as the old nature, the sin nature, the flesh, or the adamic nature, depending on the commentary or Bible version that you're using. In essence it is the 'self-life' in a <u>fallen state</u> modelled after Satan's nature.

Jesus alluded to this self-centered nature in Mark's gospel chapter 8. Quoting from the New Living Translation He says in verse 34; *"If any of you wants to be my follower,"* he told them, *"you must put aside your selfish ambition, shoulder your cross, and follow me."*

In other words, your life must go from being all about what you want, to being all about the will of God. In verse 35 He goes on to explain; *"If you try to keep your life for yourself, you will lose it. But if you give up your life for my sake and for the sake of the Good News, you will find true life."*

In other words, if you walk in the <u>old nature</u> which seeks to be its own god, you will eventually reap the chaos and destruction that comes to those who prioritize self. Galatians 6:7-8 But if you put off the <u>old fallen self-nature</u> and live in <u>the new redeemed nature</u> that God imputes, then that life that you live for God will be abundant. John 10:10, Colossians 3:9-10

> *Ephesians 4:22-24 ²² You were taught, with regard to your former way of life, to <u>put off your old self</u>, which is being corrupted by its deceitful desires; ²³ to be made new in the attitude of your minds; ²⁴ and to <u>put on the new self</u>, **created to be like God** in true righteousness and holiness. NIV (emphasis mine)*

The apostle Paul summarizes this in the letter to the Galatians Chapter 5:16-18. In verse 19 the NIV version it translates this as; *'The works of the flesh are obvious:'* (Flesh = Sarx, old fallen nature) He then goes on to list examples of what you may expect to be exhibited through either walking in the nature modelled after Satan at the fall, Galatians 5:19-21, or those following the influences of the Spirit back into the image of God. Galatians 5:22-23

Study 6: The Corruption of human identity

The 'state of being' and <u>characteristics of humanity</u> had now changed as a result of the fall. The fundamental qualities of who mankind were meant to be was <u>altered because their priorities, choices</u> and what they decided that they wanted changed.... their priorities and choices were now the lust of the eyes, the lust of the flesh, and the pride of life. Now what they were all about as people became <u>living</u> for these things, for <u>SELF</u>, rather than living to be <u>in relationship with God</u>, *pleasing, serving* and obeying Him.... now it was about pleasing SELF. We could say; You align yourself with whatever you decide to follow.

LESSON

This 'imprint and influence' distorted the <u>'identity'</u> that God had given them. Your <u>identity</u> is the characteristics that <u>identify</u> you.... particularly in terms of your perception of SELF and self-worth.... this is who you think you are, and your perceived image of self. In other words, how you see you = this self-image was now no longer established and certain in God's truth – they had followed deception, and now were deceived, insecure, and uncertain about who they were, and their worthiness.

Now mankind's identity was corrupted. In a sense you are who you think you are – the Bible indicates that your image of SELF dictates your state of being! It is powerful in terms of predicting behaviour, attitudes and responses. The information that we hold about our identity as revealed in the bible, and also in practice, indicates that this information and these beliefs about SELF are now stored in our 'hearts.' As the old saying goes: 'It's not what you think you are, but what you think, you are!'

> **Note:** In Unit 4 we will cover how to restore the broken, or out of order inner thinking that proceeds from identity beliefs in the 'heart.' We will learn how to dismantle this deceived nature by establishing God's truth in the new heart that we are given, and consequently minister God's restoration into the new nature. There are a number of words translated as heal, or healing in the New Testament. A component of most of these words is to bring to wholeness.
>
> In the case of Luke 4:18 healing the broken hearted, the Greek word used is 'Iaomai.' So, generally to heal or bring to wholeness the broken heart means to restore the fallen identity through Gods truth being received in the 'heart.' (This is a work of the Spirit of Truth communicating to the person once what a person believes about their identity is established and identified. This healing cannot normally be achieved by counselling, teaching or preaching. How this is achieved in practice is covered in Unit 4.)*

> *Proverbs 23:7 "For as he thinks in his heart, so is he. NKJV**
> **Some Bible versions translate this verse differently for some reason, when this rendering is clearly present in the original Hebrew text.*

This now distorted picture of identity is largely the power behind the fallen nature influencing you to continue to follow what Satan offers. 1 John 5:19   The heart as revealed in scripture according to the very reputable Strong's Concordance means:

2588. kardia; the heart, i.e. (fig.) the **thoughts or feelings** (mind); also (by anal.) **the middle**: --(+ broken-) heart (-ed) (emphasis mine).

Whether the Old Testament or the New Testament the 'heart' is considered to be thoughts from your centre or middle which affect your mind, and consequently your feelings and finally your decisions. (Your will.) Very significantly, your 'heart' holds beliefs which produce thoughts that in turn affect your thinking, attitudes and even your motives for what you do.

> *Hebrews 4:12 For the word of God is living and active. Sharper than any double-edged sword, it penetrates even to dividing soul and spirit, joints and marrow; it judges the thoughts and attitudes of the heart. NIV (emphasis mine)*
>
> *Proverbs 4: 23 Above all else, guard your heart, for it affects everything you do. NLT*

LESSON

Probably 95% of the ministry that we do setting people free relates to beliefs that they hold in their 'hearts' about their identity. The other 5% is to do with things believed about traumatic or deeply emotional situations that they've been exposed to. When we talk about mental and emotional disorders, or disease, we consistently find that these upsets begin with conflict about identity, and how we see and perceive ourselves. The experts tell us that behind disease almost 90 % of the time conflicted mental and emotional states are implicated. All of us we're born under the influence of the fall, so every person has a tendency to misinterpret their identity.

RESULTS OF THE FALL

We understand the outcome of the fall for mankind as being the genesis or beginning of suffering.

1. Once they knew good and evil, they knew that they had done wrong.
   Guilt, **shame** and **condemnation** entered their lives.

2. This opened the way to conflict within themselves.... their 'hearts' condemned them. (Romans 8:1 NKJV, 1 John 3:20) Significantly and importantly, this was the beginnings of mankind no longer liking and accepting themselves – (although unredeemed humanity is trying to convince themselves that they're doing alright.) This inner rejection of self is the basis of much mental disorder, emotional imbalance, ungodly responses, broken relationships, along with eventual disease and sin.

   It begins in a mind influenced by a corrupted sense of identity stored in the 'heart.' In turn this creates a lack of ease or peace in the thinking, which in turn outworks as imbalanced emotions, and finishes in the body as dis-ease. Sin is often mankind's attempt to compensate for, or a solution to, dealing with how he feels about himself.

> **Note:** Confusion about identity along with self-rejection are behind many mental disorders, emotional imbalances, and eventual disease. Your 'heart' beliefs about SELF cause negative thinking. What you think becomes a feeling or emotions which are elaborated or felt in the body by chemicals and electrical currents. When these are imbalanced, the final outworking is in the body, or outer man. So, a lack of ease in regards to identity or particular situations experienced in the 'heart,' becomes dis-ease in the physical body.

3. Mankind accepted Satan, and in so doing rejected God – having removed themselves from under Gods Lordship they now feared not being accepted by God. The result of this was that underneath mankind often;
   - No longer feels accepted, so rejection entered our lineage. When you don't feel acceptable you fear rejection, and may even reject yourself, which is self-rejection. These anxieties and negative attitudes towards self, produce negative emotions and responses that are behind many diseases and much mental conflict.
   - No longer felt secure in God's love – so we became anxious, fear entered, and unredeemed mankind as a generalization is now expecting punishment and judgement. (I John 4: 18)

- is prone to low self-image, because inside we're not liking and accepting who we are, mainly because we believe as a result of the fall that we're less than we should be, having given up our high place of service and relationship with God. We now innately have an inborn sense of inferiority, injustice, insecurity.

LESSON
These feelings and anxieties leave us vulnerable to continue to accept Satan's deceptive solutions. We want to raise ourselves up in pride to compensate for our low self-image. We rebel against authority and perceived injustice, preferring to be 'our own god.' We seek to control our environment to make ourselves feel secure. Thus, our distorted sense of identity opens us to continuing in and perpetuating the old fallen nature.

4. They were no longer okay with what they believed about themselves….or their situation. *Identity was corrupted.*

Who did this affect? Everybody from the fall on was born <u>under</u> these influences. Everyone has the tendency to misinterpret their 'identity' and be fearful in emotionally charged situations and circumstances. In part this is because we have been deceived about God and His goodness, kindness and love. The question in ministry is where did it begin for you as an individual?

LESSON
This means that as people growing up, as a generalization, every person was prone to misinterpret their identity in a negative way! This is an important key to healing. For example, Gideon. (Judges 6:12-15) In verse 12 the LORD calls him 'a mighty man of valour.' Remember God is the only one who knows our true identity. Gideon responded in verse 15 with who he believed in his 'heart' that he was. "I am the least in my father's house." He'd learnt this from someone. It was the conclusion that he'd come to through how he was dealt with and regarded growing up. He had to hear truth from God about who he really was in order to be whole, free and reach his potential. This is how identity healing and freedom comes for us all.

> **Note:** Our earthly identity or how we identify ourselves is largely formed by God's 'father image representatives' on earth – our fathers. They are to cover us and represent God to us. (Unlike God they may be selfish, absent, busy, critical, abusive, unfair, ignoring etc. We generally have a God picture based on how our earthly fathers dealt with us.)

RECAP
Sarx = the Satan <u>influenced and programmed</u> version of you! The old fallen nature, imprinted with his characteristics, attitudes and behaviour. Pride, rebellion, control, SELF seeking. *Sin began with him.* His <u>'heart'</u> was corrupted and it distorted his own created identity.

Mankind was created **originally** in God's image. The **new nature** is **a restoration**. The new nature <u>looks like God</u>, seeded by Him, birthed by His design, and comes to fulness once He is submitted to and we accept His Lordship. Romans 8:29, Ephesians 4:13

> **Note:** When ministering to people you will find over and over that they believe that they're worthless, have no value, no significance, are not cared about, are rejected and so on – all require a restoration of identity from Father God. What we term 'compensating behaviour' is when, as your 'own god,' you now seek to prove that you're worth something, acceptable, valuable.... convince yourself you're as good as others etc. (Or you attempt to mask or deny your issues with lusts, addictions, the pleasures of the world, wealth, success etc.) These 'do it yourself' attempts are the grounds for the old nature to flourish, and they mostly come from beliefs about identity in the 'heart.'

In Johns Gospel we see Jesus make this statement.
> *John 14: 30 "I will no longer talk much with you, for the ruler of this world is coming, and he has nothing in Me. NKJV (emphasis mine)*

Jesus is stating that Satan has no power over Him to manipulate Him or deceive Him as he does with the rest of humanity. The reason? He has nothing 'in' Me! No deception about His identity. Jesus knew exactly who He was, He'd heard directly that the Father was pleased with Him, and He clearly knew what His mission was. In fact, His purpose in coming to earth was to introducing grace, (redemption and forgiveness') and truth. (Sanctification, healing and wholeness) John 1:14, John 1:17

For mankind the basis of faith – that is 'trust' in Gods person and character was now distorted.

A] True faith comes through a true and right picture of God, and this was now corrupted through deception by what Satan was implying about Him.
'God's the bad guy, I'm the good guy....I'd let you eat from the tree.'

B] Our ability to receive by faith has a lot to do with us having a correct picture of our own identity and what we believe about ourselves. If we judge ourselves as unworthy for some reason, or not good enough, we don't expect Gods love, acceptance, approval or supply.

GOD'S PLAN OF RESTORATION

It's appropriate to round out our study on the introduction of the fallen nature by including God's plan to return humanity to spiritual connection with Himself. His intentions and priorities are also to make us whole by restoring our identity through receiving His truth. So, now understanding the implications of the fall we can comprehend two important elements that needed to be addressed for the revival of mankind to relationship with God, along with the restoration of our persons to His likeness.

The human spirit had been cut off from direct relationship with God, and needed to be regenerated, and the identity of man was corrupted at heart level. Consequently, we find these 2 key elements relating to the revival of humanity. The <u>human spirit</u>, and the <u>human heart</u>.

Gods plan is all about the revival and restoration of the people that He created -
> *Isaiah 57:15 For thus says the High and Lofty One Who inhabits eternity, whose name is Holy: "I dwell in the high and holy place, With him who has a contrite and humble spirit, To <u>revive</u> **the spirit** of the humble, And to <u>revive</u> **the heart** of the contrite ones. NKJV (emphasis mine)*

LESSON

So, why do we need to be revived, and <u>what from</u>? We need to be revived from spiritual death and the effects of the old nature on our identity at 'heart' level. The Old Testament word for revive/revival is 'Chayah:' which means to <u>make alive</u>, <u>re</u>cover, <u>re</u>pair, <u>re</u>store, <u>be whole</u>.

GODS REMEDY FOR THE FALL

God has promised to reset the lives of those who want to turn away from Satan and back to Himself through faith in Jesus Christ. The process entails being supernaturally given a new human spirit that is reborn, or born again, that was not born in the natural way under the influence of the natural fallen world, but rather born of the promise of God. John 3:3-8, Galatians 4:22-26, 28-31

LESSON

Formerly mankind had rejected God, now the way to return to Him is to accept Him again through His offer to pay for our sin through the sacrifice of Jesus Christ. Gods rescue plan is to reintroduce Himself and His nature into our lives.

God is a Spirit, and so the first stage of restoration is to have our human spirit reconnected in relationship with Him. We accept Him as Lord, and worship Him as God, which is something that our fallen nature did not want to do. We had preferred to follow another spirit, and chose to be our own god. Ephesians 2:1-3

> *John 4: 23-24* ²³ *Yet a time is coming and has now come when the true worshipers will worship the Father in spirit and truth, for they are the kind of worshipers the Father seeks.* ²⁴ <u>*God is spirit*</u>*, and his worshipers must* <u>*worship in spirit*</u> *and* <u>*in truth*</u>*." NIV (emphasis mine)*

Because God is Spirit our point of contact and relationship is our human spirit relating to Him as Spirit. We note from John 4:24 that we worship – or lift Him up as God – through our spirit, but also in truth. This truth relates to a knowledge of who He is, but also being made new in truth of who we really are. I would propose that our human spirit receives this truth at conversion, but our broken hearts require healing which is the process of sanctification, and our minds need to be renewed in knowledge of God and the ways of His Kingdom.

GODS' PROMISED METHOD OF RESTORATION

> *Ezekiel 36:26-27* ²⁶ *"I will give you **a new heart** and put **a new spirit** within you; I will take the heart of stone out of your flesh and give you a heart of flesh.* ²⁷ *"I will put* <u>***My Spirit***</u> *within you and cause you to walk in My statutes, and you will keep My judgments and do them. NKJV (emphasis mine)*

We observe from the passage that God replaces our 'hearts' that were hard towards Him. He gives us a 'new human spirit' which is again connected to Him. And in verse 27 He indicates that He will then put His Spirit in us. 1 Corinthians 6:17

So now we have a new <u>soft heart</u> that is open to God's workings to bring about change….. but we have a problem! The introduction of this new nature doesn't automatically delete the old nature….so now we have 2 natures in one person. This means conflict. The power of the old nature is largely driven by <u>identity beliefs</u> programmed into the human 'heart.' These need to be sanctified by truth which is an ongoing process. (Hebrews 10:14) But our hearts are now soft and receptive to the work of the Holy Spirit. Psalm 51:10-12, Psalm 139:23-24

Galatians 5:17 The <u>sinful nature</u> wants to do evil, which is just the opposite of <u>what the Spirit wants</u>. And the Spirit gives us desires that are the opposite of what the sinful nature desires. <u>These two forces are constantly fighting each other</u>, so that you are not free to carry out your good intentions. NLT (emphasis mine)

LESSON

The process of sanctification is a journey into wholeness, and restoration back into His likeness and image. (Rom 8:29, Eph 4:12) The new nature is imputed through regeneration and having our human spirit reborn. We receive a new soft heart that is open to the influences of the Holy Spirit. How we may choose to behave is transformed by knowing God's ways by the <u>renewal</u> of our minds. Romans 12:2

We continue to work with the Holy Spirit, personally on Sanctification, and corporately on the priorities and Mission of the gospel, qualified on the basis of redemption. Ephesians 2:10, Isaiah 58:6-9.

Study 7: The 'ruler' of the World

Satan now had 'dominion' over all of the areas of the Earth that Adam had been given authority over. Consequently, he rules over every person who has not been redeemed by Christ Jesus. None of us were 'born again' from the womb. We are all saved by grace through faith. Each of us must make the decision to come out from 'under' the influence of the devil.

The New Testament makes no arguments that this is the case. Jesus did not dispute that Satan could give him the Kingdoms of the World, or that he had them in His power.
Luke 4:1-12

AFTER THE CROSS

Following are some other names for Satan that indicate that his position has not changed in regard to unredeemed humanity. These references are after the completed work of the cross and indicate that the devil's position has not changed. It's the status of the believer that is different in Christ.
2 Corinthians 4:3-4 The 'god' of this age. Ephesians 2:1-3, 1 John 5:19

THE RESCUE PLAN OF GOD

The purpose of God in all of His covenants is for man to be in authority <u>over</u>; if we will submit to authority <u>under</u> the Lordship of Gods ways.

LESSON

Understanding who God is, His faithfulness and ability to fulfill His word, and His true attitude towards us is the basis of 'genuine faith.'

Study 8: The 'GOOD' News of the Gospel

Up until this point we have seen only bad news with mankind coming under the power of a cruel new master.

Interestingly, Adam, the 1st man submits to Satan in Paradise whilst surrounded with beauty, where he had everything. All that he could ever need and more. Jesus as the 2nd Adam refuses to submit whilst in the desert where He had absolutely nothing. Not even a piece of bread to eat.

LESSON
Submitting to Satan's agenda for our lives through sin, puts us under his authority, and allows him to bring about outcomes that are contrary to God's best purposes and intentions for us.

THE SIGNIFICANCE OF THE BAPTISM OF JESUS

As an act of obedience Jesus presented himself to His cousin John for baptism. John's baptism was a baptism of repentance and so this confused John as Jesus was without sin. *Matthew 3:13-17*

There are two points that we will highlight here that are very important to our story.

1. Jesus was without sin and consequently had nothing to repent of. We know however that He was going to go to the Cross to pay the penalty of death that was to be the outcome for us because of our sin. He was going to fulfill the law in full. So, as we consider this, we must examine the question; 'can sin be forgiven without repentance?'

   Luke 24:46-47 ⁴⁶ *He told them, "This is what is written: The Christ will suffer and rise from the dead on the third day,* ⁴⁷ *and <u>repentance and forgiveness of sins</u> will be preached in his name to all nations. NIV (emphasis mine)*

If Jesus were to go to the Cross to deal with our sin, without first identifying with our sin in repentance on our behalf, the work of the cross would have been void.

> **Note:** for us, repentance means 'change your thinking' and 'reconsider your ways' which will result in turning from your current attitudes and actions. The consequence of this promised by Jesus is forgiveness. *Romans 2:4*

Also see the repentant criminal receiving forgiveness from Jesus. *Luke 23:39-43*

Was one criminal less of a sinner than the other? No. One criminal had sufficient fear of God and knowledge of Jesus to take responsibility for his behavior, confessing that he was a sinner who needed saving. In so doing he was 'changing his thinking' about what was acceptable. Repentance established; Jesus proceeded to proclaim forgiveness.

 **LESSON**
It is not whether or not we are sinless that brings forgiveness, because none of us are. It is how we regard sin in our hearts that matters. We will examine in a moment how the Apostle Paul in Romans chapter 7 was struggling with areas of sin. The point is that he WAS struggling, which means that his attitude was repentant. His thinking was that he didn't want to sin, and this in turn qualified him for forgiveness through the grace of God.

THE CHANGING OF THE PRIESTHOOD

2. Another important aspect of Jesus' baptism was the changing of priesthood under the New Covenant. We see in *Leviticus 8:6* Aaron and his sons, the original priests, being baptized or washed by Moses to confirm their ordination.

Zacharias the father of John the Baptist was in the priestly line and served in the temple. So, it is symbolic that John being born of the line of priests should now be baptizing Jesus immediately before He began His ministry.

Later we know that Caiaphas the serving high priest who examined Jesus before the crucifixion tore his own robe in apparent frustration. Under the law this rending of his garment disqualified him from being high priest. *(Leviticus 21:10)*

In contrast Jesus also wore the one-piece garment of a priest. Lots were cast for His robe, and it was never torn leaving Him as legitimate to be our high priest. *Hebrews 7:12-19*

THE HOLY SPIRIT COMES UPON HIM TO BEGIN HIS MINISTRY

The Holy Spirit came upon Him at His baptism and we hear the Father expressing His pleasure at the obedience of His Son.

Notably I have read that in His culture that you were not considered a full adult until thirty years of age, so this was the appropriate time for Him to begin His ministry. *Luke 3:22-23*

Prior to His baptism we see Him doing no miracles. A part of His ministry to us was to model how we should walk in the Spirit in terms of behavior. (Exhibiting the fruit of the Spirit)
He also showed us how to move in the power of the Spirit through the gifts of the Spirit.

We note that Jesus was 'led' into the desert FULL of the Holy Spirit. But it is important to observe that after He overcame His fleshly needs and the temptation of the devil in terms of His self-realization, remaining faithful to the Word of God, that He returned in the POWER of the Holy Spirit.

> *Luke 4:1 Jesus,* **full of the Holy Spirit,** *returned from the Jordan and was led by the Spirit in the desert, NIV (emphasis mine)*
>
> *Luke 4:14 Jesus returned to Galilee in the* **power of the Spirit***, NIV (emphasis mine)*

Study 9: The New Convenant

So, we see Jesus bringing in the New Covenant for mankind. This Covenant was to be by Faith alone with Jesus bringing about a complete redemption. He fully paid for every provision for us on the cross. We have salvation, healing and deliverance from our enemies all included, and we have nothing that we can do to earn it. Jesus did it all, a finished work, and we access all of His provisions appropriating them all, and receiving them by Faith.

Romans 1:17 This Good News tells us how <u>God makes us right in his sight</u>. This is accomplished <u>from start to finish by faith</u>. As the Scriptures say, "It is through faith that a righteous person has life." NLT (emphasis mine)

APPROPRIATING GODS PROVISIONS BY FAITH

We know that God so loved the World that He sent His only son to pay for its sin, so that all could be saved. Is everyone saved? No! The opportunity of salvation is paid for everyone, but received only by those who believe that Gods Word is true in this regard. The Word says that it is there as a promise and an indication of the will of God, paid for by Jesus, but it requires faith to actively claim it for it to become a reality. E.G. *John 3:16*

And so it is with every promise of God. You do not normally come into salvation and automatically receive freedom from all bondages, broken heartedness, or the need for physical healing. When do you get them? When you know about them and accept them by faith. This often means receiving through a ministry that God has placed in His body to provide for your needs. As someone has said; 'God's goodness is for those who will accept it.'

The deliverance of Israel from Egypt is a picture for us all. In bringing them out of Egypt God did everything for them, they had to do nothing. It was a supernatural translation from captivity to freedom. In the same way God redeems us completely from sin and Satan's captivity through the work of the cross. There is nothing for us to do but receive.

But next they came to the Promised Land. For them to possess the promises that are there, they have to have an active faith with corresponding actions. God had already said that He would give them the land. They all agreed that it was a good land, but they did not all believe that God was with them, and trustworthy to be able to deliver on His promises. In much the same way after our initial salvation many of the promises of God need to be contended for by active faith. Otherwise we all agree that Gods promises are good, but being passive, deceived or intimidated by the enemy prevents us pressing in with God for the provisions that Jesus paid for. Even in this Old Testament example, the principle remains that without active faith we miss the fullness of Gods provision. *Hebrews 3:19*

WHERE DO WE NOW FIND OURSELVES?

Why has God done all of this for us when we acknowledge that all of us have sinned and lived for ourselves. I believe that God would be denying Himself, His own nature and faithfulness if He did not make a way for us. The fact is that through Adam and Eves sin and submission that Satan came to us, and we became captives sold into slavery. (Clearly sin began with Satan and his angels before mankind was created.)

So, we could say that nobody on Earth from that point on asked to be in the situation that they are in, or have the weaknesses and faults that they have. ALL fall short of the glory of God, there is no one righteous, not even one. *Romans 3:10*

We could say that every human on Earth no matter how bound, deeply deceived into sin, hurt, broken or damaged that they are, did not ask for these issues.

We say when we see someone with something out of Gods order; "something happened." We cannot judge, we do not know how they arrived at this place, or in the condition that they are in. So, God <u>cannot</u> **not** offer them grace, mercy and another chance....it would not be fair. The fact is that His very throne is established on the foundation of justice.

> *Psalm 89:14 Righteousness and justice are the foundation of Your throne; Mercy and truth go before Your face. NKJV*

God in His wisdom knows that our cooperation and submission to sin is based on being deceived and misinterpreting, or having come to the wrong conclusions about our situations.
For example, life may have taught us that we are a bad person. This then becomes 'our truth' but it is not God's truth. Nonetheless if we believe that we are bad we will most likely live accordingly.

Study 10: The Grace of God

The grace of God then is to deal with why we sin, rather than sin itself, which was dealt with by Jesus on the cross. Jesus Himself acknowledged that it was deception that caused sinful activities and asked the Father for our forgiveness. We all put Him on the cross, because we all have sinned, and it was necessary to pay the price for it all. Remember this was the plan and will of the Father to open the way for us to be able to be back in relationship with Him.

> *Luke 23:34 Then Jesus said, "Father, forgive them, for they do not know what they do." NKJV*

In this passage, basically He was alluding to the fact that they/we don't know why they/we were doing what they/we were/are doing. So, by implication He knew that He was about to pay for their/our sin. Consequentially, we could say that grace is implying:
'Father I will pay for their sin, but I will also send the Holy Spirit, who will work with them bringing truth to help them deal with why they are deceived into sin.'

> *John 16:13 "However, when He, the Spirit of truth, has come, He will guide you into all truth; NKJV*

We see two mechanisms at work through the work of the cross.

1. Redemption: The first is what we might call that which <u>God will do **for** you</u>. This work of redemption is forgiveness of sin, and the perfecting of us before God the Father, so that He can receive us, and we can relate with Him. Redemption comes to us through the finished work and ministry of Jesus, and includes all kinds of healing and freedom through faith and the ministry of the Holy Spirit. This is a completed work which cannot be added to by our own efforts or works.

2. Sanctification: The second is the process of sanctification which is an ongoing work of the Holy Spirit as we walk with Him. The cross opened the way for the outpouring of the Spirit of truth and the commencement of His ministry. This second part we

would describe as that which <u>God will do **in** you</u>. It is an ongoing work which is not yet completed in us. It includes receiving sufficient truth to access the provisions of redemption.

> *Hebrews 10:14 For by one offering He has perfected forever those who are being sanctified. NKJV*

As we have previously stated, and now reinforce, perfecting us forever is a past tense statement. Those who are being sanctified is continuing present tense. In other words, it is ongoing. So, Jesus dealing with our sin and making us right with the Father is a finished work. Possessing the land of our souls, subjecting our bodies, and walking in the authority of our inheritance is an ongoing process.

As we have said, we lost our position through deception, and it is restored in a practical way through being sanctified by the truth.

> *John 17: 17 "Sanctify them by Your truth. Your word is truth. NKJV*

Truth is a very strong theme of the New Testament appearing around 110 times. We need to base our lives around seeking Gods truth to grow into healthy children.

> *John 8:32 "And you shall know the truth, and the truth shall make you free." NKJV*

Interestingly the Bible connects evil with having a lack of truth.

> *1 Corinthians 13:6 Love does not delight in evil but rejoices with the truth. NIV*

In any case we see a just God remembering that we are dust, (created humans) and making a way for us to return to Him.

To put His justice and mercy into perspective, let me relate the following excellent story which I read in one of my devotionals.

FIORELLO LAGUARDIA; THE JUST JUDGE
Fiorello was Mayor of New York City for three terms from 1934 through until 1945.
One bitterly cold night he decided to preside as judge over a night court. An old woman was brought in for stealing a loaf of bread.

She explained that she had taken it to feed her family who were starving. As judge, Fiorello responded that he had to punish her stating that the law makes no exceptions, there must be a consequence, and payment for the offence was required.

"I must fine you $10 dollars" was his verdict. This was a considerable amount of money in the times. The rent for a house for a month in those days was around $22 and an average weekly wage was around $30.

He then reached into his own pocket and took out a ten-dollar bill.

'Here's the $10 to pay your fine, which I now remit.' He threw the $10 bill into his own hat and declared, "I'm now going to fine everybody in this courtroom fifty cents for living in a town where a person has to steal a loaf of bread in order to eat. Mr. Bailiff, collect the fines and give them to this defendant."

After the hat was passed around, the incredulous old woman left the courtroom with a new light in her eyes and $47.50 in her pocket to buy groceries! This is between $1,500 and $2,000 based on today's average wage in the U.S.
The law demanded that she be punished, suffer consequences, and pay for her actions. Justice held the environment and circumstances accountable, and required that she be extended grace.

This is a great picture of the Gospel for us. We did not ask to be born into the environment of a sinful world or our particular circumstances. Some perhaps grew up with issues such as a bad home life or generational influences affecting their lives.

A just God then says, the fine must be paid, but I will pay it.

Not only did you do nothing other than be born into this world to earn this free gift of forgiveness', but I am also going to bless you with every spiritual blessing in the spiritual realms. Just like the old lady in the story we come before the judge with nothing but guilt and empty handedness. However, just as she did, we leave pardoned and blessed beyond our wildest imaginations. We have a fair judge, and a Gospel or Good news that seems too good to be true. But it is! *Ephesians 1:3-8*

SUMMARY
Before we move onto Unit two, let us summarize the outworking of the New Covenant as it relates to us and our lives in an ongoing manner:

1. Redemption: 'That which God does **for** us'
   A completed work, finished and paid in full
2. Sanctification: 'That which God does **in** us'
   An ongoing work of the Holy Spirit
3. Mission: 'That which God does **through** us'
   This comes as we understand our redemption,
   and as we cooperate with the Holy Spirit in the
   work of sanctification, it opens the way to works of faith…

   James 2:17-18 ¹⁷ In the same way, faith by itself, if it is not accompanied by action, is dead. ¹⁸ But someone will say, "You have faith; I have deeds." Show me your faith without deeds, and I will show you my faith by what I do. NIV

UNIT TWO

The Church and the Holy Spirit

Introduction
Let us begin recapping in broad terms three themes that we find in the New Testament in regard to our walk with God:

1. REDEMPTION – 'What God will do <u>for</u> you'
2. SANCTIFICATION – 'What God will do <u>in</u> you'
3. MISSION – 'What God will do <u>through</u> you'

Study 1: God's intentions for mankind

1. REDEMPTION
We have covered this largely in Unit one. We saw how Jesus Christ paid the price for us for our sin and its consequences. As a result, we now belong to Him and are able to access by faith all of His benefits. Jesus' work is finished, and we receive through faith by the ministry of the Holy Spirit. *Psalm 103:2-4*

2. SANCTIFICATION
Some people believe that when you are born again and receive the Holy Spirit that God has finished the work in you. As a result, much of the Church remains passive, deceived, captive and broken. The truth is that receiving the Holy Spirit is the <u>beginning</u> of His ministry to you and through you. *John 8:32, John 16:13, John 17:17-18*

3. MISSION
This relates to the mission of the New Testament church.

The church being the 'ekklesia' as it is in the Greek language, which means the community of believers or saints. Together as the body of Christ we are to be doing His work on Earth. So, in essence we are to continue the ministries that He was doing, as His ambassadors or representatives.

The needs of the World are the same today as they were in His time when He came to us as the 'Son of man,' healing the sick, setting the captives free, and healing the broken hearted. Certainly, these items were central in His own earthly ministry, and were the activities that He commissioned the early 'disciples' to continue. *John 20:21-22*

THE SPIRIT OF THE LORD AND THE ANOINTING
What we must observe here is that the work of God is always about helping people. Gifts or the 'anointing' are not about us personally, to make us feel good or be impressive to our fellow man. We can be sure that the Holy Spirit will make our faith driven activity a reality, as we operate in the revealed will of God. *Mark 16:20*

Study 2: Living According to the Spirit

John 16:7 "Nevertheless I tell you the truth. It is to your advantage that I go away; for if I do not go away, the Helper will not come to you; but if I depart, I will send Him to you. NKJV

Jesus considered that we would be in a better place if He returned to heaven and sent the Holy Spirit to us. In His flesh body, manifested as the son of man, He was limited by problems such as distance, and exposure, in terms of how many people He could help. He taught the disciples how to live according to the Spirit in regards to behavior and attitudes.

He also trained them in how to work with and be led by the Holy Spirit and to allow Him through them to set people free. He did no recorded works that I am aware of prior to His own baptism and the subsequent filling of the Holy Spirit.

We can confirm then that He did no works as a man, but only began to fulfill His calling as the 'word made flesh' when He allowed the Holy Spirit to work in and through Him. Clearly, His ultimate intention was for many disciples to be trained to minister to the needs of a hurting and captive humanity just as He did. *John 16:7, John 16:13*

LIVING AS THE ANOINTED CHURCH
The criteria for us to be the church that God is pleased to anoint, is for us to be led by the Spirit as Jesus was. *Luke 3:22*

Having received the Holy Spirit, the next thing that happened was that He was led by the Spirit into the wilderness, being 'filled with the Holy Spirit.'

> *Luke 4:1 Then Jesus, being <u>filled</u> with the Holy Spirit, returned from the Jordan and was led by the Spirit into the wilderness, NKJV (emphasis mine)*

In the wilderness He dealt with that which we might describe as the 'self-life.' This is in terms of putting what you could have, or want for yourself, aside in favor of being where the Spirit wanted Him to be.

Later as we know the devil came and tempted Him offering Him the same things that he had tempted Adam and Eve with in the beautiful Garden of Eden.

The devil tempted Him to turn the stones into bread. Eve saw that the food was good to eat. The devil let Him see the kingdoms of the world and their glory. Eve was impressed by what she saw. *1 John 2:16*

> *Genesis 3:6 So when the woman saw that the tree was <u>good for food</u>, that it was <u>pleasant to the eyes</u>, and a tree desirable to <u>make one wise</u>, she took of its fruit and ate. NKJV (emphasis mine)*

As we know each time Jesus was tempted, He used the written word of God as His reference point for which spirit He was going to align with. So, the devil's final temptation was using the written word of God in order to get Jesus to bow down and submit to him. Having dealt with what the World offered, the elements of the 'fallen self-life,' and also the devil who works through the first two, Jesus returned in the 'power of the Spirit.' *Luke 4:14*

This all happened immediately before Jesus announced the beginning of His ministry and the confirmation of the Prophetic word of Isaiah 61, that a person who came in the flesh, would make the Word true by the working of the Holy Spirit through Him. *Isaiah 61:1-2, Luke 4:18, Acts 10:38*

WHAT DOES ALL OF THIS MEAN TO US?
So, why is the anointing of the Holy Spirit on the Church today? It is to empower us to do the works of Jesus today by the manifestation of the Holy Spirit working through us also? *Mark 16:20, John 20:21-22, 1 John 1:20*

HOW DO WE WALK IN THE 'ANOINTING' ON US?
We know that the Holy Spirit uses people by working through them and giving gifts as He decides is appropriate and commensurate to their sanctification, development and character. *1 Corinthians 12:11*

Jesus showed us the way. He began, having received the Holy Spirit, to now be led by the Spirit. *Romans 8:1 + 14, Galatians 5:16-18, 1 Corinthians 6:19-20*

Then we know that all things that we need will be added to us and everything we could need for our enjoyment will be given. *Mathew 6:33, 1 Timothy 6:17*

Study 3: Old Testament prophecy of the Holy Spirit through Jesus

To really comprehend the work of the Holy Spirit through the Church we firstly need to understand His work through Christ. Remember, Jesus as a man showed us how to work with the Holy Spirit. There are characteristics of the ministry of the Holy Spirit which should become increasingly evident is us as we follow the Spirit in sanctification. *Isaiah 11:2*

The passage is teaching us that what is known as the sevenfold ministry of the Holy Spirit or the seven Spirits will rest on Jesus and work through Him. There are various references to the seven Spirits in the book of *Revelation 1:4, 3:1, 4:5 and 5:6*. They together represent the activities or manifestations of the Holy Spirit that we would expect to see through a believer.

THE FRUIT OF THE SPIRIT
We have already described that the fruit of the Spirit is largely directed towards considering and preferring others. *Galatians 5:22-23* In contrast the works of the flesh or 'fallen self' nature is all about self-gratification, self-promotion and self-realization. *Galatians 5:19-21*

THE MINISTRY OF THE SPIRIT
The fruit of the Spirit then is evidence of the nature of the Holy Spirit changing our attitudes and behavior. There are also attributes of the Holy Spirit that equip us or give us the tools to minister to others; hopefully we are able minister in the right spirit and motivation. Having received healing and freedom ourselves, it is a normal consequence, to now become aware of the needs of others, and to want to give out that which we have 'freely received' ourselves. *Mathew 10:8*

This list of spiritual attributes or equipment should become increasingly evident in our lives.

The Holy Spirit then works through us in our work for others as revealed in *Isaiah 11:2* in the following ways:

1. The Spirit of the LORD – we understand this to be the Revelatory Spirit, as seen in prophecy. It knows the mind of God for a situation. Let me propose that in the NT this manifestation of the Holy Spirit is revealed as 'the mind of Christ.'

> *So, we could propose that this Spirit is the knowing of what the Lord is thinking about a situation. Walking after the Spirit of Christ becomes asking Him; "what do you want me to do or say here Lord?"*

2. The Spirit of wisdom
3. The Spirit of understanding
4. The Spirit of counsel
5. The Spirit of power (or might)
6. The Spirit of knowledge (to some degree perhaps this refers to the knowledge of God, and the ways, statutes and precepts of God)
7. The Spirit of the fear of the Lord

Symbolically placed in the 'temple' was what is known as the 'Menora.' This was a candle stand with seven arms made of pure gold. These arms bore the candles which were representative of the seven spirits of the Holy Spirit. It is common to find these spiritual manifestations of the work of the Holy Spirit in isolation or grouped together in places throughout the scriptures. *Deuteronomy 24:9, Proverbs 1:1-7 + 8:12-14 + 9:10, Psalm 111:10, Mark 6:2*

Study 4: Jesus and the Gifts of the Spirit

We are always looking to Jesus as our model for all that we do. If He did it, we want to do it. If it doesn't look like something that He would have done, or how He acted, then we should not be drawn into it. Being in nature God, of course He worked perfectly with the Holy Spirit to complete the works of the Father for those in need around Him.

Consequently, as the Spirit of the Lord was on Jesus, He demonstrated the entire sevenfold ministry of the Spirit in His own earthly ministry.

He prophesied frequently. We see Him understanding what people were thinking at times. *(Matthew 9:4 + Luke 17)* He gave counsel and taught about the Kingdom with an authoritative knowledge of God. He had knowledge of, for example, the history of the Samaritan woman at the well. He displayed power regularly with miracles. In the garden of Gethsemane, He exhibited the fear of the Lord, in preferring the Fathers will over self. And notably, as mentioned previously, we see people attributing the signs that He was performing to wisdom and not merely power. *Mark 6:2*

THE GIFTS OF THE SPIRIT

We have just detailed the seven Spirits that represent and manifest the work of the Holy Spirit through us. Now we look to the New Testament gifts of the Spirit, moving beyond the gospels and into the epistles. We see clearly the work of the Holy Spirit manifesting the 7 Spirits through the church as He wills. We would we be surprised if the gifts did not match up producing the same prophesied attributes and activities here, as described throughout the scriptures, and collated in *Isaiah 11:2 and 1 Corinthians 12:4-11*

So, the gifts are the practical outworking of the seven Spirits. Let us list them here and make a comparison:

OT	NT
Spirit of the Lord	Prophecy
Spirit of wisdom	Word of wisdom
Spirit of Knowledge	Word of Knowledge
Spirit of power	Working of miracles (Greek 'power')
Spirit of counsel	Different types of healings

Note: If you discern something you understand that which you are looking at

I think by now that we have established what the working and anointing of the Holy Spirit looked like on Jesus, and should therefore look on us, His church. Let us now examine what the New Testament teaches us about the PURPOSE of the presence and anointing of the Holy Spirit upon us.

In terms of our personal growth and sanctification the Holy Spirit is working in us to conform us to the likeness of Christ. *(Romans 8:29, Ephesians 4:11-13)* In regard to our calling He is working through ascension ministries to equip us for the work of the ministry, each fulfilling our role in the body of Christ.

THE PURPOSE OF THE SPIRIT OF THE LORD UPON US

We have noted already that the Holy Spirit and His anointing is on the church for exactly the same reason as it was on Jesus. Namely to fulfill the MISSION of reaching, saving, healing and freeing captive people that God loves.

Study 5: Physical and emotional healing

We see the heart of God in commissioning Jesus to do 'good' by healing those <u>under</u> the power of the devil. *Acts 10:38, 1 John 3:8*

Jesus taught about the Kingdom of God, and then demonstrated its benefits by healing the sick. He then 'discipled' and trained His followers into doing the same. We consider this to be a 'hear,' 'see' and 'do' process. Hear about the Kingdom, see me do it, and then go and do it yourself.

THE HOLY SPIRIT IN US

As we have stated Jesus did not begin His ministry on Earth until He was filled with the Holy Spirit. For Him this occurred concurrently with His water baptism which is something which happens occasionally.

> *Luke 4:1 Then Jesus, being filled with the Holy Spirit, returned from the Jordan and was led by the Spirit into the wilderness, NKJV (emphasis mine)*

This 'filling' with the Holy Spirit happened immediately before His correction of the fall in His confrontation with the devil in the wilderness. This was followed by His announcing of the fulfilling of His ministry in Luke 4:18. Notably Jesus' appeared to immediately go out and look for His church in the form of Peter and the others, to begin the training and discipling process immediately. This is a very good indicator that His purpose and intention was always to train His church how to work with the Holy Spirit to fulfill the Fathers will.

He taught His disciples that the coming of the Holy Spirit, also known as the Spirit of Christ would work from within them. *John 14:16-17, 1 Corinthians 6:17, Ephesians 2:8-10 + 3:20, 2 Corinthians 4:7*

> *1 John 4:4 But you belong to God, my dear children. You have already won your fight with these false prophets, because the Spirit who lives in you is greater than the spirit who lives in the world. NLT (emphasis mine)*

In this regard we can join with Jesus in acknowledging that God prepared our bodies for His inhabitance, to do His will in the Earth. Hebrews 10:5-7

Study 6: Receiving the Holy Spirit

Jesus often created pictures or used analogies to explain spiritual principles in a way that was easy to understand. At one time He used the example of not putting New Wine in Old wineskins. My wife and I used to own a vineyard and well understand that new wine ferments and expands, and it needs to be contained in a way that allows for this growth. The 'type' of the New Wine is that of the Holy Spirit poured out. I believe that Jesus was saying that if He were to put the Holy Spirit in your hard, unregenerate human spirit that is not sensitive to God or the Holy Spirit that you could not contain His presence. *Matthew 9:17*

He is indicating that your human spirit must be made new, born again first to be able to cope with the expansion that the Holy Spirit will bring. So, scripture indicates that He works on three fronts in His regeneration of mankind. He firstly puts a new human spirit in us. Then He puts a teachable, sensitive heart in us…. remembering that this is the centre of our soul. And then He puts His Spirit in us to facilitate and empower all of His works.

> *Ezekiel 36:26-27* ²⁶ *I will give you a new heart and put a new spirit in you; I will remove from you your heart of stone and give you a heart of flesh.*
> ²⁷ *And I will put my Spirit in you and move you to follow my decrees and be careful to keep my laws. NIV (emphasis mine) *[Note: my Spirit is in capitols letters creating a distinction from a new human spirit in verse 26]*

HOW TO PRACTICALLY HELP A PERSON RECEIVE THE HOLY SPIRIT

Some people simply pray for people to receive the Spirit. Others lay on hands. Personally, I often don't even pray for people to receive. I normally explain to them that this is Gods idea and desire, and that Jesus already made them right with the Father so that the Holy Spirit can come into them. *Acts 10:44-45*

> The point is that we don't need a formula, we often only need to activate the gift.

ACTIVATING TONGUES

Many years ago, I was praying with a Chinese lady who wanted to be baptized in the Spirit and speak in tongues. I had convinced her that God wanted her to have the gift and had shown her from the Bible where it explained that this was for today. The problem was that I had never led anybody into the Holy Spirit Baptism before. The thought came into my mind to pray in the Spirit short sentences, and have her imitate what I was saying, and that she would trip over her tongue and receive her own prayer language. When I followed this prompting that is what happened, and I have been leading people to speak in tongues the same way ever since. At times this will be large groups from the front of a meeting, other times individually in prayer lines where often as many as 20, 30 or more people will be filled one at a time.

Some people get their own tongue very quickly, others are very good at remembering and imitating what you have said. Eventually however, if you persevere some words that I have not said in my prayer language begin to creep in. Let me reiterate, many other people do this in other ways. This is simply how I do it and offer it if you do not know what to do, as a means to help get people going. The main thing is that they receive.

THE MINISTRY OF THE HOLY SPIRIT THROUGH US

In terms of ministry, a person comes to you with a problem; it is God who has the answers and power to resolve it. Our part is to be equipped to be the little piece of fuse wire that makes the connection between their need and Gods power and promised provisions. In this sense we make His Word 'flesh,' or in other terms give it an expression in the natural realm. We do this through being a 'door' aligned with the Word of God that the Holy Spirit can confirm and make manifest His abilities through.

We too, will become people full of grace and truth. Someone has said that there is no junior Holy Spirit. In other words, we all receive the same Spirit. The question is, are we letting Him work through us, is the door open....and in some measure, how much of us has He got use of in terms of cooperation, submission, knowledge and understanding of His ways and will? *John 1:14*

In the Old Testament we see reference to us being a spiritual entry point for God into our realm. It has been well said that both God and Satan are looking for access to the Earth to manifest their nature and have an expression. We are therefore referred to as 'gates' and 'doors' that are entry points for God to come into our environment and bring change. As we behold Him and obey His will in faith, He has His expression. *Psalm 24:7-9*

Study 7: The God Dimension

Having realized that God will do His work coming in through us, we then need to open our minds so that He can have as much access as possible to do His will in the Earth. In order for us to reach our potential in God through the Holy

Spirit, we have to begin to think in another dimension. The Earth is a created program that has rules and limitations. But God is outside of those and is not limited or confined to the basic principles of this Earth. *Colossians 2:8-10, Mathew 19:26, Mark 9:23*

JESUS MOVES THE THINKING OF THE DISCIPLES
The point is that God is above the limitations of the world. In the New Testament we see Jesus trying to get the disciples to understand this, in order for them to be able to launch His church with supernatural signs. In Matthew chapter 14 we see Jesus doing a miracle by feeding 5,000 men and also women and children with 5 loaves of bread and 2 fish. There were 12 baskets of leftovers. Again, for natural man this is ridiculously impossible. Notably Jesus then 'made' the disciples get into the boat and cross the lake without Him.

> *Matthew 14:22 Immediately Jesus **made** the disciples get into the boat and go on ahead of him to the other side, while he dismissed the crowd. NIV (emphasis mine)*

Why did He do this? He was trying to get them to think beyond what was possible. At 3am He came to them walking on the water…defying and totally disregarding the natural laws of buoyancy. Evidently Jesus was trying to alter their thinking about the limitless abilities of God, to move them into His dimension. I believe that this is why He allowed Lazarus to die, so that He could raise their faith and lift their expectations. *(John 11:14-15)*

The disciples were amazed that the words of Jesus carried such supernatural power. Again, Jesus used this to move their thinking towards understanding that they could also speak through faith and release power from Gods dimension.
Mark 4:39-41, Mark 11:14 + 20-25

UNIT THREE

The Healing Streams of God

THE RIVER OF GODS PROVISION
Before moving into 7 healing streams that God provides, let us briefly detail 7 areas or problems that require Gods ministry through the Holy Spirit:

1. Spiritual freedom - clearly our own human spirit needs to be reborn and set free from sin - often people struggle with demonic spirit bondages
2. Emotional wholeness – many diseases stem from imbalanced feelings
3. Mental problems - a high percentage of mental issues are inner belief based
4. Relational issues - these come as we interact from our perceptions of self
5. Physical healing - our bodies are the end of the line in terms of hormonal balances in relation to our inner thought life (if these thoughts and beliefs are not at ease we have; dis-ease)
6. Sexual disorder – our sexuality often needs to be healed and reoriented
7. Addictive bondages – these often begin as our bad solutions to our pain or are 'self'-pleasing issues connected to our perceived need

> *Psalm 46:4 "There is a river whose streams make glad the city of God, the holy place where the Most High dwells." NIV*

> *Philippians 4:19 And my God will meet all your needs according to his glorious riches in Christ Jesus. NIV*

Now we have the 7 basic problem areas that mankind suffers with. We have 7 Spirits that God uses to deal with these areas. And now we are going to look at 7 Healing Streams that the Holy Spirit works through to meet every need.

Healing is largely a matter of putting things back into Gods order. In other words, becoming whole, in the sense of being restored by Him, and becoming in His likeness. As we have described physical wellness comes as a result of the affect of the Holy Spirits ministry to our spirit and soul. *3 John 1:2*

This concept of freedom and healing coming through wholeness is held in the words translated from the Greek language as 'saved' and 'salvation.'

Saved = 4982. **sozo**, sode'-zo; from a prim. sos (contr. for obsol. saos, "safe"); to save, i.e. **deliver or protect** (lit. or fig.):--**heal**, preserve, save (self), do well, **be (make) whole**. (Emphasis mine: reference, Strong's concordance)

Being saved then includes being *delivered* from captivity, being *healed* of areas where the devil has had ground, and being made *whole*.... all of which are usually the same thing. As we come into mental, emotional, relational and spiritual wholeness our bodies reflect the same.

This wholeness in Christ is a result of deliverance from the power that Satan has had over us through our deception, and our consequent submission to, and cooperation with him.

Turning from this submission and cooperation comes from our 'repentance' and changing of our thinking. Acts 3:19 The meaning of 'repent' from the Greek language is noted below. Repent = 3340. **metanoeo**, met-an-o-eh'-o; **to think differently** or afterwards, i.e. **reconsider** (mor. feel compunction):--repent. (Emphasis mine: reference, Strong's concordance)

THE 7 STREAMS
Stream 1 'Faith principles'

In its most fundamental form faith and believing in God is to be persuaded or convinced that you can trust in God. If He has said something, then we expect that it will be so.

Believe = Greek *Pisteuo*; to have faith (in, upon, or with respect to, a person or thing), commit (to trust), put in trust with. *Faith* = Greek *Pistis*; persuasion, i.e. conviction.

God has limited Himself to working through faith in the Earth. Why has He set these limits? I believe it is because the first sin, and the basic reason that mankind fell was their lack of belief and trust in the nature of God. We could say then that we receive all of the promises of God through faith in His nature, which was demonstrated by Jesus who healed 'all' who came to Him. *John 6:28-29, Romans 4:20-22, Romans 1:17*

As we lay this foundation for the Stream of healing by faith, we see that in Jesus' hometown they could not believe, and this meant that they could not receive. Familiarity stifled the flow of faith which was required to release the power of God in their situations. *Mark 6:3-6*

LESSON
If we can convince people that God is trustworthy and willing and able to meet their needs then anything can happen. *Mark 10:27, John 14:12*

GIVING FAITH

Once someone has experienced God healing people, it is very difficult to convince those people that He won't. This applies to emotional healing, deliverance, or physical healing. Some people have stronger faith in some areas than others because they mainly work in one of these streams.

LESSON
Our personal faith is infectious and other people are impacted and moved by it if we are convinced ourselves.

PERSISTENT FAITH

Healing and deliverance is a journey that has miraculous moments here and there. Sometimes patience and perseverance are developed as we 'contend' for the faith. *Jude 1:3*

LESSON
Persistence in believing will always produce a result. Faith will have its outcome.
RECEIVING FAITH
Jesus often asked questions such as *do you believe that I can do this?* He also made comments such as *your faith has healed you, according to your faith* and so on. He was looking for faith to receive in the person whom He was to minister to. Of course, He had perfect faith Himself, but without them being able to receive it would be like trying to tip water into a jar with the lid still on.

LESSON
Accurately teaching the word of God or sharing stories of what God has done can often raise faith to receive in people and produce results beyond what we would ourselves have expected.

FAITH AND BEING 'FULLY CONVINCED' AT 'HEART' LEVEL

Being fully convinced, I believe is something in the heart rather than mental assent or wishful thinking. At times we have 'heart beliefs' that prevent us from believing that God would want to prove His word in or through us. We will cover this in more detail in following sessions. Let us say though that this could be because we believe in our 'hearts' that we are not worthy, not really loved, not cared about, or good enough for God to touch, depending on what was programmed into us as children. Healing of beliefs in our hearts can open up new realms of faith.

> *Mark 11:22-23* ²² *So Jesus answered and said to them, "Have faith in God."*
> ²³ *"For assuredly, I say to you, whoever says to this mountain, 'Be removed and be cast into the sea,' and* **does not doubt in his heart**, *but believes that those things he says will be done, he will have whatever he says. NKJV (emphasis mine)*

LESSON
Many times, we need truth for our own 'inner heart beliefs' or the inner beliefs of the hearts of others, in regard to for example, worthiness to minister or receive, before we can have faith that God will move through.

DEALING WITH DOUBT AND UNBELIEF

So how do we deal with our doubt and unbelief? In two Corinthians chapter ten and verse five we see that we are to demolish and destroy arguments that set themselves up against the knowledge of God. The Greek word here that is translated; as *arguments* is *logismus*, and it means; computation, i.e. (fig.) reasoning, imagination, thought. *2 Corinthians 10:5*

There is no working out the word of God, it can only be believed and received. Think about it. Jesus walks on water, talks to storms, drachmas appear in fish's mouths, He feeds five thousand with next to nothing, axe heads float, water becomes wine, seas part for the Israelites to cross, donkeys talk to their riders ... shall I go on. These cannot be argued or worked out.

The point is that you cannot reason out something that you will never be able to understand. the word of God and His promises are technically not logical or possible. They cannot therefore be worked out; they can only be received.

Smith Wigglesworth who very clinically dealt with his own unbelief, proclaimed his well-known default position. *God said it, I believe it, that settles it.* In other words, there is no more to think about, and nothing to work out; I trust His integrity, promises and ability without question. He also made the statement that; *carnal (worldly) reasoning will always land you in the bog of unbelief.*

LESSON
The issue is very often not whether or not we have faith, because we have all been given a measure which will grow if we feed it. The problem most times is that we concurrently have wrong beliefs which produce doubt and unbelief. These need to be resolved in order for faith alone to be our default position.

HAVING 'GIVING FAITH' WITHOUT POSITIONING THOSE IN NEED FOR 'RECEIVING FAITH'

Reading the great healing Apostle Smith Wigglesworth, I noted that there were occasions where he would go to minister in a home and would not immediately pray for the sick person. He commented once that *there was not an atom of faith in the house.* He would proceed to minister the Word of God in order to deal with the environment, and then he would pray sometimes the next day and get his result. It's important that we observe faith before ministering. *Acts 14:9-10*

LESSON
It is vitally important to build an environment of faith based on truth, so that the people are positioned to receive.

TIMES WHEN YOU MAY NOT 'FEEL' FAITH

When you are used to God working in a particular way your expectation is set and you may not feel any special faith. Perhaps you are tired, but you are still convinced that God will work.

LESSON
Faith does not need to be felt emotionally, although often you do feel it as your emotions are the outworking of your beliefs.

BELIEVING FOR YOURSELF

Many times, it is more difficult to believe for yourself than it is for others. This is probably because you have experiential knowledge of your symptoms being present each day. God has placed healing gifts in the body for a reason and they can help us to receive. Even Smith Wigglesworth suffered from appendicitis and almost died. It was a praying woman of faith and a young man who came and addressed the problem that brought about his healing. He was apparently unable to believe and come to faith for his own cure.
1 Corinthians 12, 1 John 5:4

LESSON
At times you may need the ministry of others to help you receive for yourself.

HOW SHOULD HEALING LOOK?

Many people don't receive their healing because they believe that it should look some particular way, or that they should feel this or that. I would estimate that with most of the people that we see healed physically through our ministry nothing obvious happens. This can be true also of deliverance or baptism in the Holy Spirit. *John 4:46-52*

LESSON
God heals many different ways. He does not always work the same way and has a variety of expressions depending on the person that He is working through, or the environment.

FAITH VERSES UNBELIEF

Faith puts us *under* God's provision and outcome. This is evidenced by Abraham who was fully convinced that God could do that which He said He would do. As we have said, once we have our convictions about God's promises and intentions for us, we need to leave the details to Him in terms of how it will look and when it will take place. Doubt, unbelief and skepticism put us, or keep us under Satan's outcome, which will not be positive, changing or redemptive in nature.

> *Matthew 21:21-22* ²¹ *So Jesus answered and said to them, "Assuredly, I say to you, if you have faith and do **not doubt**, you will not only do what was done to the fig tree, but also if you say to this mountain, 'Be removed and be cast into the sea,' it will be done.* ²² *"And whatever things you ask in prayer, believing, you will receive." NKJV (emphasis mine)*

Each of us has been given a measure of faith. So, having faith, however undeveloped, is not the problem as we only need a mustard seed of faith. The issue then is usually not how much faith we have, it is how much unbelief. The Bible says that healing is Gods idea and not ours; therefore, we don't have to talk Him into it! He already promised, paid for it, and commanded that we minister it. If we simply receive without doubting it is ours.

LESSON
The expectations of what God will do for people is a strong indicator of their believing in regard to faith. At times you can see faith, as a look of expectation, other times you see unbelief.

CHOOSING FAITH

Whether you want to receive your own healing or help in the ministry to others you need to take captive, and deal with your doubt and unbelief. Once you have decided to refuse to even think about the possibility of God not being true to His word, it can be helpful to meditate over and over on His nature. *Psalm 103:2-13*

LESSON
It is God who does the healing. We cannot understand how He does it, we can only know that He does. We don't, therefore, need to know everything about what we are praying for in the stream of faith healing.

SUMMARY

The most important work then in any kind of healing ministry is to position the subject under Gods provision, submitted to Him and trusting in His ability and promises. Remember, whatever we submit to has power <u>over</u> us. *Daniel 3:17- 18, Romans 6:16, 2 Peter 2:19b*

Stream 2 'Under the anointing'

The second healing stream that I am proposing is the anointing, which is the presence of God, and can be the tangible power of God. It can come as the result of faith that has risen through spiritual gifts, testimonies, teaching or an act of faith for example. Equally faith can come as a result of the anointing or presence of God in a meeting. *Luke 5:17*

We have already pointed out that the *Spirit of power* is one of the seven Spirits that are a working or presence of the Holy Spirit. Clearly, *the anointing* or presence of God is also tangible at other times, such as, worship services, prayer meetings or ministry sessions to the hurting and broken, as well as for many people who feel His presence with them.

THE ANOINTING, IN THE SENSE OF POWER FOR HEALING

There are two words translated in the New Testament as power. The first word is *exousia* which means *authority* type power. The word power in the following text is *exousia* which means *authority* type power.

> *Acts 26:18 'to open their eyes, in order to turn them from darkness to light, and from **the power** of Satan to God, NKJV (emphasis mine)*

The Greek word for literal power in the New Testament is *dunamis* which means literal or miraculous power, force or might. An example of *dunamis* power would be the literal power of God working in and through us that we observe from the following passage in Ephesians.

> *Ephesians 3:20 Now to Him who is able to do exceedingly abundantly above all that we ask or think, according to the **power** that works in us, NKJV (emphasis mine)*

LESSON
So, the distinction is that *exousia* power as authority is like a badge that we wear, an authorization from the kingdom of God. However, *dunamis* power as literal power is a manifestation of *the anointing* of the Holy Spirit, in or through us.

ATTRACTING *THE ANOINTING* OR PRESENCE OF THE HOLY SPIRIT

How strong the presence of His anointing might be in a meeting is not something that we can control, although we can observe. It does however appear that where there is hunger for His presence, expectation, humility and genuine worship you can certainly expect a strong manifestation. At times people are spontaneously delivered or healed when the anointing of the Holy Spirit comes upon them. Remember we are just the door or channel that God comes in through, He has His entrance into an environment, and what happens next is as the Spirit wills.

LESSON
The Holy Spirit comes as He pleases. When He comes in as the power of God through us, we mostly cannot predict what He might do or how He might touch a person. We are gates and doors to His Kingdom provisions.

SEEKING THE 'ANOINTING'
The Holy Spirit seems to be particularly attracted to obedient people and humble people. We know that Jesus had the Spirit without measure, so He is always our model in all things. We can look to Him for the secret to the anointing. Most of the great healing ministries of the past understood that the way to having God come increasingly through you, was a process of getting yourself out of the way. *John 5:19 + 8:29*

The late Apostle of Faith Smith Wigglesworth explained this process of walking increasingly as a clear channel for God in this way; *All of me, none of God - less of me, more of God - none of me, all of God.*

LESSON
People that we may term as 'anointed' are usually those that have yielded themselves to the Holy Spirit. They have removed self-preference, wanting to do what pleases God. This makes them a wide channel for God to come through. This is not something that was imparted to them in a prayer line.

LAYING ON HANDS TO RELEASE THE ANOINTING
Finally, laying on of hands is a channel for the power of God to flow through. Some people feel it and others don't. That is not the point. Why does the laying on of hands work? Because Jesus said to do it! Jesus still laid on hands where there was unbelief. *Mark 6:5-6*

We can see why Jesus taught about the Kingdom, and what God wanted for them before He ministered. He raised faith first through people having a right understanding.

The streams often overlap as they run into the same river. For example, the anointing or presence of God brings faith, but equally faith ushers in the presence of God.

LESSON
The power of God will flow through the laying on of hands. Some people will receive this, and in others you will sense resistance because of their beliefs.

Stream 3 'Gifts'
Gifts raise faith in the supernatural ability and intervention of God into our situation. Often people covet gifts so that they will appear to be someone, or better than other people. God is looking for people who will seek gifts because of a genuine motivation to see people receive His help and provision. In this case they are expressing gifts because of love for Him and for people. This places you 'in the Spirit' in the sense of being aligned with the nature, purpose and ministry of the Holy Spirit. It makes you a genuine candidate for Him to use you, choose you and gift you.

A BASIS FOR THE GIFTS OF THE SPIRIT
As a foundation for our study let me refer to the gifts of the spirit as listed in *1 Corinthians chapter 12:1-11*

USING THE GIFTS
As we have said *spiritual gifts raise faith*. Some are very gifted or *pre-wired* by God for

spiritual gifts and it is easy for them, while others of us are *hard gainers*. The thing to know is that we can still get there and help people; it just might take some of us a little longer to learn how to position ourselves to hear from God.

STEPPING OUT
Moving into the realm of using gifts in faith you often have a strong sense of an element of risk. After a while, you find that if your heart and motivation are right that God will always come through. Some people like to make spiritual gifts a part of their identity and worth and feel that if they operate in them that they are somehow superior to others. The truth is that anyone can be used if they make themselves available. God will use anyone who is willing to help and is prepared to trust Him.

THE INNATE ABILITY TO CONNECT TO THE DIMENSION OF GOD
We could perhaps use the analogy of the modern 'smart phone' to help us understand how the Holy Spirit works within in us, as a pathway to access another realm. Firstly, a smart phone is a machine with various feature and capabilities already put in it by the designer. So, it can operate as a unit on its own without connection to outside resources.

Secondly, it has a receptor that can connect it to the power of the air and receive messages and so on from outside of the unit. In much the same way we have programs, or things that we have learnt that can operate in our soul without outside sources. We also have a spirit that has the capacity to pick up from outside sources.

When the Holy Spirit comes into us and joins to our human spirit we are now connected to and have direct access to God's dimension.

So, in a sense the Holy Spirit is like a receptor in us, that is door to the spiritual Kingdom of God. As with a smart phone we can go 'online' with God and receive information and power that are coming from Him as the source.

With spiritual gifts, we deliberately connect with, and go 'online' with God to receive a message or instruction that comes through us but did not originate with us. John 4:23-24

HOW CAN I RECEIVE A WORD OF KNOWLEDGE OR PROPHECY?
You begin by making yourself available to God and looking to Him to put something into your mind to help or encourage someone. So, we begin by giving our mental faculties to God for His use. The old saying is that; *God talks how you listen.*

LESSON
We can be looking for some big lightning bolt supernatural experience or word from God. The truth is that most times we have communication from Him in a simple way through our senses. We can test if it is God or not by asking ourselves a question. Did I deliberately come up with that through my thought and effort, or did it just come into my mind or I sensed it when I turned my attention to Him?

How to work with the Gifts of the Spirit
WORDS OF WISDOM
A *'Word of Wisdom'* is probably more common than people realize. Have you ever been sharing with someone and you hear wise words and understanding come out of your

mouth? You may have attributed it to your own mind and knowledge, and yet, you know that you did not think it through to come to those conclusions. Consequently, I think that *Word of Wisdom* is one of the more common, and unintentional manifestations and gifts of the Spirit. Unlike other gifts it is probably more often than not, not deliberately reached out for. It is very often just there when we need it.

WHO CAN WORK IN GIFTS, HOW DO YOU QUALIFY?
Jesus said that if we ask for bread God will not give us a stone. *(Matthew 7:9)*

So, it begins with desire to further the work of God. Good ground for us is a church environment where the gifts are taught, and the work of the Holy Spirit is valued. Depending on your calling, you are often drawn towards a particular gift which you can see will be valuable helping you achieve your task. For example, and apostolic person or an evangelist might be drawn to word of knowledge to facilitate healing ministries and so on.

LESSON
We do not receive from God by trying hard. It is the practice of giving Him our attention and being aware of what we are receiving.

SO HOW WILL THE HOLY SPIRIT SPEAK TO US?
Some people think in words, others in pictures. So, the Holy Spirit may put things into our minds in the following ways:

Thoughts, pictures, impressions, sudden understanding, scriptures and so on.

A friend of mine who is a well-known international prophet says that sometimes it begins like the faintest impression, but as you look at it more detail will begin to appear. It is like a photo developed in a dark room. As you isolate it and close out other things that could detract from seeing it clearly form begins to appear.

LESSON
When we are faithful with little, we can be given much. So, it is good to develop a gift, this could include study from others about how the gift works.

So, we go through a little process that looks something like this; (eventually it happens automatically when we are in a situation that demands gifts)

1. Reach out for inspiration from God…. open your mind and give Him your attention. (this can be likened to 'going online' with the internet, connecting up)

2. Something comes into your mind that is not the result of conscious thought. (In other words, you did not think, *what can I come up with*, there was just something there, in the mailbox, so to speak. You have mail!)

3. The message or word is examined. If it is prophecy, you will be looking at, *what is God wanting to communicate to this person?*

4. Now you step out and bring the message/ or word. How you do this will depend on your personality, but you should be natural and not try to assume some form or 'wear someone else's armor,' just be yourself, otherwise you are not basing what you are doing on truth. If you are not trying to be falsely spiritual, the Holy Spirit will quickly take and confirm the word to the heart of the hearer.

5. The word is then received by the person and confirmed by their response whether or not it is correct and for them. Some people will have an emotional response as the Holy Spirit touches something deeply inside them.

6. Now, if received, it falls to the person to respond to the word in an appropriate way. A friend of mine puts it this way: 'If God is giving you a word to do with the plans that He has for you then you can take it as: *an invitation to become, God prophecies to your potential, it is not a done deal.*' You still have to walk with God into your destiny and at times sow into where God wants to take you, which requires faith.

Prophecy will not be condemning, it will not be demanding that you try harder or telling you that you are not doing enough, it will be encouraging, strengthening and comforting.

> *1 Corinthians 14:3 But everyone who prophesies speaks to men for their strengthening, encouragement and comfort. NIV*

Fundamentally *prophecy* is receiving a communication for a person or people from God. A *word of knowledge* is going to also be inspired information that will normally relate to a condition that the person has. This could be a physical problem, or an emotional, relational, financial, or other kind of circumstance that God is wanting to resolve. It is received in the same way as prophecy, with the differentiation that you are not looking for what God is wanting to communicate to the person, but rather what their problem is so that He can meet the need.

LESSON
Some people will be more drawn to one gift that another. This often relates to the particular 'tools' that they may need to outwork their calling.

ACTIVATIONS
We often have to '*activate*' people by getting them to give God the use of their faculties and minds, turning their attention to receiving from Him. We do this with simple exercises, taking very small steps and giving God the opportunity to put something in our minds.

STEPS TO ACTIVATING PROPHECY
1. Have your group break into pairs, preferably people that they do not know, or know well. Have them face each other, with each of them facing a wall.
2. Now you have them meet the Holy Spirit halfway, so to speak, by giving him some kind of landing pad...by giving them something fairly simple to reach out for. So, this means that they are not just standing around waiting for something to come into their mind.
For example, we ask the Holy Spirit to put a person from the Bible on their minds. Then we ask them to ask God why He put this particular character in their minds, and what is He saying about the person being prophesied over because He gave them this person.

3. We have them take it in turns sharing what they received with each other.
4. We then repeat the process asking the Holy Spirit to bring to mind items such as a scripture, could be an activation, or words of a song another, something from nature, (E.G. Jesus called Peter a 'rock' and prophesied that because of this solidness He was going to build His church on him) and so on. You can make up your own. By the time your group has done three or four activations in a row other thoughts that haven't been propagated will begin to come to mind. Eventually with practice and repetition they will be able to reach out, and God will just put something in their minds without prompting. Some will be more gifted and pick this up more quickly than others. Often once the thoughts begin to come there is a spontaneous flow of thought.

We first saw activations of this type modelled through the ministry of Faylene Sparkes

STEPS TO ACTIVATING WORD OF KNOWLEDGE

1. I will quite often ask if there are people in the meeting who have never given a word of knowledge. I will usually ask 3 to 5 people to come out the front and to line up facing the congregation.
2. I will then ask the Holy Spirit to imprint a physical complaint on their minds. It could be something like a particular back problem, or a knee injury or perhaps some kind of sickness.
3. Once they have called out the complaint that has come into their minds, *(and remember it will seem like their own thoughts, and could be words or a picture, or even feel something sympathetic in their own body)* We are then looking for detail to raise faith.
4. So, now I ask them if they have a slight leaning to one side of the building, left, or right? Once they have chosen a side, I again ask them that if they had to pick would they think the person was at the back of the meeting, middle or front.
5. Now we have the complaint and where we feel that the person might be sitting. Then we check to see if there is a sense of what gender they might be. If they don't have a leading about where they are sitting or about gender, we do not push, but most people do have a sense.
6. Now we announce something such as; there is a lady sitting down the back on this side of the building who has a kidney problem.

Over the years I have been amazed at how often following this process to activate people who have never given a *word of knowledge,* that the person and complaint is exactly there. God is faithful! Sometimes in large churches I have seen the members of the church get very excited as the subject of *the word* puts their hand up…. proving to them that gifts of the Spirit can work easily through any of them.
Nearly always everyone who participates receives a word from the Holy Spirit.

7. We have the people who have been identified come out to be prayed for by the person who received the word. The exciting thing is almost every time the person getting prayed for receives healing for their affliction.

The first time that I saw an activation of this type was through the ministry of Ron Strode.

IN THE SERVICE OR OUT OF THE SERVICE

We have just described how people might receive during a service; they could even wait on the Lord for something whilst sitting in church. Another way that you can receive from the Lord is to open your mind to *a word* before the meeting even begins. If you are a minister you can be asking the Lord for something even as you lay in bed in the morning. At times this affords time to let it develop in your mind and you may receive a great deal of detail which can release significant faith. Words of knowledge can raise faith in a meeting and open the way for a lot of healing.

> **Note:** God is not the author of disorder. You need to be submitted to the authority of the leaders in whatever environment that you find yourself in. It is important that you have permission to operate spiritual gifts in places where you are not in charge.

LESSON
Praying in the spirit as a part of your daily routine develops a sensitivity to the presence of the Holy Spirit which makes it easier to access the gifts. They are His gifts, not yours, so you need to make sure that you give Him plenty of use of your faculties to help you receive.

DISCERNING OF SPIRITS

Different people seem to have different ideas about exactly what discerning of spirits is as a gift. To discern is to recognize or find out and carries the sense of being able to distinguish one thing from another. In this context, discerning of spirits is understanding what you are looking at. *(Spirit of Understanding. Isaiah 11:2)*

This could apply to demonic influence on a person's life, or whether or not their own human spirit is cooperating with worldly or satanic precepts. We see Jesus exercising this gift, naturally seeing which spiritual influence the disciples James and John were under.

> *Luke 9:55 But He turned and rebuked them, and said, "You do not know what manner of spirit you are of. NKJV*

OTHER GIFT SUMMARIES

Here we will briefly comment on the remaining gifts in the 1 Corinthians 12 passage.
<u>Gift of faith:</u> We have already mentioned a supernatural faith that is beyond our normal faith that can be present at times.

<u>Gifts of Healings:</u> Some people consider that this applies to the fact that each individual healing is a gift, which could well be the case. There are in addition to physical healings, healing of the broken hearted, healing of relationships and so on. So, I think that healings plural may apply to these different works of the Spirit in bringing healing to different areas of the human person.

<u>Working of Miracles:</u> Some translations say the *working of miracles*; others use terms such as *miraculous powers*. In the Greek language it certainly refers to the operation of literal *dunamis* power. *(Spirit of Power. Isaiah 11:2)*

This is power that most commonly comes through the hands of a believer, and is not the result of cognitive effort. It is simply there.

<u>Different kinds of tongues:</u> This is generally accepted as a tongue that is different from your normal prayer language, and is a form of prophecy which is usually interpreted by another believer who is given the meaning of the message brought in tongues.

Stream 4 'Repentance'

Many people do not want to *change their thinking or reconsider their ways,* which as we have stated is what *repent* essentially means. They are happy being in control of their own lives and doing what they want. And yet an unrepentant heart is often a large blockage to receiving healing of any kind. *Proverbs 26:12, Galatians 6:7-8*

You can imagine somebody who reads in the Bible that drunkards will not inherit the kingdom of God, but they persist in drinking a bottle of whisky a night. Why would they be surprised if they end up with liver disease? Is that what God wants for them? No.

I have never seen God not be prepared to free someone from an emotional, physical or spiritual problem regardless of the condition of their lives. So, we are not confusing repentance with only being able to be healed if you do everything right, never sin, and are perfect. The fact that you come to God wanting His help to change is repentance. However, many do not come, being content in their own solutions and so do not receive their freedom …. or perhaps want healing so that they can get into more mischief. *James 4:1-3*

A simple example of a lack of repentance that can block God's provision is unforgiveness. Jesus clearly stated that if you will not change your thinking and reconsider your ways in terms of forgiveness of others, that you will not receive forgiveness yourself. Remember 'the message' is repentance and the promise of forgiveness goes with it.
Mathew 6:14-15, Mathew 18:34-35, Luke 24:47

WE CAN SEEK GOD FOR HIS TRUTH AND HELP TO ACHIEVE REPENTANCE

Repentance is the desire to follow God's ways not necessarily the ability within yourself to achieve it or having already attained it. Very often we need God's help to accomplish repentance, and the changing of our thinking, and reconsidering our ways is an ongoing journey. It begins with accepting the fact that we are out of order with God's ways. We confess and agree with how He sees our issue and take responsibility for our part in it.

> *2 Timothy 2:25-26* ²⁵ *In meekness instructing those that oppose themselves; if God peradventure **will give them repentance** to the acknowledging of the truth;*
> ²⁶ *And that they may recover themselves out of the snare of the devil, who are taken captive by him at his will. KJV (emphasis mine)*

LESSON
We need to be aligned with the ways of the Kingdom for the provisions of God to flow freely to us. Perhaps we could liken it to disconnecting the drainpipe from the roof of your house, and then wondering why our water tank is not full. We must have the pipe both connected, and properly lined up to receive the supply when it comes.

GOD LOOKS AT THE HEART AND ENCOURAGES US TO REPENT

> *Romans 2:4 "Or do you despise the riches of His goodness, forbearance, and longsuffering, not knowing that the goodness of God leads you to repentance?" NKJV*

We could suggest then that repentance is an attitude of the heart that God is looking for, as opposed to having no weaknesses or shortcomings. The criminal on the cross acknowledged his deserving to die for his sins. Significantly he regarded the person and power of Jesus and His Kingdom, whereas the other criminal did not. *Luke 23:39-42*

He is looking for us to choose Him as a response towards His goodness and the freedom that He brings to us. *John 5:14 + 8:10-11*

REPENTANCE AND EXPECTATION
Evangelists running healing meetings early last century would look for expectation of healing in the eyes of those coming for prayer and considered this to be visible faith. They were fairly certain in those days that those who had no intention of attending church or ever serving God need not to expect to get healed. Our hearts could condemn us because we have no intention of changing our ways or following God. *1 John 3:21-22*

Stream 5 'Sanctification'/ [Righteousness?]
As we are conformed to the likeness of Christ, as we have mentioned, we will also be conforming to the Word of God. This holds health benefits for us, for example, we no longer respond holding bitterness, resentment or unforgiveness. Instead of releasing negative hormones into our bodies, as we grow in love, grace, joy, acceptance, positive feelings and attitudes we release healthy chemicals into our bodies.
Proverbs 3:6-8 + 4:21-23, Psalm 92:13-14

LESSON
As our thinking is made Holy through sanctification, then the end of the line is our outer person or body which conforms to our thought life. Perfect thoughts, beliefs and consequent actions result in physical health.

SIN AND SICKNESS
Another element of sanctification, through receiving God's truth and conforming to His word, is knowing the truth about redemption and God's promise of healing. Sin and sickness are linked and so when we examine the scriptures, we see them both being dealt with at the same time. *Psalm 103:2-3, Mathew 9:5-6, Peter 2:24*

Stream 6 'Spiritual release'
We will cover this subject with all of Unit 5 being devoted to it. We can state here however that many problems, including the spiritual, mental, emotional, relational, sexual, addictive and often physical issues can have a demonic component.

Often what *we believe* opens the door and leads us towards giving *a place* to the devil.

> *Ephesians 4:27 nor give **place** to the devil. NKJV (emphasis mine)*

Place *in the Greek language = topos > means a location, or position. We could say by extension, somewhere to stand or to operate from. There will be more detail on this in Unit 5.*

Offering a place can be our solution to our deceptive perception of reality, and this causes us to choose the sin that the World offers. *1 John 2:15-16*

In the event that a spirit has come through a breach, via a weak mental or emotional moment, a demon may be present to hold onto this weakness. Our thinking and beliefs release hormones and neurotransmitters in order to chemically elaborate the feelings or responses to our thoughts that we call emotions. When these hormones and belief-based emotions are imbalanced then our physical self will be prone to disease. Considering that demons amplify, intensify, and replay beliefs producing emotions, we see that they can greatly accelerate, worsen and promote an environment producing the likelihood of disease and other issues.

Often, we see physical healing come when a *spirit of infirmity* (weakness) is addressed. The *ground* or *terrain* that it has many times are the deceptive *beliefs* that are held, which eventually produce disease.

Of course, disease can be present because of emotional imbalances without demonic interference, but it may not be as serious, or it may emerge more slowly as we age. Obviously spiritually influenced cultural environments such as high sugar and high fat diets, alcoholism, drugs, and so on contribute to the ability for the diseases to prosper and proliferate as the body's defenses are broken down.

Stream 7 'Truth Encounters'

Unit 4 is entirely devoted to explaining this important stream which has implications for bringing healing and freedom to all of the 7 major problem areas that afflict mankind. A *Truth Encounter* is when the Holy Spirit sets a person free from a wrong belief that is held in their *hearts*. The distinction between the *heart and mind* will be explained in the next Unit.

As we proceed to Unit 4 we will illustrate that the *heart* has beliefs that produces thoughts.

Dealing with these are critical to our wholeness in every area.
Proverbs 4:23, John 8:32, Hebrews 4:12

UNIT FOUR

Part 1: Truth Encounters: A Biblical Perspective

INTRODUCTION

When the man in Mark chapter nine brought his mute son to Jesus for freedom, Jesus asked him this question,

> *"How long has this been happening to him?" And he said, "From childhood"*
> *(NKJV, Mark 9:21).*

Another example noting beginning points would be the woman who was bent over with the Spirit of Infirmity in Luke chapter 13.

> *"And behold, there was a woman who had a spirit of infirmity eighteen years, and was bent over and could in no way raise herself up" (NKJV, Luke 13:11).*

Something happened eighteen years ago that was an entry point for the spirit, and apparently nineteen years ago she did not have the problem. It became clear to us that Jesus was looking for the origin of the issue, the *beginning point*. This indicated that there was some event or experience which was the starting place, or source and origin, for what was going on now. In other words, the *beginning point* for ministry is an individual being asked to remember and *describe* what had happened at a particular time in their lives?

Study 1: Truth Encounters and 'The Fall of man'

Why does the truth make us free? We begin by considering how man came into bondage. Every activity, good or bad, that occurs in the Earth is a result of what people *believe*. The result of their beliefs plays out in their choices and what they decide that they want to do.

For everything to work in harmony, beginning with the internal workings of our bodies and extending to our relationships with God, others and even ourselves, we require TRUTH AT EVERY LEVEL OF OUR BEINGS.

Satan continues to work very hard to prevent this from happening, opposing God's perfect ways for mankind. In *Genesis 3:1* we see the devil bring Adam and Eve under his counsel by deception. The deception came about by creating a perception about God's love, integrity, goodness and provision for them. 'Really,' implied that God was not caring and was in fact keeping something good from them. Clearly this was *not the truth*.

We can say that what we *believe* and perceive to be 'true' is the basis of all wrongful behavior and activity within the Earth today.

Activities may seem right to us and good at the time and we often justify our acceptance of wrongdoing. For Adam and Eve, this *false perception* created by Satan produced doubt and, as a result, they did not interpret the situation correctly. This *misinterpretation* led to a *conclusion*, from which they made a *decision* which produced an *action*. The action was disobedience, and rebellion against the Word of God. Throwing off Biblical laws and limits is known as sin.

We could summarize this simply by saying that sin comes through *misinterpreting the truth* of a situation and, consequently, what is actually best for us. For Adam and Eve, they saw that the tree *was* good. But in truth it was not good for them. They were much happier before, enjoying all of the many things God had given them in innocence and without guilt.

The devil continues to work in exactly the same way with humans to this day. He deceives us about who God really is and His attitude toward us, and then programs us with wrong beliefs about our own identities. Through this he manipulates humanity to serve and submit to him. His deception is behind every problem and area of suffering that is known to man. Truth then, becomes the basis of freedom from captivity; it is the basis of faith which releases all of God's provision. It is the tool that sets us free and places us back *over* the influence of the deceiver that man has submitted to and come *under*.

Study 2: Understanding the Biblical meaning of the 'Heart'

Before we can fully appreciate the ramifications of receiving truth in the processes of sanctification, healing and freedom, we first need to study where truth needs to be applied.

THE MINISTRY OF JESUS

John 16 says that "however, when He, the Spirit of truth, has come, He will guide you into all truth." NKJV, (John 16:13)

The application of this passage relates to the Holy Spirit guiding us into 'ALL' truth. All means every area that requires truth. We tend to read this as meaning doctrinal truth, revelation, and understandings for our minds. This is certainly a part of how we will know the truth that will set us free. For example, hearing the good news of Christ Jesus can bring us redemption. Renewing the minds of believers is a high priority for the modern church in an information-based world. There is no doubting that this is very important for learning and following the ways of God.

THE HEART

There is another area of our being that is however largely neglected by the modern church. This part of our person also requires truth and is often directly related to us receiving wholeness and freedom. Once He had received the Holy Spirit, Jesus announced amongst other things that He was going to 'Heal the broken hearted,' and 'set the captives free.' *Luke 4:18* What He introduced to us was meant to be the beginning of the *Luke 4:18-19* ministries for mankind and not the end. *John 20:21-22*

Jesus promised that when we know the truth it will make us free. Specifically,

> *"And you shall know the truth, and the truth shall make you free." NKJV (John 8:32)*

What is the Biblical function of the 'Heart'?

> *"And you shall love the LORD your God with all your **heart**, with all your **soul**, with all your **mind**, and with all your **strength**. This is the first commandment" NKJV (Mark 12:30, emphasis mine)*

Here are four clear and distinct areas that the Bible reveals as individual in function. In this passage your mind is also singled out and the word that it is translated from, means, your capacity and faculty to be able to reason, understand, and imagine. It has the ability of conscious thought leading to conclusions. It is very much a conscious activity and would include deliberately memorizing and voluntarily storing information. We could summarize the *mind* as your thinker or your computer which has the ability to store or access information.

We come now to what the Bible refers to as our heart. For the sake of the study, I will quote the function and operation of the *heart*, as translated from the Greek directly from the very reputable Strong's Concordance.

> *2588. kardia; **the heart**, i.e. (fig.) the thoughts or feelings (by anal.) the middle: --(+ broken-) heart (-ed) (Emphasis mine).*

It appears from the original language that the scripture is referring to a deeper area of the personality that holds thoughts which produce feelings and behavior. I am proposing that these thoughts and feelings are coming from beliefs that were once conscious thoughts or beliefs involuntarily learnt by experiences and events. They were significant conclusions or interpretations arrived at in the past that are stored or *taken* to heart. These thoughts, beliefs or feelings have usually come as a result of the programming of life, as deliberate training or experiential beliefs stemming from events.

We may no longer know them as beliefs or thoughts but rather as feelings, behavior or responses to particular situations. This is further confirmed in the Bible with the statement that the word of God is able to access this deeper place. *Hebrews 4, verse 12 states,*

> *For the word of God is living and active. Sharper than any double-edged sword, it penetrates even to dividing soul and spirit, joints and marrow; it judges **the thoughts** and attitudes **of the heart**. NIV (Hebrews 4:12, emphasis mine)*

So evidently our hearts have thoughts and attitudes that need to be discerned or judged. Our heart, or *middle* as Strong's concordance describes, has a lot to do with how we live, act and react. Might I suggest that the heart is the middle or centre of the soul, that is, the centre of the mind, emotions and will. And that most of our decisions or acts of our will proceed from the influence of these inner thoughts/beliefs and emotions.

> *"You brood of vipers, how can you who are evil say anything good? For out of the **overflow of the heart** the mouth speaks." NIV, (Matthew 12:34, emphasis mine)*

It is a principle that often the words that come out of us locates us in terms of what our inner beliefs are. In other words, often we say things that we do not consciously think through. Or if conscious thought is involved, it is influenced by what we believe in our hearts. The New Living Translation presents it in this way:

For whatever is in your heart determines what you say. NLT, (Matthew 12:34b)

Let me suggest some of the outworking's and implications proceeding from the *beliefs* held in the heart. In fact, we have found that every kind of problem known to man can be found beginning here. As a sweeping statement, this includes things that we suffer as a result of the condition of other people's hearts. This is clearly confirmed in scripture:

"Above all else, guard your heart, for it affects everything you do." NLT, (Proverbs 4:23)

Study 3: The role of memory

VOLUNTARY AND INVOLUNTARY MEMORY

Voluntary memory
One type of information is that which that we have decided to consciously learn and then retain through repetition. This could include the 10 times table or the scriptures. We could also have memory that affects us through learning from Worldly things that we have decided to expose ourselves to.

Involuntary memory
Involuntary memory is *beliefs* that you have taken into your *heart* that were not intentionally or purposefully learnt. They have been learnt through life experiences. For example, your father leaves home when you are a small child. You come to the conclusion that you are not important. You don't deliberately try to remember this. It is something that you now believe from interpreting the traumatic situation and may or may not be able to put it into words.

Identity beliefs
We could summarize that the most damaging *heart beliefs* are those that are to do with your identity, or who you are as a person. They are *self-beliefs*. They are almost always learnt before the age of 10 years old when you are deciding who you are, and this is confirmed by both science, which regards your brain as in plasticity at this age, and scripture. *Proverbs 22:6*

Remember our definition of 'the heart' as being *thoughts and feelings* from our *middle or central part*. These may come to us involuntarily through experiential learning in, for example, feelings of rejection received in a historical event, or perhaps fear, anger or inferiority learnt through life. These beliefs have become 'automatized' and so we no longer necessarily know them as conscious *thoughts or beliefs*; we may now know them as only *feelings, emotions or responses and behavior*.

Automatized thinking
As an adult, most likely if you exit your shower or bath and begin to dry yourself with a towel, it will not be a deliberate conscious exercise. You are possibly thinking about how your day will go or something else. At one time when you were learning how to dry yourself, it was a deliberate conscious effort involving your mind. Now if you involve your conscious thought with something like, "do I dry this arm or this arm next?", you might find that your minds involvement creates confusion with your processes that are now automatic. Many of our responses, actions, feelings and even sins come automatically from the conclusions and

interpretations about life that we *already* hold in our hearts. Jesus very emphatically stated that many of our actions come from the prior encoding of this deeper place. *Mathew 15:18-19, Luke 11:39*

Situational beliefs
A *situational belief* is one that has come from an event or theme in life that has programmed you to believe something which could affect how you feel about life in general. A sample of identity beliefs includes: *'I am not loved/lovable, I am worthless, not good enough, not important, I am a nothing, I don't matter,' etc. etc.*

A sample of situational beliefs includes: 'There is no one there to protect me; I won't be able to do it, I am trapped and could die, I am out of control' etc.

Repetition
At times heart beliefs are taken in through being exposed to or hearing the same themes repetitively. A Biblical example can be found with God telling Joshua five times to be strong and courageous. He seems to be saying; 'you need to meditate on this, take it to *heart*, and make it your default position, because when you see those angry guys with spears coming over the hill you will need to have your default position and response settled way down deep inside of you. Then you don't need to think about it because you have it as an *automatic* response.'

Critical moments or events
Information deeply encoded in *significant* emotional or traumatic *events*, including moments of weakness, or episodes containing fear or extreme stress, are taken to *heart* and *remain*. Most seventy-year old's will not remember what they had for breakfast on their first day of school. There is no reason for your brain to store in memory that information as it has no real bearing on your life. They may however remember beliefs recorded through interpreting events related to the anxieties of the day, and the acceptance of others in a new environment.

We have found that anything that you can remember from your childhood was a significant moment in either a positive way or negative way. Later events will only potentially confirm what you already believe about yourself or the situation. These times will be interpreted by what you hold as truth. For example, if you believe that you are not important, then events where people seem to be ignoring you will be accepted as this is happening because I *am indeed not important*.

Study 4: Grasshoppers and faith

"For as he thinks in his heart, so is he. "Eat and drink!" he says to you, But his heart is not with you." NKJV, (Proverbs 23:7)

This passage indicates that how a man sees himself will be reflected in how he lives. His beliefs may even transmit from his inner being as either confidence or timidity that can be observed.

Notice that this passage does not state as the man thinks in his mind. He has a conflict between his mental conscious choice and desire to behave a particular way, and what is going on for him in terms of his believing at heart level.

As *he thinks in his heart,* so is he. A profound old saying puts it this way: **'It's not what you think you are, but WHAT YOU THINK, you ARE!'** In other words, you will live your life according to what you think about yourself. *Proverbs 4:23*

A great example of this in the scriptures is that of the Israelites. They all agree that it is a good land that God has for them. So, what is the problem, what holds them back from entering into this promised life walking in the provision of God? It is in fact how they see themselves, and what they project about their identities that can be readily observed by those around them.

Remember, they grew up as slaves, treated as lesser human beings. Consequently, in their low self-image they saw themselves as inferior and small in comparison to their masters.

> *Numbers 13:33 "We even saw giants there, the descendants of Anak. We felt like grasshoppers next to them, and that's what we looked like to them!" NLT*

In like manner some of us grew up being told that, l*ittle children should be seen and not heard.* What we learnt through this was that we were insignificant 2nd class citizens who had no right to speak.

Study 5: 'Strongholds' and spiritual warfare

Many years ago, we were ministering through Micronesia and our host took us for a tour around the Island of Guam. He showed us the concrete bunkers that the Japanese had built before the coming battle in order to hold the ground or territory that they occupied. The Bible says in Ephesians chapter 4 and verse 7 to not give the devil a place. The Greek word translated as 'place' is the word, *topos*. It means a place, a location, a position, a spot or a home.

In much the same way as the Japanese made strongholds **before** the battle began, the devil establishes **a place** in our *belief systems* through deception and misinterpretation while we are still children.

Many people believe that when they are feeling bad or anxious that they are under some kind of spiritual or demonic attack. Most times what is actually happening is that *beliefs* that the person already holds are being stressed or triggered through the environment or situation that they find themselves in. Perhaps they are confused by Paul's later statement in Ephesians regarding wrestling spiritual powers. *Ephesians 6:11-12*

In fact, he is more likely to be making reference to the fact that, although you are dealing with humans, flesh and blood, it is the negative spiritual dynamics projecting from them onto you that is your problem. In fact, he is more likely to be making reference to the fact that, although you are dealing with humans, flesh and blood, it is the negative spiritual dynamics projecting from them onto you that is your problem. In other words, it is not the people themselves that are attacking you. It is the spirits manipulating the people through *their* areas of deception which give place and cooperation with the powers that you are actually dealing with.

Jesus floated the concept of human participation with spiritual inspiration at various times in the gospels. It is wrong believing that opens us to being potential unwitting hosts to unholy spirit. This is exemplified in the following passage:

> *Luke 9:54-55 (Emphasis mine)*, *"You do not know what manner of spirit you are of."* NKJV

Study 6: Beliefs produce feelings or what we term emotions

We have seen that the Israelites were unable to take up their destiny because of beliefs of inferiority which produced feelings of fear and inadequacy. If they had instead been programmed by life that they were equal or if they had received healing from their previous beliefs, they would have felt confident and full of faith! But alas the Spirit of truth had not yet been poured out as in our times.

THOUGHTS AND FEELINGS

A feeling or emotion is the result of a belief that has been accessed. In fact, it is your chemical bodies' version of what you believe. So, a thought or belief and feelings or emotions are one and the same. Some time ago I was reading a book where Charles Finney made the statement that *'feelings follow thoughts.'* You do not simply have a feeling because you have a feeling. It is emanating from something that you already *believe*:

- If you believe that nobody loves you, then you will feel sad.
- If you believe that no one cares about you, you may feel angry.
- If you think that there is no protection for you, your emotion will probably be anxiety.
- If you believe that you will never ever be able to be what people expect you to be, then you will feel overwhelmed and hopeless, which is the basis of endogenous depression. Endogenous meaning, having an internal origin. The Bible says it is from the heart:

> *Proverbs 12:25 says,* "Anxiety **in the heart** of man causes depression, But a good word makes it glad." *NKJV, (emphasis mine)* **[remember heart is thoughts and feelings from your centre!]**

A feeling or emotion is a chemical elaboration of a belief through the release of hormones or neurotransmitters. It is a *thought or belief* that your body makes into a *feeling or emotion* through these chemicals.

Study 7: The example of the Apostle Paul's dilemma

In *Romans chapter 7:15-25,* we see a battle going on in the 'members' or different areas of the Apostle Paul's being. This is the case for many people in the church today. Let us summarize the problem in this way. Their spirit is reborn of the Holy Spirit, a new creation, *(John 3:5-8)* so they are now connected to the Father and the Kingdom of God, but there are areas where wrong believing still has 'a place.'

Paul is not suffering from some kind of personality disorder. His Spirit is alive to, and wanting the things of God, so his mind is also committed to this course of action. However there already exists *contrary beliefs* held in his *heart* producing automatic feelings and behavior.

In order to understand this clearly, in the following verse let's make his spirit led man and mind to be in bold letters, and his 'flesh' person (which I propose is his unsanctified *heart* and body, sometimes called the sin nature, or Adamic, Carnal or fallen nature) to be underlined.

> *"I don't understand myself at all, for I really want to do what is right, but I don't do it. Instead, I do the very thing I hate."* NLT, (Romans 7:15, emphasis mine)

The problem then is the belief that is held in the unsanctified or unhealed part of the heart. The Spirit of truth has to bring truth, healing and sanctification to this belief before that area of the heart can come into harmony under the covering of the Spirit. Otherwise it will continue to contest what kind of behavior is most appropriate as a response to life situations. This appears to be the kind of dilemma that Paul was found in.

> *"For I delight in the law of God according to the **inward** man. But I see another law in my members, warring against the law of **my** mind, and bringing me into captivity to the law of sin which is in my members."* NKJV, (Romans 7:22-23 emphasis mine)

This tension between what Paul wants to do, and what his old nature leads him to do makes him miserable. Remember that Jesus clearly states that sinful behavior comes from the heart, that is the inner thoughts and feelings. King David acknowledged this as the source of his own sinful activities. *Psalm 51:5-6* His prayer was that God would create in him clean thoughts and feelings from his centre. *Psalm 51:10, Psalm 139:23-24*

> *"Oh, what a miserable person I am! Who will free me from this life that is dominated by sin? Thank God! The answer is in Jesus Christ our Lord."* NLT, (Romans 7:24-25)

Study 8: Sanctification, healing and freedom come through truth

We have already quoted the verse *that the truth will make us free.* This freedom begins by acknowledging that our captivity comes through what we believe that is not truth. Such as not understanding sound doctrine in regards to our minds but also importantly what we hold to be true at heart level. It is clear that sanctification comes through truth from God.

John says, "Sanctify them by Your truth. Your word is truth." NKJV, (John 17:17)

That is a fairly unchallengeable and straightforward statement. Our minds are renewed by truth and our hearts are healed and released from captivity to wrong beliefs in the same way. If then, sanctification comes through truth, it is fair to deduce that being guided into truth by the Spirit of truth is the way of sanctification at every level. *John 16:13*

This is why we have come to refer to this ministry as 'Truth Encounters.' It is when we have an encounter with the Holy Spirit and He reveals truth to us. He speaks to us as sheep who hear His voice and we are changed.

It appears from the Bible that the very reason for the coming of Jesus was to bring us the grace of God, and then restore us to wholeness through the truth. The ministry of the Spirit of Christ then in this era is vital in every way. *John 1:17*

Study 9: What is a Broken Heart and who are the broken hearted?

We have already identified from the Greek language in the New Testament that the heart is *beliefs or thoughts* that are manifested or matched by corresponding *feelings or emotions*. In the Old Testament the word that is translated as *heart* from the Hebrew language *Leb*, and it also relates to your centre, your intellect, will and is widely used for feelings.

The central place of motivation for your inner thoughts, which produce feelings and influence your decisions and responses, is your *heart* and the *beliefs* held there.

BROKEN?

In the Gospel of Luke chapter 4 we see the statement that the Spirit of the Lord is upon Jesus to Heal the Broken Hearted. I think that we have thoroughly dealt with what *the heart* means, but what does it mean for a heart to be *'broken?'* We have related in an earlier unit that the word heal used on this occasion also means *to make whole. Luke 4:18-19*

I think that we can deduce that if our *thinking and feelings* are not *whole* or as they were intended to be, then they are *broken* and need *healing/fixing*. We have already established that this is done by receiving truth from the Spirit of truth. The Greek word 'suntribo' translated 'broken' literally means *broken, crushed, shattered, or bruised*. This reflects the results of experiences that have impacted our identities and broken our *self-image and self-perception*.

Whether you are a little bit broken or you are completely shattered, you are still broken because you are not in the working order that the designer intended. You are not whole. The application here is relating to the state of your heart. If your *beliefs and feelings* are in any way not as they were intended to be, then you are broken. So, we are all broken hearted in some measure!

Now we can see clearly why God desires *truth in our hearts. Psalm 51: 5-6* It relates directly to our journey into wholeness and freedom from captivity in every area of our lives.

Many people have had their self-image *broken* down through negative statements and constant criticism. Others are *crushed* under the burden of expectations to perform and please others. Some have had their lives *shattered* through such traumas as physical, verbal, emotional or sexual abuse. Still more have had their sense of well-being bruised through anxiety about being loved and valued. All of the *beliefs* resulting from this treatment and programming, constitute the brokenness of the human person in *the heart*. The Greek word 'sozo', normally translated as 'saved' on examination carries a much fuller meaning. As well as saved, it includes *to be healed, to be delivered and to be made whole*.

IMPLICATIONS OF A 'BROKEN HEART' AND CAPTIVITY FOR WRONG BELIEFS

Let me outline again seven of the basic problems that assail mankind. I will not address them in detail here, but you will see that each of them is directly impacted by what we *believe*.

1. Spiritual bondage
This relates firstly to remaining unsaved and a slave to the ruler of this world. Our blindness and lack of knowledge regarding our situation keeps us submitted to this spiritual being.

2. Mental soundness
Beliefs producing fear and anxiety are tormenting and can lead to all kinds of *masking* behavior. The vast majority of mental problems that are observed begin with *beliefs* at a *heart* level with chemical imbalances being the outworking.

3. Emotional peace
If our minds and thoughts are not at peace then our feelings and emotions will also be out of order. You do not simply have an emotion; remember it is a *thought* coming from a *belief* first.

4. Relational wellbeing
If you have mental inner thought issues along with emotional damage, your responses will also be out of order in relationships, making it very difficult to have harmonious interactions.

5. Sexuality
We have even found that in order to come together fully in sexual union there are often beliefs that need to be dealt with first.

6. Addictive problems and besetting sins
Addictions are usually related to masking behavior or coping mechanisms for *heart based*, unresolved emotional issues. They are in effect our solution to our pain or anxiety which lay us open to setting up chemical cycles, associations and bondage to habits to cover our feelings.

7. Physical health
Our bodies are the end of the line in terms of our *thought life*. How you think about yourself and life will have a direct effect on your health in either a positive or negative way. The medical world tells us that around 90% of diseases have a mind, emotion, body connection.

Study 10: Physical healing through healing the broken heart

When we have a thought or belief it goes to the part of the brain called the hypothalamus. This part of the brain oversees, amongst other systems, the central nervous system and the endocrine or glandular system. These glands release hormones into our bodies that are involved in many body functions. In terms of your chemical/physical body, hormones make your world go around.

E.G. If you begin to think about your favorite food, your hypothalamus will begin to perform the relevant functions to get your body ready to eat. You may now find your stomach grumbling as the hormones involved begin to prepare your gastric system.

So, if you are thinking happy thoughts it will make you healthy, but if you have negative identity beliefs you will eventually get sick. We say that if your mind is not at peace or at ease, you are open to *dis- ease* in your physical body. *Proverbs 17:22*

> *3 John 1:2 says, "Dear friend, I pray that you may enjoy good health and that all may go well with you, even as your soul is getting along well." NIV*
>
> *Proverbs 4:20-23 "Pay attention, my child, to what I say. Listen carefully. Don't lose sight of my words. Let them penetrate **deep within your heart** for they bring life and **radiant health** to anyone who discovers their meaning. Above all else, guard **your heart**, for it affects everything you do." NLT, (emphasis mine)*

We have many stories that we can relate of physical healing coming as the result of being set free from negative heart beliefs and inner brokenness.

THE POWER OF LIFE AND DEATH

> *Proverbs 18:21 "The tongue has the power of life and death, and those who love it will eat its fruit." NIV*

This proverb suddenly becomes very powerful in its potential power to break *a heart*. For example, in its simplest form, when a child is told that they are stupid, useless or in some way inadequate, it becomes a part of the programming of the identity or self-beliefs within their hearts. The echoes of these beliefs are literally a breeding ground for negative emotions eventually leading to disease and finally premature death. Not only might they impact on the length of life, they will almost certainly have an effect on the quality of life. Fortunately, Jesus promised us that He came to set the captives free in order for us to have abundant life to the full.

If we have been crushed by negative words, it will be difficult to have a *cheerful* heart that releases healthy hormones. A *heavy heart* that has been crushed this way will load our human spirit down in its ability to empower our bodies to function properly. *Proverbs 18:14*

EVERYTHING STARTS WITH A THOUGHT

I have concluded that everything begins with a thought that is shaped by what we *believe*. The *beliefs of the heart* are most powerful in terms of their implications because we do not usually know what they are or how to rectify them without the Holy Spirit. *1 Corinthians 2:10-11*

CONCLUSION

The Bible relates that revival is something that happens in the human heart. A *revival* is when enough hearts are changed to impact a city or nation.
The Bible often refers to us in type as a temple, or even a city. The Old Testament gives us many pictures of believers being used to rebuild the broken walls etc. Meaning help restore the broken-down personalities of humanity. E.G.

> *Proverbs 25:28 "Like a city whose walls are broken down is a man who lacks self-control." NIV*

Further study on this concept can be made in the following passages: *Nehemiah, Isaiah 57:17, Isaiah 58:6-11, Isaiah 61:1-4*

PART 2: Ministering Truth Encounters

INTRODUCTION

We are going to begin to look at the practical aspects of knowing what to do to connect a person with the Holy Spirit for a 'Truth encounter.' Although we are spending a lot of time talking about the ministry, we could sum up the whole process in a couple of lines.

> We are looking to identify that which we <u>believe in our hearts</u> that is causing some kind of issue and asking God to set us free by bringing His truth to our inner parts.

This ministry is aimed at purposefully, deliberately and diligently at bringing specific areas, issues and hurts to the feet of the Father for His truth. He has said that *my sheep hear my voice*.

Study 11: Accessing the Heart via the mind and emotions

SCREENS, ICONS, PROGRAMS

For the sake of an illustration, let us imagine your conscious mind as a screen; perhaps as a television (TV) screen. In today's world there can often be up to 100 channels or more on our TV. On a normal TV set, you can only view one channel or program at a time. Your conscious mind is much like a computer in this respect, having been designed to be a sequential processor, or in other words to focus on one task at a time. In a ministry session then, we are tuning into the fear, rejection or whatever other channel in order to view and connect with it.

As we begin to concentrate on, and embrace our fear or other issues, bringing them onto the screen of our conscious minds, we will have a chemical bodily response that we call emotion or feelings. We can now begin to look for *the belief* and inner thoughts producing the emotion. Whether we present with a negative emotion and identify *the belief* producing it, or have a negative belief and let ourselves feel it, is immaterial. The important thing is that we connect them both on the conscious screen of our minds. Usually people will come presenting with negative emotions such as anxiety, fear, anger, rejection, bitterness and so on. Some people will look for help because of how they are reacting in relationships or to life. As you listen to their story or problem you will most likely hear the beliefs behind the emotions come out in words. I usually have a piece of paper or a notebook with me, and record statements that I believe may be connected to *beliefs*. Jesus said that we will hear the overflow of the heart from the mouth: *Matthew 12:34b states,*

> "... *for out of the overflow of the heart the mouth speaks.*" NIV (Emphasis mine)

DEALING WITH MULTIPLE BELIEFS

Rounding out our illustration of a television screen, let us consider the multiple channels again. Most of us have a significant number of *channels* that need to be *reprogrammed*. By way of example, someone may come presenting a problem of fear. They may have a fear of rejection, failure, flying, abandonment, or lack of protection or provision and so on. Each of these fears is a *different belief* and stem from various historical events. You can only have one of these *channels or programs* running in your conscious mind at a time. It is necessary to go through them one at a time and switch them off individually, so to speak.

We have a handful of questions that we use over and over to help people identify that which they believe. Sometimes we will be visiting fear channels, other times switching of all of the rejection or bitterness channels. On occasions we will be finding the beliefs behind sin. Some people will be very emotionally connected and receive the ministry easily. Others will have defenses and objections or be people who want to resolve their own problems with their minds and have not been able to.

COMPUTER SCREENS
Most people today have seen a computer screen. We can use this as an analogy to further examine how our conscious mind operates. On most screens are little pictures called *icons* which have some kind of symbol depicting the program that they represent. The program is in the unit stored in a deeper place. On my computers you have to click a button twice with the pointer on the *icon* to open the program. The point is that these icons connect you to programs that are there underneath whether you open them or not. In the case of operating the computer most of these are opened as a deliberate act. This is largely the case with accessing our *heart beliefs* with our *minds*.

In summary then, as a tool to help our understanding, we know that when people look to us to connect them to God for healing, we need to get them to go through the exercise of connecting, consciously and deliberately, with information that they hold in their hearts. Some are hesitant to do that and you may need to spend some time working through getting them to look at the problem, and bring it up onto the screen of their conscious mind. Quiet rooms and a one on one session are ideal for this where possible.

> **Note:** We can only minister to whatever a person is wanting help with. It is entirely up to them. God will not make them get ministry and neither should we. Our job is to offer healing if they desire it. This is between God and the person; it is not our place to judge, only to be equipped to help when possible.

Study 12: Sources of & Influences on Heart beliefs
THE GENERATIONAL PRINCIPLE

Have you ever wondered why, in a neighborhood, some of the residents are alcoholics, while others will never have a drink in their lives but are drawn like a magnet to horror movies, drugs, violence or pornography? This is the outworking of the *visiting* on the family line. The visiting in Exodus 20:5 is like a *drawing to*. On face value, it almost seems as if the father's sin in a particular area, becomes an area where the children will be tested to see if they love God and prefer His commandments and ways. Will they seek Him to be free from their sins and weaknesses? *Exodus 20:5-6, John 14:15*

POSITIONS ON GENERATIONAL PRINCIPLES
Let me give you three distorted positions that Christians often hold pertaining to generational principles:

1. It was 'all done at the cross.'
This doctrine proposes that Jesus ended the penalty of the curse and so there are now no effects on Christians. This is a *positionally* true statement. Jesus did pay for our freedom from the curse of the law; hence all of His part was *done at the cross*. But we need to know that all of these promises are under the New Covenant which is mediated and accessed by faith.

In the event that this were automatic and operative without the faith component there would be no sick Christians, no mental, emotional, relational issues, physical problems or sin addictions to be dealt with. It is reasonably obvious that this is not the case. All of these maladies one way or another relate to the curse of sin through our generations all the way back to Adam. The truth remains though, that Jesus did pay for the curse that passes through the generation lines, and largely we appropriate that provision of freedom through the ministries of the Holy Spirit. Water baptism is an ideal time to pray against dynamics coming through the family, as you are choosing to put the old life behind. *Galatians 3:13, 1 Corinthians 12*

2. All of your healing and freedom will come through dealing with generational issues.
This group has you renouncing everything that you can possibly think of. Personally, I have not seen freedom come to many people using this model. If your generational influences have become your personal sin then you need to confess, repent, be ministered to and set free. I have seen people with issues that could be easily ministered to, endlessly and fervently going through books renouncing all kinds of sins of their ancestors with no results. The truth is that Jesus DID take the penalty of that curse for you. Now by faith and through the ministry of the Holy Spirit you can be set free. Self-effort in renouncing will not yield much without Him.

3. The children eat sour grapes.
In arguing that generational influences are not relevant to Christians, people often quote the book of the major prophet Ezekiel in order to imply that generational principles are no longer in effect. *Ezekiel 18:1-3*

If these people were to look further to the same account in the book of Jeremiah, they would see a fuller explanation of this. Remember, they are both prophetic books speaking of a time to come. *Jeremiah 31: 29-34*

Clearly, the expanded Jeremiah passage refers to the new covenant of provision through faith which was established for us by Jesus. You will find this in the book of Hebrews Chapter 10 in the New Covenant directly quoting Jeremiah.

Jeremiah 31:33-34 is the same as *Hebrews 10:16-17*. We can deduce that the prophetic biblical statement that was made by Jeremiah and Ezekiel regarding 'sour grapes' referred to the covenant mediated by faith that we are now under. It was not something for their times.

HOW THEN SHOULD WE REGARD GENERATIONAL PRINCIPLES?
As we have already established, Jesus paid the price for our freedom from generational influences. We consider co-laboring with the ministry of the Holy Spirit as a part of facilitating that freedom in a person's life. Because Jesus has already paid for their release then we can now simply consider generational influences as another potential source for their problem. We are simply ministering to the *beliefs* that are now held as a result of generational factors.

When we are dealing with emotional and *heart-based* healing, regardless of the source the ministry is the same, although we may observe that the source is generational. The ministry is actually appropriating the freedom from the curse that was promised under the New Covenant.

DELIVERANCE FROM GENERATIONALLY TRANSMITTED WEAKNESSES
Although not directly related to our 'Truth Encounters' subject, I will mention here that at times, deliverance of an evil spirit can go along with ministry to generational problems.

HEREDITARY DISEASE
If you attend doctors for some kind of chronic illness or disease, they will usually ask you if it is in the family. Physiologically they may test and observe some kind of genetic predisposition for the onset of the disease. We have already previously discussed studies that propose that as many as 90% of diseases stem from emotional imbalances.
I would like to suggest, and have noted over many years, that what often actually passes through families are particular emotional problems that create an environment for that specific malady. For example, hereditary self-rejection will give opportunity for autoimmune problems to proliferate in a family line. So, dealing with rejection which has led to self-rejection will remove the predisposition for further generations to suffer. I have observed other troubles e.g. bitterness and resentment in families that suffer from illnesses such as cancer and arthritis.

EPIGENETICS AND SECULAR SCIENCE
Incidentally, modern secular science confirms the biblical generational principle. Most of that which the modern world is discovering relating to people can be found in your Bible which was written thousands of years ago by the creator of everything! It is already well documented that disease can be hereditary or generational. Epigenetics is an area of science that is stating that habits, behavior and addictions, for example, are also transmitted through the family.

The choices we make – the foods that we eat, the things that we watch – can affect how DNA is expressed. When we have kids, we pass on the sequence to them. So, if we become addicted to stuff, we can pass along to our children gene instructions that make them more vulnerable to addictions. So, take pornography addiction, for instance, since it's the fastest growing epidemic in today's church. According to a recent study, 68% of Christian men are addicted to porn. Most likely, they are unaware of the hereditary ramifications of viewing porn. It doesn't happen generally with one exposure to pornography. It's the repetitive volitional exposure to pornography that will cause this type of gene expression change to happen". Neuropsychologist, Dr. Timothy Jennings

In practice, we have usually found that the parents of men addicted to porn have also had the problem. Christians are not exempt from these principles and temptations in the World, but we do have the option of freedom. This is just one example. We acknowledge that whether we are dealing with *beliefs* that need truth, or sin problems that need deliverance or other ministry, generational sources are something that we need to be aware of.

CONCEPTION
Our next source is at conception.
In the following passage, King David ties his weakness and subsequent iniquity with Bathsheba to sinfulness that he received right at conception. Notably, in Psalm 51, verse six, he cites the solution and best defense against self-deception and sin as being *truth in the inner parts,* or *heart* as some translations render it. *Psalm 51:5-7*

As a source, I will not spend much time on conception as it is relatively unusual for a belief to be birthed right in that moment. However, it is good to be aware of the possibility. At times you may minister to someone who has always felt defiled or dirty. It may turn out that they were conceived in an event such as rape or incest. As they focus on the feeling, and belief if applicable, the Holy Spirit will set them free.

None of these sources of beginnings are places that you deliberately look for or suggest. It will usually come from the person that you are working with.

PRENATAL, 'BEFORE BIRTH'

I have digressed a little here and there but we are looking to find the beliefs that we hold in our hearts that are not God's truth or perspective. In the case of taking in beliefs *prenatal* or while we are still in our mother's womb, we need to realize that these *beliefs* were initially feelings. Later, when we have words, we can describe the feelings with words. The words are a verbal explanatory version of the feelings or emotions and are one in the same. There is a great deal of science and evidence that indeed a child is impacted by that which both the mother *and* father are thinking and doing whilst the child is still in the womb. *Luke 1:41*

This is an area that you may commonly find yourself ministering in. Again, it is vital that you do not suggest this as the source. When you have exhausted all other possibilities of where beliefs may have begun, and there are no memories then this is a *possible* source. There are other reason why people may not have memories, such as repression or dissociation.

A feeling of not being wanted in a prenatal setting may later be described in words as the belief that no one wants you or perhaps that you are unacceptable. Put simply, rejection is non-acceptance. I have noted, over the years, some predictable beliefs emerging when a child is not accepted when they are known by the parents to be present: 'I don't belong, I am an intruder, I shouldn't be here, I am not wanted, I am not loved, in the way...etc.' There of course can be other reasons coming from memories and events that can cause you to hold those same beliefs.

OTHER KINDS OF BELIEFS FROM PRENATAL INFLUENCES

It is very much the case that we can receive any kind of belief that the mother is feeling. If a father has left the mother because he found out that she was pregnant, she will most likely feel she is not *important* or valued. The child may grow up believing that men will not be there for them and that they do not value you or treat you *as important* or valuable. This is likely to be a possible root to behavior such as *extreme self-importance* and is behind issues such as narcissistic attitudes. The point is that we can be very vulnerable to the thoughts and feelings of our parents in the prenatal setting.

KEEPING IT SIMPLE AND HELPING LOCATE A PERSON CLOSE TO THEIR BELIEFS

Whether prenatal or from another source, as ministers, you can make an educated guess as to what a person may have been thinking in a given situation or circumstance. You can propose what might be believed, and offer it as a suggestion. People actually know what they feel if they are honest. They will either say *yes, I do, no, not really, or that's close, but it is more like this or this!* You have simply landed them near their belief. People come to you to help them identify whatever it is that they believe is causing their problem. Basing your suggestions on what you would expect could be reasonably taken in as a belief can make a session dramatically shorter.

A FINAL NOTE IN RELATION TO PRENATAL MINISTRY IF IT PRESENTS AS THE SOURCE.

Spiritually, God intended for us to be accepted, valued, received and loved right from our very beginnings. A rejective spirit is from another kingdom which is not the kingdom of God. In the event that our commencement to life and relationships was under rejection there is often a spirit there which also needs to be dealt with.

> **Important Note:** I never think about evil spirits when I am ministering in a Truth Encounter. I am focused purely on finding the beliefs. If there is one present, after studying Unit 5 you will become aware that it is involved. Don't go looking for spirits. The spirit is usually involved in the sinful responses or reactions to the hurtful belief. Once the hurt is resolved the person no longer needs or wants to respond in this way, which is a gift of repentance. (2 Timothy 2:25 KJV)
>
> Examples of this could be issues such as; bitterness, unforgiveness, rebellion, pride, self-pity, anger, ungodly control, fear and so on. Any of these issues can be present with or without demonic stronghold or amplification.

Study 13: Memory

Most of the time when we are helping people, and indeed the majority of their problems, are going to be found in *beliefs* learnt or interpreted as *conclusions about their identity* stemming from situations found in their *memories*. We will therefore examine how these *beliefs* may be deposited in the *heart*.

Some people question whether or not accessing memory in a ministry setting is a valid activity. If I asked most people what John 3:16 says, they would quickly respond; 'God so loved the World....' How do they know this? They remember it. How to find your way home, sit on a chair, speak, or do anything at all, is based on learning and remembering. Memory is therefore related to every single action that we perform, including breathing.
Some people say that you shouldn't spend your whole life looking into the past. I agree that we should be moving on and working for the Gospel. But we also need to set aside specific times where we deliberately deal with issues from our past.

In terms of negative beliefs and emotions, it is a critical part of the healing process. The initial memory where a belief is taken in, is the place with the most detail for accurately examining and i*dentifying the conclusion and consequent belief* from the circumstances taken to heart.

It is good to note that memory does not simply relate to the past, it also has implications for the future. For example, if someone has had an event where they were perhaps publicly embarrassed, they will now be on the lookout for potential places or situations where this could happen again. This will then be a source of low-grade anxiety and will often be present in gatherings. All fears or responses to particular stressors have their beginnings in memory of some kind. The possible exception to this may be a fear that has passed through the generation line.

CRITICAL EVENTS
The first time that we do anything is a significant moment in terms of encoding information about how we perceive that activity. Our early impressions of how we perform in areas such as the school environment for example, are a common place of memory where people arrive in a session. How our parents and teachers regarded and assessed our efforts will affect the way in which we view our person and ability to perform and meet requirements. This certainly has impact when we are deciding about our *identity* as a child, and while our brain is plastic and impressionable.

TRAUMAS AND EPISODES

A number of years ago we were conducting our healing school and a Chinese lady came into the session with her husband. All the way through the teaching she would cough every few seconds, not being deliberately disruptive, just unable to prevent it. The next day she made an appointment to be on the ministry list to receive some help. As we interviewed her it came to light that she had been in an accident her chest was being crushed, and this was the beginning point for her coughing. She was a very brave lady and connected with the *fear belief* proceeding from the trauma, which was as I recall; *I am going to die*.

As she remembered the event and connected with the belief and feeling, we invited the Lord to bring His truth. In this instance, because she was connected with the event, a spirit of fear of death was exposed and manifested, and then came out. At the same time God communicated to her regarding the trauma belief. She was free and sat quietly throughout the day, finally testifying to her healing in the evening service.

EPISODES

By *episodes*, I am referring to individual events where beliefs were the conclusions arrived at in that critical moment. For example, sexual or physical abuse which are usually extremely traumatic in nature. Your parents, forgetting to pick you up for school, might be a one-time episode where you conclude that *you're not important, and really don't matter*. But it may not be traumatic, because even though you are feeling hurt because of the omission, you are having a great time with the other kids in the playground.

SEXUAL ABUSE

To be abused sexually is a traumatic episode which can affect many areas of the personality. From the damage and brokenness involved, there emanates rejection, fear, confusion, degradation and low self-image. This could range from being touched by a friend of the family or relative right through to penetrative sex with a small child. Having ministered to a great many of these victims, I can offer hope that God will faithfully set you free. I also offer a list of possible beliefs that are commonly present with people who have been offended against in this way.

Inferiority
I am dirty, unclean, not like other people, ruined, a nothing, or, I'm bad.

Confusion
I am overwhelmed, and don't know or understand what is happening.

Guilt
Somehow this is my fault. I have done/caused this.

Insecurity
People cannot be trusted, there's nobody to protect me.

Fear
This can be in the form of being overwhelmed physically and emotionally and not understanding what is happening. Beliefs such as; *I cannot cope, it is too much to bear, I am trapped, overpowered*, may also be present.

REPETITIVE THEMES

God Himself encouraged repetition as a means of making our beliefs permanent memory, or our *default position*. For example, we recall Joshua being told five times to be strong and courageous. In other words, meditate on your responses until they are an automatic neural pathway. God is saying here that you need to set up a *default position on* how to react when you are under attack. Then, you no longer need to think it through, it is already decided who you are and how you are and for that matter how God views you. Repetitive themes from childhood, when our brains are *plastic,* malleable, and particularly impressionable, become long term beliefs that we hold. Many people have only ever experienced criticism and disapproval, being programmed over and over again with their shortcomings and failings. *Deuteronomy 6:6-9*

In defense of all parents I would like to add that most fathers and mothers love their children. They would not deliberately hurt their families and would certainly have done things differently if they had understood the ramifications. In some measure the church is responsible for having failed to teach its members how to protect their children in this vital area.

UPGRADE INFORMATION
We don't want to confuse the healing of our *heart beliefs* with the renewing of our minds. There are many things that we learn through life that are not deeply recorded. We are talking here about areas such as *identity beliefs*. This is for God to free us from. But if we simply have wrong beliefs about how to do life then receiving improved information will renew our minds.

Let me say here that most of the changes in how we live and see things come to us through reading our Bibles or hearing the word taught. If this were not so, then why would we even bother to preach and teach. All that we are talking about here relates to areas and issues that we cannot overcome through better information.

There is a great old story of a lady who was cooking a roast. Her friend was watching her and asked her; *why do you cut the roast in half before you put it in the oven? The lady replied; I actually don't know, my mother always did it that way so I will have to ask her!* When the question was presented to the mother her response was; *Oh, I only have a small oven, so I have to cut it in half, but you have a big oven and that is not necessary for you!*

The lady just received better information on how to do life. To keep this ministry in balance and perspective, there is still a preeminent place for Biblical advice (Counseling) and Bible teaching.

Study 14: Types of Beliefs

Other ministries use different names for identifying types of beliefs. Over 20 years of working in this area we have found that they commonly fall into one of the following categories. It helps to know what type of belief you are dealing with because you then understand the kind of circumstances in a memory that you are looking for, and whether it relates to how you perceive yourself, or more how you regard a certain situation.

IDENTITY BELIEFS - ABOUT SELF
Identity beliefs relate to that which you perceive about who you are and how you are. Rather than a lengthy discourse let me suggest some common beliefs reflecting how one's identity is seen:

"I'm not loveable, I'm unacceptable, not enough, less than others, stupid, a nothing, dumb, ugly, a failure, a loser, useless, weak, I don't matter, am not important" and so on. Notice that they are all beliefs relating to your identity, they are about 'self.'

Sample story

Imagine someone who has come to you is reporting how much anxiety they are going through. How I would deal with it may run something like this;

Fred: I have a terrible problem with anxiety.
Me: Can you give me an example of how it affects you?
Fred: I was at work the other day and heard the main door behind me open; I had an anxiety attack and reached for my pills.
Me: If you stop and think about the situation for a moment, what was it that you were worried about when you heard the door open?"
Fred: Thoughtful pause; Mmmmmm...I was nervous that it may have been the boss.
Me: And if it was, what are you worried about happening?
Fred: He may have come over and looked at my work!
Me: And if he did, what do you think could happen?
Fred: He might tell me that it was no good.
Me: I am sure that that is not a good feeling. I want you to close your eyes and feel what it is like for him to tell you that your work is not good enough, and let your mind connect you with other historical places where you have felt just like that.
Fred: Pause; I have just remembered that when I was in kindergarten, I was doing a painting with some other kids and the teacher was coming along looking at everyone's work. The first person was Mary and the teacher said that Mary's painting was so creative, and then Johnnie's was so neat and all in the lines. When she saw mine, she said, it was the biggest unrecognizable mess that she had ever seen in her life!
Me: As you look at that criticism and rejection, I want you to look for the conclusion and belief about yourself that you came to.
Fred: With some emotion; I'm useless, not as good as others.
Me: Let's ask the Lord what He considers to be true about you being useless and inferior. Just concentrate on those beliefs and feelings and listen.
Fred: Pause; He said, why would He have called and chosen me if I was useless. He said that all of His children are created equal, they have different gifts but none are better than another. I have just remembered that I was the best reader in the group!
Me: So how do you feel about people discovering that you are useless and not as good as them now?
Fred: Honestly, I feel that I am fine just as I am. And I am just the same as everyone else, the same only different, different in a good way, unique!

Identity beliefs also have a bearing on our relationships and how we respond, react to, and deal with others. They also reflect on how we relate to ourselves, and ultimately God.

SITUATIONAL BELIEFS

As the name suggests, these are beliefs which have come out of a situation and may or may not relate to your identity. Phobic beliefs fall under this category. An example of this type of belief might be something such as having panic attacks in small spaces where you feel captive, such as an elevator. As you focus on the feeling you might, for example, identify that the anxiety about small spaces might be that you will not be able to breath. As your mind does a data match with other places holding those feelings you remember as a small boy playing football at school. You managed to get hold of the ball and five or six boys jumped on you and held you down. In that moment you were crushed, trapped and struggled to breathe. As you focus on the situation, we ask you what will happen if you can't get away and breathe. The response is; "I can't breathe, I am going to die!"

There is nothing here relating to identity, it is all to do with the situation. As we have the person embrace the *fear feeling and the belief* that they are trapped, can't get away, and are going to die because they cannot breathe, we ask God for His truth.

OBJECTION BELIEFS

These are beliefs where for some reason there is an objection held that stops the person from proceeding to the memory or receiving from the Lord. At times people will come into a session and you can observe that they are very tense. Sometimes I will simply suggest something along the lines of; *do you believe that you won't be able to do this ministry?* or *Are you afraid that I will be disappointed if you cannot do this?* They often look a bit surprised but respond with a ready; *Yes! How did you know?*

We need to deal with the fear of failure memory first. This may be a place where they may have disappointed someone by not being able to do what was expected, or perhaps a place where everyone else could achieve and they could not, or something similar. These types of beliefs will prevent them from entering fully into a ministry session because of fear of failure.

GOING TO THE DEEP PLACE WHERE THE BELIEF RESIDES

This ministry can be carried out anywhere and at any time. For the best possible results, I find that a quiet room, in preferably a one on one situation affords the person receiving ministry the best possible opportunity to concentrate without distraction. I do remember situations such as ministering to a man who was suicidal on the side of a very busy street. There were noisy cars and motorbikes' roaring past, but the man seemed to be unaffected, and to my amazement, was able to focus on the source of his pain and receive his freedom. Normally we try to have a quiet room. Having heard their story and made a few notes about areas that may need ministry I encourage them to go to what I call, *periscope depth*. In other words, close their eyes, shut out the outer world and concentrate on the inner deeper place of the *heart*.

SECONDARY MEMORIES HOLDING THE SAME BELIEFS

Often people will not go directly to the first memory where the belief was interpreted and encoded. For example, someone who believes that they are not as good as other people may have memories later in life or even recently that seemed to confirm this thinking. Ultimately, as we have previously stated, their *identity beliefs* will have begun before the age of 10 years old.

Very commonly, the beginning point for a ministry session, is the report of the subject having been triggered in a relationship or particular situation. In the event that the emotion from the belief is strong in the current relationship, but not so strong in the initial memory, you can have the person switch backwards and forwards from the strong feelings from the present time to the event held in memory state. This will help to identify and accept the accuracy of the thoughts and feelings coming from the original source.

COMMON BELIEFS, DIFFERENT PERSONALITIES

After a period of time doing this ministry, you begin to find repetitively that there are some very common beliefs that people hold and you deal with over and over again. What does change is the differing personalities of the people that you are working with. Some people are very emotional while others have little emotion and are largely cognitive, mind-based people.

The key to the healing is identifying the belief, not the degree of the emotion. Someone who experiences feelings intensely may struggle with emotions daily. A more stoic person may simply get on with life but have issues, such as anxiety, or belief-based behavior such as the need to succeed, being regarded, or being right. The emotional person may have a dramatic time in the ministry session and express a great sense of relief and freedom.

The more cognitive person may only feel enough to identify and resolve the belief. They may not report much more than that the belief no longer feels true. Just because they lack the euphoria does not mean that they are not free. They are more likely to experience what has happened in terms of how they see life, their sense of peace and wellbeing, and notice that old responses and reactions have disappeared when certain stressors are present.

WAYS IN WHICH WE REMEMBER
1. Emotionally:
Fear, anxiety, rejection, grief, unworthiness etc. We access memory by connecting with the initial places that hold these feelings.

2. Pictures:
Memory events from very early life may just be a vague impression rather than a clear picture. Some people have incredibly vivid memories with amazing recall of detail. This can relate to the level of trauma and corresponding strength of the picture. Some people can have memory pictures that are not connected to emotions. They may have pushed the emotions down because they are too frightening or painful to look at.

3. The body:
(Somatic) headache, stress, breathing, tension, stress, muscles, nausea, aches and pains, etc. Have you ever had that sick, dread feeling in the pit of your stomach? This is a probable body memory connecting you to a belief learnt in a previous situation. In a ministry setting you would have the person focus on this feeling and look for other places where they may have felt the same.

4. Senses:
Smells, sounds, taste, and touch etc. A commonly used example of this is music from your past which may make you feel happy or sad. The song is associated with a time in your life which may have been positive or negative. It may relate to bringing you to a visual event that contains something significant. Some people do not like to be touched or hugged. It connects them to times where touch may have meant something negative. You can have them focus on the thought of being touched and this will often bring a memory to them which contained these feelings.

5. Words:
Some phrases or unkind nicknames may be joined to unpleasant memories that are to do with the shaping of heart beliefs.

Sample questions
As you begin to work in this ministry, or even examine your own thoughts, you will find that there are only a certain number of questions available to use and I suggest some here. You can of course be creative and come up with your own.
"What will happen if … ?" (e.g. …'you have to fly overseas').

> **Note:** We call fear the what if spirit! so what will happen if? is a good basic question for fear, anxiety, stress or insecurity. (Fear is the expectation of something negative happening)

"How does it feel to think that...?" (e.g. ...'there is nobody to protect you').
"How does this make you feel ... ?" (e.g. ...'to think that you don't matter').
"Why do you think ... ?" (e.g. ...'no one cares about you').
"What does this mean about you ... ?" (e.g. ...'that everyone else is able to succeed').
"What does it make you ... ?" (e.g. ...'if you are the person who is ignored').
"What do you believe is true about you ... ? (e.g. ... if someone has perhaps, learnt that they are stupid in an event).

Typical belief samples
Fear: "This or that could happen!"
Anger: "They don't care about me!" "This is not how things should be!"
Rejection: "Nobody wants me, I don't belong, am not a part of this."
Stress: "I can't cope!" "It's hopeless." (Depression)
Sadness: "I am not loved."
Rebellion: "It's not fair!"
Performance anxiety / inferiority: "I cannot do what others can do, or what is expected."
Insecurity: "People aren't doing what they should be doing."
Bitterness / resentment: "I will not forgive them for what they have done" or at times, "what they have not done that they should have!"

All of these kinds of perceived beliefs affect relationships and often produce sin responses and reactions.

THE DEMEANOR OF THE MINISTER
If you are going to be effective in this ministry you will need to become a good listener. Slow to speak and quick to listen is great wisdom. You hear what a person is saying to gather information and note cues that may point to beliefs. In addition, you are looking to God for prompts, inspiration and information. If you are not yet mature as a Christian, or indeed free from your own issues, you may have a need or tendency to be vocal about all that you know and think. This may not inspire the vital trust that is needed for a person to share their most intimate details. The need for confidentiality is absolutely critical.

POSITIONING
The most important area of any healing or freedom ministry is to have the person aligned to receive from the Lord. Jesus taught about the Kingdom of God before He ministered. It is vitally important that people understand what the issue is, and what God offers in terms of resolving your problem. Therefore, explaining or teaching about the ministry is key. This can come in the form of your own explanations, a work up book, video or audio teaching.

We have found that God will not usually override a person's free will and choice. Consequently, He will only do for people that which they want and choose. This can be frustrating for some new ministers. They can see the answer to the problems and try to push people to deal with their issues. Jesus only ministered to those who came to Him. Given that He was preaching repentance, and many did not want to reconsider their ways or change their thinking about their lifestyles, possibly many did not come. Our job is to teach what God has made available as best we can, and then be equipped to serve Him in helping those who come.

COMMON REASONS WHY PEOPLE MAY NOT COME FOR MINISTRY

1. Ignorance
They simply do not know about this opportunity for freedom or they have received a distorted picture of it from some source.

2. Fit
It does not fit into their theological or ministry method framework.

3. Pride
Pride is the most common reason. Many people are full of their own opinions and views. Having some knowledge, they become *puffed up.* (Proverbs 26:12) They want to fix the problem themselves without help from others, working it out in their own minds. Remember the Pharisees who considered themselves above the common sinners. Jesus at one time rebuked them for searching the scriptures because they thought that the written word alone would provide eternal life. *(John 5:39-40)* Pride says, *I will fix me! in a sense, following on from the temptation in the garden to be as or like God!*

4. Control.
We have already discussed that many people want to be in absolute control of their lives. For some of these persons, to be able to trust another with the deep things of their lives is very difficult.

5. Fear.
There are those who are simply too afraid of what might happen, what you might think about them, or what they may have to face to consider opening up for help.

6. Denial.
Some people simply will not accept they have problems, or they may have a part in faulty relationships. These people expect that their own emotional well-being would be fine if everyone around them did what they think they should be doing.

SHOPPING LISTS

By the time a person has listened to teaching on Truth Encounters or has done a work up session, they should have a basic understanding of the ministry process. Many by now may have noteworthy memories coming to them. Anything that is a memory is significant or it would not be remembered to begin with.

We now ask the person to begin to put on their shopping list the areas that they may suffer with and are looking for freedom in. This can be known problems, such as never feeling that they are worth anything, or perhaps a fear of storms, or it can be a set of reactions that they have to specific situations or in current relationships.

We can summarize the areas of responsibility in the sessions along these lines;

Our part:
- To teach or instruct them in understanding the ministry.
- To help them identify and clarify the beliefs in their hearts.

The person's part:
- To be willing to seek out and note their issues.
- To be prepared to embrace and accept their beliefs, emotions and memories.

The Holy Spirit's part:
- To guide and inspire the minister and the person in the session.
- To reveal God's truth and bring freedom.

WAYS THAT GOD MAY COMMUNICATE WITH PEOPLE

An old saying says that *God talks how you listen.* He made your brain and soul exactly how He intended it to be. Some people think in words, others in pictures or impressions; let me offer some of the common ways that God might communicate truth to you.

1. In words:

I tend to think in words, so mostly when God uses my mind to communicate truth to me it comes in words. Interestingly I have noticed that as I have become more and more free that I also receive pictures and impressions at times either for myself or others. Some people get stuck here because they are waiting for flashes of light and a booming voice, or an audible word from outside your body. I explain it this way. My computer is set up with the fonts, letter styles, writing size and so on that I like. If I were to give it to you and ask you to write me a note, when you returned it to me, I might exclaim; *that is just my writing!* That's true; you just used my faculties or equipment to communicate your message to me.

In the ministry room, having identified the heart belief, I simply encourage people to let their minds go. When they hear something, occasionally people might explain that it just seemed like their own thoughts, but they heard this or that. We test and see whether or not it is God by looking at the old belief. Perhaps a person may have always thought that they were dumb. It felt true to them. Now they look for the belief and cannot find it, or it is no longer true; it has always been true to them, but it is now gone.

2. Pictures or impressions:

Many people think in pictures. I remember a man who was suffering from a rejection belief of some kind. When this man spent time with his own children, he would put his face up against their face as a sign of love and affection, indicating acceptance and connection. The man was focusing on his belief and feeling that he was rejected, and God gave him a picture, an impression of the Heavenly Father putting His face against the mans. Needless to say, he was deeply touched and moved, now set free from the knowledge of Gods affection for him.

3. Scriptures:

Very often the Holy Spirit will use a scripture that people know well in their *minds* and apply it to issues and beliefs present in their *hearts.*

4. Realizations:

An example of a realization could perhaps be that of a child coming into a room where mother and father are having a heated argument. In that moment the child believes that it is somehow their fault. Looking back and exploring the memory through the eyes of God they now realize, as they see more of the picture that was not as emotionally intense, that the parents were already fighting before they entered the room. So, how could it be their fault? God will at times bring freedom in this way through realization. I have also seen at times people being set free at the moment where they realize why they believe what they believe, and where it came from, and for them that is the healing.

5. Sensations, feelings, knowing:

God is indeed very creative in how He communicates with us. Some people report simply feeling love. Still more, report that they just *know* that the beliefs they held are not true. I remember asking one lady after a session what she now thought of God. She thought about it for a moment, and then replied; *He's clever, He's very clever!* Amen. Our God is indeed very clever.

6. Through our senses
One lady that we ministered to had come with the presenting problem of struggling to believe God for provision. She was actually a woman of great faith in most areas of her life. However, as a child she was never sure that they were going to have food to eat, and the belief that she took to heart as a result of that anxiety was at the root of the problem. Immediately after we asked God to communicate His truth to her, she asked a question; *who has got the bread? I can smell bread!*

After assuring her that no one had bread I asked her what the smell of bread meant to her. She reported that it meant that; *there will always be enough.* For her this resolved the issue, and as a result of her new expectations of God providing, over the next few months her family situation changed dramatically. Through our senses seems to be a much less common way that God uses, but it happens from time to time.

WARNING
Many ministries have gone off the rails and brought the ministry into disrepute by suggesting how God should communicate with them. For example, I have heard of people suggesting to picture Jesus in the memory. This is potentially a recipe for disaster, licensing possible deception. I have had people report seeing Jesus in their memories perhaps two or three times in 20 years of ministering *Truth Encounters.* Even these were many years ago, and I cannot be sure that they had not been exposed to other ministries who practiced this and, as a consequence, thought that this was what was expected.

Study 15: Problem areas that you may periodically encounter

CONSCIOUS OBJECTIONS
We have already discussed that some people will simply not want ministry for some reason; they might propose that they are a new creation so there is nothing left to do, and point to the finished work of the cross. If you cannot help them negotiate these conscious objections then you simply acknowledge their free will and choice.

Some ministers feel that now that they see the problems for what they are, and know the answer, that they need to push people to go to God for healing. God Himself does not force anyone to do anything; it is not in His nature. We see this in how Jesus dealt with the disciples recognizing their free will and choice. *John 6:66*

SUPPRESSION
If you suppress something then you restrain, subdue, repress, or hold it back; like a sneeze, a cough or a yawn, at an inappropriate moment. When we are talking about suppressing memories, we are saying that you have chosen to not permit yourself to look at it for some reason. Perhaps it holds guilt, shame, rejection or some other unsavory emotion in it. So, we restrain it from coming onto the screen of our minds, pushing it back, as a willful act denying it, and eventually over time, we have repressed it to where we can no longer readily access it. The neural pathway that connected us to the event has gone from a strong four lane highway with street lights, to a broken-down potholed dirt track. It is now barely

accessible, and we do not want to go to it in any case.

Usually if people have chosen to remember memories no more as an act of their will, then to see those pictures they now *have to choose* to see them again. They are still there, in storage, it is just that the connection to them has become weak.

DISSOCIATION

I have a wrist watch that has written on the back of it, Waterproof to 30 meters. I have often wondered what happens at 31 meters when the pressure becomes too great. Theoretically at least the outside circumstances become too great for it to deal with and it is overwhelmed, crushed, and broken. *Proverbs 18:14*

Not being able to cope with, or bear a situation, can cause the mind to overload and disconnect from the event. Modern homes often have a circuit breaker on the electrical system in case the wiring is overloaded and damage might occur. If this looks like happening, it simply breaks the connection that allows the power to flow into the situation. Mentally we seem to have the same kind of protection in our wiring. If something is happening to us that we cannot bear, then the mind disconnects or dissociates from what is going on.

There is generally some kind of fear or overwhelming belief that prevents the person from connecting with the memory such as: *I will be out of control, I will die, I won't be able to cope, it's hopeless, it's too much to deal with, I cannot let it be true,* and so on. These beliefs need to be dealt with before the person will allow themselves to connect with and enter into the memories.

PERSONAS, MASKS AND DENIAL

The Pharisees and teachers of the law adopted a religious image which presented themselves as Holy men who were right with God. Many people who feel that they are not good enough as they are, will adopt some kind of mask or persona that they feel will make them acceptable.

You need patience and love to have them trust you sufficiently to take the mask off and own their inadequacies. These images often are not based on truth in regards to who they really are.

Denial and self-justification are another possibility for hindrances to helping people receive ministry. If they feel that they have, for example, *every right to be angry,* then they will not be prepared to look at what it is in their lives that has been tapped into producing the response. Many people deny that they have any issues at all. It is everyone else that is at fault! As the saying goes; *everyone is messed up except for you and me, and now we mention it, I am not that sure about you!*

IS THIS COUNSELING?

We do not consider this type of ministry to be counseling. We are not giving instructions regarding efforts that people should undertake to resolve their problems. We simply teach them about what God will do for them if they want to receive from Him. Then, if they choose to connect with the beginnings of their presenting issues, we assist them in defining that which they believe in their hearts. Rather than this being something that they can do, these sessions are all about letting God do what He promised to do in setting them free.

FLOW CHART
The ministry process:
A person comes to you with a problem. This could be a mental, emotional, relational, addictive, spiritual, sexual or physical issue.

↓

They may have been *set off* or *triggered* by a life situation producing for example: anxiety, anger, sadness, bitterness, resentment, guilt, inferiority, rejection and so on.

↓

Your role is to help them focus on these feelings and reactions and to identify the beliefs which they believe at *heart* level, and which they may no longer immediately consciously access.

↓

The key components that you are trying to connect here are: The emotions, the beliefs producing the emotions, and the matching memory pictures. (No pictures prenatal, perhaps a feeling or a sense of something)

↓

You have them focus on the presenting feelings and using questions help them to discover the beliefs producing the emotion, OR

↓

If they have a belief, such as, *I just never think that I am good enough*, have them connect with the feeling that should be associated with such a thought. (The emotion often comes up as the story is related or the memory is accessed and described.)

↓

Request that they let memories come to them or willfully look for the memory picture, if they don't already have it, which contains the thoughts and feelings. (With some pictures that are remembered, it is not always immediately obvious as to why the beliefs have been interpreted here.)

↓

Having refined and identified the belief that was learnt, invite God to bring Truth. (You can be creative in how you request this to avoid being repetitive, but using phrases such as, *Lord, would you like to show Fred how you see this situation? Lord, would you touch Fred by revealing your Truth to replace what he perceives as the truth here? Lord, what would you like Fred to know about the belief that he holds?* and so on.)

I offer this guideline as an example of how a ministry could flow, to help with what you are looking for, where you are looking, and how you look. In practice it all happens quite naturally and organically as you listen to a person's story and ask questions when appropriate. The Holy Spirit really will inspire your thoughts. When you first begin, feeling like you don't know what to do is a common, expected part of stepping into something new.

REVISION AND RECAP
1. As you begin to minister to people struggling with spiritual bondage, mental disorder, emotional, physical, or relational issues what is the main thing that you are looking for?
   Answer – You are trying to identify root heart beliefs that the person generally is not consciously aware that they believe.

2. What will these beliefs relate to?
   Answer – These will mostly be in regard to perception of identity and beliefs about SELF. At times these will be beliefs connected to certain situations or circumstances.

3. Where will we find these beliefs?
   Answer – The beginnings of identity beliefs will be found in memories consistently before the age of 10 years old. Many times, some of the negative beliefs that a person holds have been interpreted or concluded in the womb. Most beliefs relating to traumatic or emotionally charged situations will usually also be found in the formative years when we're most vulnerable.

4. Which memories will be the most significant?
   Answer – The initial memories, or the first time that something was believed. After the belief is in place it is used to interpret later events. For example, once you been rejected and believe that you're not good enough for some reason, you will conclude that any further rejections are for the same reason, based on what you already believe.

5. What is a 'qualifying statement?'
   Answer - A qualifying statement is the reason that we believed what we believed in the memory. In fact, it is often why we need the initial or first memory. For example, "I'm a bad person <u>because</u>" …. of whatever you did in the memory. It explains why you believe what you believe. (As opposed to believing in your heart that you're a bad person, but not really knowing why. It gives the reason for your perspective and consequent deception. Once you know you can then be set free by Gods truth.)

6. How do you begin a ministry session?
   Answer –
   A)   We make sure that the person understands the ministry process.
   B)   We listen to their story and note heart-beliefs that may be evident.
   C)   We ask about their issues, or current troubling events.

7. How do we find what these beliefs are?
   Answer –
   A)   we have the person embrace thoughts and feelings and look for matching memory events in early childhood. Pre ten years old. (If there are no memories it may have a prenatal origin, or there could be suppression or disassociation)
   B)   We ask questions to help them identify what they believe.

Steps to a ministry session
Let me present three common access points, or pathways to initial memories that a person may come in for ministry presenting with:
1. They may already have a memory with negative or unresolved content. If this is the case the memories can be directly accessed and explored. The person is attempting to connect with the feelings that were present and identify what was believed about their identity. (Or possibly the situation)

2. They may have something in their current situation that is a stressor, or trigger mechanism. It's a present time event that produces negative reactions, feelings, or responses. Usually some kind of relational conflict, or anxiety. It taps into existing beliefs that were taken to heart in early memory events. They interpret the current event through whatever is already believed.

3. They may have something negative that they have always known that they have believed or felt about themselves (identity) or certain situations. They need to search for the memory where they learnt this

WHERE TO FROM HERE?
In many of units after unit 5 of this publication, I examine being able to discern or understand where the different types of beliefs that are producing specific feelings, attitudes or responses are coming from. Some of these issues are matters such as rejection, rebellion problems, low self-image, fear and so on. At the end of each of these, I will attach scenarios of typical cases relating to those particular issues. In Unit 5 we will study the ways in which spiritual influences interact with, and are implicated, and connect with beliefs.

When are influences spiritual? Always. We are primarily spirit beings in a spiritually manipulated world. So, we are going to try and clarify how this affects us. for

UNIT FIVE

Principles for understanding demons or evil spirits

Study 1: Spiritual dynamics and setting the captives free

We do not go into a ministry session looking for demons, generational problems or entry points from any other source. If we come from a *methods*, or t*his is what you do, follow this process* type training, we will often gravitate to being directive and preempting what the problem might be. I have seen ministries that work through a particular list of *demons*, or *we break this or that* as their standard ministry model, and, many times, they see very few or limited results.

We begin with *what is your problem?* Along the way we may become aware of demonic power being involved. Even when these spirits are discerned, our primary interest is the *ground, terrain, activity,* or belief that gives them place and not the spirit itself. The devil and His demons are completely and utterly totally defeated and there is no other way to regard him.

Luke 10:19, Colossians 2:15

We can accurately say then, that for a believer, the devil is not the problem, rather it is the area of our t*hinking or inner believing* that gives him ground and deceives us into moving our will to participate with him. So, we really are not *demon focused,* instead we are targeting the presenting problem that a person carries, being aware that at times it might be empowered and amplified by an evil spirit. Our mission, in co laboring to set the captives free, is to resolve wrong believing and areas of deception working under the ministry of the Spirit of Truth. Examining beliefs at a heart level is the quickest way that I have seen to expose the ground held by many evil spirits. The beliefs themselves may be the ground for the demons, or the resultant sin choices and behavior may give them place. *Luke 11:20*

WHAT ARE DEMONS OR EVIL SPIRITS?

By observation however, we can say that they are bodiless spirits. The terms *demon, evil spirit, or unclean spirit,* according to the famous Bible teacher Derek Prince, are interchangeable. To be demonized is considered to have or be under the influence of an evil, unclean spirit or a demon. Although *demons* often *possess* or have control of areas of the human personality or body, in truth, a believer is redeemed and *possessed* only by Christ. The control of these areas is certainly by degrees ranging from one part of the person having strongholds, through to many areas. Mostly demons are not always manifested or seen all of the time.

For example, people may have an unresolved problem area that appears only on rare occasions when particular circumstances present and trigger the belief response. This response from the belief may or may not have a demon attached to it. In summary then we could say that usually the demons hold areas of a person in the soul or body.

People who carry demonic spiritual dynamics will often have an almost magnetic spiritual atmosphere that you need to avoid being pulled into. It is trying to illicit a reaction in you to have some measure of control over your behavior. For example, rejection rejects, pride will make you feel inferior, rebellion will treat you unjustly and disrespectfully to try to create the same responses in you that gave the spirits place in the host.

We can say that we need to be aware of the spiritual dynamics of people that we are dealing with and that discernment is our best defense against receiving or responding to someone else's junk. We can see it many times as being something beyond the normal levels of a person's problems, to the amplified or unnatural tangible invisible influence of an unseen entity. If you are aware, you can often see the presence of a spirit on a person as a facial expression of for example, grief, low self-image or lust.

You can also see them in body language such as pride and arrogance, perhaps rebellious or aggressive attitudes. At times you will be aware that speech coming from a person is demonically influenced even though there is not complete control of the voice as in cases of heavy demonization. In these cases, it will be more of a mixture with the person's own personality and there will not likely be a complete voice change. This could be something in the order of; *I hate you!* or *I'm such a loser!* where the intensity of the emotion or statement may be an indicator of a resident spirit.

ACTIVITIES OF DEMONS

The late Derek Prince compiled the following list of the activities of demons from both scripture and personal involvement with deliverance ministry. In my experience it is completely accurate.

1.	Demons Entice or tempt.	*(James 1:14)*
2.	They deceive.	*(I Timothy 4:1-2)*
3.	Spirits enslave.	*(Romans 8:15)* [This would include besetting sins]
4.	They torment.	*(2 Timothy 1:7; 1 John 4:18)*
5.	Demons drive or compel.	*(Luke 8:29)*
6.	Evil spirits defile.	*(Titus 1:15)*

LESSON
Demons work to deceive, oppose, destroy and rob us of peace and produce disharmony and division at every opportunity.

Study: Unholy spirits, are they inside or outside?

SPIRITUAL INFLUENCE FROM OUTSIDE

Spiritual pressures that come from outside of us largely come through the programming of the world. This could be in the form of cultural dynamics, for example, the western world is highly sexualized in our times. As a consequence, we are bombarded with ungodly sexual themes and images which proceed from demonic influences. These are *coverings* or spiritual powers that have found cooperative people or groups to work with and follow them. This submission gives them power. In the case of Jesus' dealings with Satan through Peter, Jesus pointed out that the access came through Peter's *man* thinking which was programmed into him by the world system. Notice that Jesus did not say *come out*. Peter did not have a demon inside him, rather he was submitting to the spiritual environment and training coming through his society. *Matthew 16: 23*

Further references to cooperating with spiritual influences' from outside of the body can be found in *Job 26:4 (NLT)*, and *Luke 9:55 (NKJV)*. In the Luke account we observe Jesus instructing His disciples that they did not understand what manner or type of spirit that they were cooperating with, rather than casting it out.

CAN SATAN ATTACK YOU AT WILL?

Many Christians seem to have the idea that Satan can attack you out of a *clear blue sky* so to speak, anytime that he wants. This thinking suggests that he can attack you at will without some kind of agent to work through or exposure to some kind of medium or prior programming to tempt you. Their concept proposes that the devil might suddenly decide to attack you with fear, or to hold you back in your walk, just because he chooses to. In my experience I have never seen anyone attacked by fear who was not presented with a potentially anxiety inspiring situation, or more commonly holding a previously existing fear belief from a historical source.

To believe this would be to believe that someone who has never suffered with bitterness or lust for instance could suddenly be attacked with resentment for no reason or struggle with immoral thoughts. To take this further, this kind of thinking proposes that you could, without contact with another human being, or any kind of advertising, exposure or encouragement suddenly be overcome by a power drawing you into alcoholism, drugs, violence, and the occult or horror movies. This is absurd really, but there are a lot of people who spend time on *spiritual warfare* against a non-existent threat.

Believing that the devil can do this is giving him much more power than he actually has. He is roaming around, but he tempts through media or temptations to cooperate with him through some kind of peer pressure or reaction to offences from other people. Jesus preached repent, in other words change your thinking about what you allow yourself to join with and be exposed to, saying that the Kingdom of heaven is at hand to cooperate with. *Isaiah 14:16*

Normally in the first instance, even God does not approach a person who has no knowledge of Him without the use of a person. *Romans 10:14*

In conclusion, we could say that as we resolve our fallen nature tendencies by dying to that which the world offers, and deal with deceptive beliefs held at a heart level, the devil has no place from which to bother us. The only power that he actually has, is in what he has already trained you to believe, such as to live in fear, or, that you are not acceptable and so on. These *beliefs* give him access to how you respond to life and deal with others, which now gives him opportunity to provoke or tempt others through your ungodly activities and attitudes towards them. The Apostle Paul knew that the people's eyes were closed to the deception and activities of Satan, and that this was the source of his power over them. *Acts 26:18, Ephesians 2:1-3*

RANDOM ATTACKS FROM SATAN

Am I saying that God or unholy spirits cannot put thoughts in your mind from outside your person? No. What I am proposing is that it appears that neither God nor His opposer randomly put thoughts into your mind without *eliciting or evoking your attention* by some means. If you watch a horror movie and then have bad dreams in your sleep it is because you gave Satan your attention and handed him your mind. He is going to try to get to you through the world system, people, and through your existing beliefs.

In much the same way we choose to communicate with God in prayer and seek Him for His counsel. So then when we open ourselves to His input, we ask, seek, knock, then we receive something, otherwise we probably won't hear much. Once we have committed our lives to Him, He has every right to give us His thoughts if we are looking to Him and giving Him our attention. Of course, if His Spirit resides *inside* of us and we are one in spirit with Him then he has full access to our faculties all of the time. In much the same way, if we have a spirit *inside* of us holding onto an area of our thinking then that demon will be a constant influencer towards those kinds of thoughts.

Attacks that come from the devil will usually come through people who are submitted to him in some area. This could be in the form of someone rejecting or being violent towards you and range through to a fellow teenager showing a schoolmate pornography on a smartphone. Either way his attack has not come from nowhere but rather evil spirit has found a manifestation in the natural realm through a door or gate. Both God and Satan are looking for a manifestation in the Earth. We truly do need to make our focus worshipping God. Our behavior and attitudes being *doors and gates* for His Spirit only, giving Him a manifestation in the Earth.

> *Matthew 16:18, Psalm 24:7*

We need to come to the truth about whose spirit we are allowing to work through us, and often that requires receiving truth in the inner parts or heart before we are able to know what manner of spirit that we are of. *John 4:24*

SPIRITUAL INFLUENCE FROM INSIDE

When a spirit finds a way inside a person it has much greater influence over them, and becomes entwined in the personality or body. This is true of the Holy Spirit indwelling a believer as well. Obviously, there is no comparison between the power of the Holy Spirit and a demon, but in many ways, the Holy Spirit also limits His power in us, and through us, to willful cooperation. Whether speaking of the Holy Spirit or an unholy spirit we could say that when they are inside, they have greater access and influence on our thoughts and faculties. The Holy Spirit normally comes inside when the person is ready and open to His presence. He does not force His way in. On the other hand, a demon will take any opening possible to find a way into a host person. Because of the presence of the Holy Spirit, we can have *the mind of Christ* if we choose to listen. Let me propose that whether you are a Christian or not, if you have a demon inside you, then you can have the mind of that evil spirit using your faculties as well. It is not that the evil spirit is more powerful than the Holy Spirit; it is that you choose to follow it for some reason.

A major part of our freedom and protection from evil spirits, whether they are inside or out, is by responding to the divine influence of the Spirit of Christ and receiving healing, deliverance and wholeness from His ministry. If demons are influencing us from outside of the body the Bible instructs us to resist them. If they are operating inside the body, we are to cast them out in the name of Jesus Christ. *1 Thessalonians 5:23, James 4:7, Matthew 8:16*

I hear people say that a Christian can't have a demon. I think the question is more like can a demon have a Christian, or at least an area of one? And evidently the answer is clearly yes.

A DEMON UNDER EVERY BUSH

Some people who are excessively demon focused may be looking for a *demon under every bush!* Whilst that may be true to some extent, it is not a healthy way to approach this area of ministry. The other end of the scale is to ignore the possibilities of demons altogether and come up with some unbiblical theology that excludes them. Let me propose that not only can a believer have a demon, but in fact deliverance from them is our bread or a provision for us that is not available to those without faith. *Mark 7:25-30, Matthew 10:1, John 10:10*

To say that a Christian cannot have a demon is a bit like saying that they cannot have sin or sickness. The overwhelming evidence is that they both can and do, although the intention of God, as modeled by Jesus, is that ultimately, they should not have either.

Study 3: The Strong man's goods

EXPOSING THE ENEMY THROUGH TEACHING

It has been proposed that fully one third of Jesus' recorded ministry to people in the gospels was dealing with demons in some way. We know that before He ministered, He often taught the people.

WHAT ARE THE STRONG MAN'S GOODS?

A strong man's *goods or possessions* are those things which he holds that strengthen his position. The Greek word translated as *goods or possessions* is *huparchonta*, which also means *that which one has*, or *his property*.

> *Luke 11:20 But if I drive out demons by the finger of God, then the kingdom of God has come to you. 21 "When a strong man, **fully armed,** guards his own house, his **possessions** are safe." NIV, (Emphasis mine)*

Let me suggest that he is fully armed with areas of deception that protect those areas that he considers his property, possessions or goods. These possessions that give him a *place* are the beliefs that we hold that cause us to serve him and participate with him. For example:

- A spirit of bitterness will hold hurts and beliefs resulting from being hurt or abused.
- A spirit of rebellion will hold beliefs relating to injustice.
- A spirit of pride will hold beliefs relating to inferiority.
- A spirit of self-pity will hold beliefs to do with nobody caring about the host and so on.
- The one who is stronger is the Spirit of truth, because truth overpowers the power of deception just as light dispels darkness.
- So is the spirit the problem or, is the property or possessions that he holds that give him a place, the issue?

> *Ephesians 4:27 "... nor give **place** to the devil." NKJV, (Emphasis mine)*
> *Ephesians 4:27 "... and do not give the devil a **foothold**." NIV, (Emphasis mine)*

Giving the devil a foothold or a place to stand, through what we believe and the resultant way that we act, is the true nature of the problem. Again, we look to the original Greek language and see that *foothold* and *place* come from the word *topos* which means a location, a home, or even an opportunity. So often through what we *believe* we consciously or unconsciously yield a portion of our personality, soul or body for the demon to stand on.

Being *fully armed* relates to his ability to protect his position. For example, if his possessions which give him place are *beliefs* relating to inferiority then his ability to defend those beliefs are the pride response that comes from those beliefs. Now he is safe because the host will not go to anyone for help because their pride will not allow them to be *under* another person. Remember this is because the solution to inferiority that the devil suggests is to make you *over* or *above* everyone else in pride. This means that you believe that you know more or better and have more wisdom than anyone else. If we continue to use the same examples the *fully armed* component of injustice beliefs is the rebellion reaction. Now the person is captive because they cannot submit to another.

In the case of a control spirit, the person's insecurity is the issue. To trust another would mean that they are no longer in control, and this is the defense of the strongman and so on. This is why ministering to the *root heart belief*, rather than trying to cast out the demon by attacking his defenses is a far more effective and permanent way of dealing with the spirit. He is now weak and easy to cast out because he has lost his *possessions* which gave him a *place* and so this is also a gentler approach for the person.

Many times, the spirit is attached to sinful behavior, attitudes, reactions and responses that are retaliatory by nature. The name of the demon is the name of ungodly sinful activities such as unforgiveness, resentment, bitterness, ungodly control, rebellion, pride, hatred, self-rejection, fear of rejection and so on. I need to point out that all of these can and do exist without the presence of a demon inside the host. Either way the *beliefs* need to be dealt with to remove the areas that the devil can work through from outside, or that are strongholds of evil spirits on the inside.

Two of the main ways that the demons have a *place* then, is firstly by holding people captive to pain and hurt coming from heart beliefs. Secondly, they are from responses that you believe will resolve the issues proceeding from these beliefs. This could, along with the emotional reactions that we have described, include things such as lustful or immoral activities, violence, addictive behavior, theft, lying, criticism, and so on.

How right was Louis Pasteur when he made an observation relating to the destructive power of the unseen enemy that we now know as germs! *The germ is nothing, the terrain is everything!* In a spiritual sense we could replicate this principle by saying that the demon is nothing, the environment or *beliefs* that give him place are everything. The only hold he has on us to use us, manipulate us, and keep us in bondage is some area of deception or wrong believing in the mind, heart, or both. The *germ is nothing* and consequently our focus is not on him, he simply *flags* the real problem. Once we know the type of *root belief* and likely circumstance that it was learnt in, we can deal with the terrain.

LESSON
The best way to take away *the armor* of the 'strongman' is to remove his possessions that give him place. The armor is usually the ungodly responses that come from *the beliefs* that he possesses.

THE 'DUNG' GOD
Jesus described Satan as *Beelzebub* which means the *dung god, or the lord of the flies*. This gives us a great perspective on how God regards demons. They are nothing, they are just like

flies. The only power that they have is whatever you are deceived into giving them, which is why when you know the truth it will set you free. I think that most of us who started out with a *cast out the demons'* focus, and neglected healing the broken hearts, would agree with me that many times we would shoo away the flies on Monday only to find that we had to do it again a week later. Some people would stay free, or have a measure of deliverance but many, even though they may have had powerful deliverances and manifestations, would return bound again.

Whereas when we take the *Truth Encounters* model, we see them completely free in the area ministered to, and are often not even aware if there was a demon there or not, because we took his goods in which he trusted in. It is much gentler for the person than attacking a fully armed spirit if we remove that which he trusts in. In short, clean up the dung and there is no further reason for the flies to be there. They need food and the dung heap as their place. The fly is nothing; the dung is *everything*!

SWEPT AND EMPTY
When Jesus used the picture of that which the spirit considers to be *his house*, or *place that he inhabits*. He states that if this abode, which is based on the possessions of the demon is left empty, then it is likely that the evil spirit will return. Why is this?

Let me propose that the property of the demon that gave him place was the *deceptive beliefs* that the host or person held. So, if the house is left empty and not filled with God's truth through the ministry of the Spirit of truth, then there is nothing stopping him from returning. If knowing the Truth will set you free, and if this is done by the Spirit of Christ, then you will remain free indeed. *Matthew 12:43*

LESSON
If we have not cleaned up the dung,* then the flies will stay around, or return if we have shooed them away. *The dung is the wrong beliefs that are evident as we are measured against the word of God. For example, if we believe that we are not loved or loveable, when the Bible clearly says that we are.*

REPENTANCE AND DELIVERANCE
Once a spirit has established a strong hold on your hurts or sinful reactions, he is going to *replay them* as inner thinking or addictive and often repetitive behavior. He is also going to *amplify* your responses and the intensity of emotion that you hold. People with demonic powered beliefs may often not be able to control their feelings and have an inordinate response in how they react to stressors. The word translated as *repent* from the original Greek language is *Metanoeo* and it means to *think differently* or *reconsider*, or to change one's mind. Jesus came to destroy the devils works, but His message was repent. In other words, if we don't come to accept that what we're doing is out of order then Jesus cannot pull down that which the devil holds us into because we choose to continue in it. *1 John 3:8*

> *2 Timothy 2:24 "And the servant of the Lord must not strive; but be gentle unto all men, apt to teach, patient, ²⁵ In meekness instructing those that **oppose themselves;** if God peradventure will give them **repentance to the acknowledging of the truth;** ²⁶ And that they may recover themselves out of the snare of the devil, who are taken captive by him at his will." KJV, (Emphasis mine)*

Study 4: Names of demons and touching the spirit realm

Some people feel that they need to know the names of all the demons and get them right before they will leave. You can simply say something such as; *you spirit that is attached to this or that, leave in the name of Jesus.* As we read the scriptures, we see the story about the lying spirits in *1 Kings 22:21-23*. In this passage the prophets were looking to say what the Kings wanted to hear in order to receive their acceptance and favor. The usual reason that people tell lies is a fear of rejection and it is the most common reason that I have found that causes people to lie.

What I learnt from studying and meditating on the passage is that the spirit was not a *lying spirit*, it was just a generic nondescript spirit. It was only able to attach itself to that which was yielded to sin, in this case lying. It could not go and be a spirit of lust or bitterness because that was not the area of the personality or body that was being made available to sin. So, the name of a spirit is simply the area of the person that they hold. If it's bitterness, its bitterness, lust, lust, lying, lying and so on. It exists there because it has access to the person in some way, often through their unwitting yielded ness in following sinful behavior, attitudes and responses.

Many in the church seem to have this idea that the devil already has spirits with special names, functions and job descriptions in stock, that he can send at will to attack people. When they run through generation lines, they seem to be able to promote the same *beliefs* and ground to operate on that was in previous generations. As a result, you may see for example issues such as ungodly control, lust, unforgiveness or rejection run through families, with corresponding mental, emotional and physical maladies, until someone receives freedom from Christ Jesus.

TOUCHING THE SPIRIT REALM

Let me suggest some areas where we may create openings, and if there is demonization that goes with it then the following list of examples could all be the names of demons. We could address them as; *you spirit that has been involved in holding Fred into 'rebellious' behavior.* (This assumes that we have dealt with the injustice *beliefs* already or concurrently.) These are some sample areas of the human person that spirits may influence or affect:

- Emotional breaches;   fear, bitterness, rejection, inferiority Etc.
- Mental problems;   doubt, unbelief, fantasy, withdrawal, insanity. Etc.
- Moral issues;   pornography, fornication, adultery, lying, theft. Etc.
- Relational disharmony;   mockery, criticism, judgment, religion, rejection Etc.
- Spiritual alliances;   the occult, false religion, witchcraft. Etc.
- Physical bondage;   addictions, lusts, altered states, violence, infirmity.

These are all potential areas of exposure to the spirit realm if we touch it or there is an opening through which it can enter. You will note that virtually all of these are tied to thoughts coming from *beliefs*, which precipitate and present in decisions. This should re center us on the need for truth at every level of our being so that we can make good protective choices.

LESSON
To know what kind of demon or evil spirit we are dealing with we simply look at its function and the area of stronghold in the person.

Study 5: Breaches

INTEGRITY

Most probably when you hear the word *integrity* you think of a business man or similar who conducts their dealings in an upright and trustworthy manner. The word integrity actually means; *the state of being entire, or whole.* As an example, if you could imagine your skin as a God given barrier to protect you from the elements as well as various bacteria and diseases. While my skin holds its unbroken integrity and remains whole you could pour, for example, hepatic B virus over my arm and I would not be harmed. But if you created a small cut or opening in the wholeness of my skin then I would become infected and get sick.

We have already mentioned that the word for being *saved* is *sozo* and that a part of the meaning of that word includes to *deliver or protect* and coming to *wholeness*. The more whole we are in regards to truth about God, ourselves, how to deal with others, and the spiritual world that we have, the more delivered we are. This is our best protection against possible infection from the spiritual realm and this is why children are the most vulnerable, because they have the least amount of truth and understanding. They need our spiritual protection and instruction to bring them up in the counsel of the Lord.

The most whole person who ever walked the Earth was Jesus. He stated that because the devil had no *wrong beliefs in Him* in regarding Himself, *(identity)* how Father God saw Him, or why people were used as instruments of the devil to try to get to Him. Because of the level of truth that He had inside He was without sin; the result was that the devil couldn't touch Him. Wholeness is our best protection.

> John 14:30 "I will no longer talk much with you, for the ruler of this world is coming, and **he has nothing in Me.**" NKJV (Emphasis mine)

When we have a break or breach in our spiritual or emotional integrity, it is a potential entry point for a spirit. This could be a time of fear or trauma. It could be a time of abuse where our understanding of the situation is overwhelmed and we are out of control. It could also be at a time where we are on drugs or drunk, and our normal resistance and mental integrity is weakened, and now we do something sinful that we would not normally do. In a ministry setting we are aware of possible breaches in our wholeness of some kind that may have given place to a spirit. We are looking to repair the breach in the walls of the human personality so that the people again have normal resistance to spiritual inroads.

> *Isaiah 58:10-12, Isaiah 61:3-4*

Walls were intended to keep the bad things out and protect the good things inside. In much the same way a healthy soul carries its own protection. Some spiritual and emotional building materials that are used to strengthen the walls of the human personality and keep the temple in good condition are such items as; love, acceptance, grace, truth, value, significance, encouragement, worth, freedom, respect, honor, forgiveness, kindness, protection and so on.

LESSON
Our best defense against spiritual inroads is wholeness. If we don't get our issues dealt with others around us will suffer as a consequence.

INTEGRITY TO INTEGRATION

Once a spirit has breached the integrity of a person through some means and come inside, it will entwine itself with your personality in that area. From experience I would say that a demon is limited to work in you in the area or place that has given it ground. By this I mean that a spirit that causes you to be violent has no ability to lead you into false religion or lustful behavior. Its function and area of influence is limited to that which has given it access and place. *Romans 6:12-13, James 1:14-15* Although many times a spirit will come to us as a result of the sins of others which have created breaches in us, in the preceding verses we see that at times the demon has come as a result of opening a door through our willful cooperation.

LESSON
We can open a door to a spirit by engaging in activities that are beyond Gods created order. (I am not suggesting for a moment that every time you sin that you are going to receive an evil spirit, although at times this can be the case, but it is certainly possible with deliberate repetitive sin.)

ENTWINED

Let's continue examining sexuality as an easily understood area of our person that can be open to demonic activity through some form of immorality. Once engaged in lustful behavior the spirit inside has entwined itself with your sexuality and you have, to some measure, become one with it in your thoughts in regards to sexual matters. As a result, the sexual ideas, desires or tendencies you have are now all influenced by the demon inside of you.

We could say that it has come in through some kind of breach in the integrity of your person and has now moved to being integrated with your sexuality. If you are unaware of this influence then you now think that it is only your *thoughts and ideas* that move you towards ungodly sexual activities. So, you do not hesitate to go ahead with this behavior because you simply think that it is what you alone want.

The same could be said for retaliatory or revengeful thoughts that you may be having if you hold unforgiveness. You simply think that it is what you want, and what will please you, and so you don't hesitate to act out further in sin. This could apply to any area of distorted behavior or attitudes that we are in bondage to, and that are *replayed* or *amplified* as an expression. We need to discern it by identifying that which is out of order with Gods intentions for our attitudes and actions. This is done by measuring these thoughts and deeds by the Word of God and the counsel of the Spirit of God. *John 6:63*

It is often difficult to receive deliverance and separation from an integrated spirit until the person understands, to some degree, the concept that a part of their thoughts are not actually them. After all, why would you want a part of yourself cast out?

Once we have integrated with a spirit, we can use terms such as participating with, following, or cooperating with the ungodly internal entity. We have to begin by changing our thinking about it in repentance and then fall out of agreement with our working with it as a basis for being set free.

LESSON
Separation begins with seeing and understanding the true source and nature of the problem, and choosing willfully to be disconnected from it.

PHYSICAL OR MENTAL PROBLEMS

Once a demon has integrated and amplified, for example emotional issues, you can expect some kind of outworking in the physical body and or mental health areas. Remember, dealing with the connected *inner beliefs* is the basis of the freedom and not merely shooing away the flies. The imbalanced emotions follow deceptive inner thoughts and finish in the body.

LESSON
Demons often magnify inner heart beliefs producing imbalanced emotional and unhealthy hormonal balances that lead to, or hasten disease or weakness in the body.

INFIRMITY

Strong's concordance informs us that the Greek word asthenia from which we have the word infirmity contains the following meanings: Feebleness (of *body or mind*); malady; frailty: *disease*, infirmity, *sickness*, *weakness*. Luke 13:11

We can conclude that whenever we are praying for a disease, sickness or malady that has outworked as a weakness in the body, there is a strong possibility that a s*pirit of infirmity* is holding the body into that condition. It has most likely taken hold when the physical integrity or wholeness of the person was weakened and breached through trauma, or longer-term hormonal imbalances caused by emotional 'dis' ease from faulty *heart beliefs*, or some other kind of breakdown of the body's normal defenses such as immune problems.

People are healed after a simple prayer commanding the spirit to go. Many times, the emotional components of the disease need to be ministered to, and also beliefs emanating from trauma dealt with to take away the ground that the spirit holds. If we don't do this then, although the spirit is gone and healing may result, we have left the door open, so to speak, and they may end up with the same or another sickness. If people prayed against the spirit of infirmity more, and the recipients of the prayer understood what this meant, we would see many more people being healed. Not surprisingly this can extend to physical injuries where a weakness has occurred through events such as accidents. We could say; *you spirit that has come in through weakness leave* and expect the same results.

INSANITY

The majority of this publication is directed towards how to become increasingly sound of mind and whole of body. To be insane simply means to be unsound in mind. We see various mental illnesses which have a spirit of insanity involved. People such as drug addicts' risk being open to this problem through opening the door by voluntarily going into altered states that make their mind not sane, not sound or whole, and seeking unreality as a means of pleasure, escape from life or emotional pain. *Hosea 9:7 (NKJV), 2 Timothy 1:7 (NKJV)*

POSSIBLE ENTRY POINTS

We have already covered some of these major topics in detail.

- Trauma or loss of mental or emotional integrity
- Sin responses, or reactions coming from emotional pain or abuse such as, unforgiveness, bitterness, hatred, or rebellion etc.
- Sin solutions stemming from efforts to resolve emotional pain; Lusts, excessive use of substances such as food, alcohol, drugs, or escape into media and unreality, immoral

relationships, addictions etc.
- Involvement in the Occult, witchcraft, or false religions as being the worship of other gods.

GENERATIONALLY INHERITED SPIRITS

In a sense all sin is generational, because for mankind it began with Adam and Eve, and has traveled through the generations up to this point in history. Often the drawing to the family weaknesses opens us to also committing the same sins and giving place to the devil through our own submission and compliance.

'SOUL TIES'

Another area that we have not touched on and has become popular in church jargon, is an opening for demonic entry that has been dubbed a *soul tie*. Although difficult to find under that terminology in most modern translations, the principle refers to some kind of connection of the soul whereby some ungodly element passes from one person to another.

If we replaced the term *soul tie* with the word *relationship* then you discover that the whole Bible from cover to cover is talking about the interaction of the souls of humanity, and the consequent impact that it has upon us. A godly *soul tie* or *relationship* then would be something such as parents ministering love and acceptance to their children, or believers building each other up and encouraging one another. But clearly there are many negative things that can be imparted to us from the souls of others in relationships. *1 Corinthians 6:16 + 15:33*

Perhaps at the least end of the soul tie scale we could suggest something such as a boy in year 4 at school looking to a lad in year 6 who he thinks is *very cool*. The older boy swears and uses bad language so as a result of the younger boys' agreement and coming in line with wanting to be like the very cool year 6 lad, he also begins to swear. So, something ungodly, sin, has just passed through their relationship. In this case, when the younger boy gets a little older, he decides that actually it is not cool to swear and decides to stop. This change of thinking or repentance as we know it, then breaks the tie.

At times, if the connection is stronger then, the relational joining can be an opportunity for a spirit to pass. This could be through an illicit sexual relationship, where a spirit relating to the one flesh joining sits over the connection, holding them together. People report suffering from depression or having suicidal thoughts or lust problems that they have never known before, but that their partners in the ungodly act suffer from. Therefore, demonic transference through the ungodly relationship or interaction of souls is a very real possibility.

If someone is struggling with some kind of *relational* or *soul tie* to another then their part in their freedom is to voluntarily disconnect from any memories of the other person. For example, I have ministered to a number of men who have had previous sexual partners who, now married, feel as though when they are having marital relations with their wives that there are 3 of them in the bed. These men are usually still allowing themselves to think about this past partner from time to time which keeps the tie alive. Our advice with any kind of soul tie is for them to remember them no more. This means pleasures, adventures together or whatever memories might bind them, and get rid of any articles that might promote these thoughts and remind them of the past.

The critical element of breaking the tie is not the spirituality of the minister or the power of God, it is the will of the person to disconnect. If they are genuinely prepared to do that, then if you feel that there is a spiritual power involved then you can address the spirit that binds them together, or anything that is known of that has come to them through the other person. Again, *breaking soul ties* or *generational links* is not the first place that I would go as a method, but rather is something that you deal with as it comes up in the course of resolving areas where they require the Lord's healing and freedom.

LESSON
A common way that a spirit may find an entry point is through relationships and joining with others in sin, or a connection through an ungodly event with another person being acted out on us.

TRANSFERENCE

Some people fear that a demon can simply pass to you for no reason, and this is very much not the case. As we have already described there has to be an opening in the wholeness of the person. This could be through someone willfully opening the door, through to something such as an ungodly tie or cooperation and alliance in sin with another person. It could also come as transference through the generation line or through an opening such as submitting to significant fear. This fear could come through the violent or abusive behavior of another acted out on you, or fear generated through some kind of occult ritual or witchcraft type behavior.

The idea that you could be near another human and without some kind of breach in the integrity of your person, that a spirit could just pass to you is not the case. *Proverbs 26:2*

LESSON
A spirit cannot simply come into you without some kind of door, opening or exposure to something that creates an entry point.

MANIFESTATIONS

Some people get hung up on the type of things that they expect to see when a person is delivered of an evil spirit. They may feel that there should be loud shrieks or the person slithering across the floor. There is a wide variety of manifestations that may happen ranging from those types of lively encounters to seeing nothing at all, with the person simply reporting that something left, they feel free, lighter, peaceful or joyous. This is in part to do with the type of spirit that you are dealing with, and sometimes how much you have undermined its position before you have told it to go.

Sometimes upon commanding them to leave you may see an unexpected eruption of emotion which can be quite deep if the pain has been traumatic. A spirit may rise in their throat and come out with coughing or some other kind of appearance such as involuntary deepened breathing. The more dramatic manifestations are often connected with involvement in activities such as witchcraft or the Occult. We leave all of those things to the Holy Spirit as the finger of God. Our job is just to be obedient as God's mouthpiece and command them to go. Don't be surprised by what happens or doesn't happen, the main thing is that the person is free.

LESSON
You will probably never experience a demon leaving a person that you are helping if you don't command it to go in Jesus name. There will not necessarily be a big

manifestation with most 'garden variety' demons if you have done the healing work or there is genuine repentance if it is a sin issue. On rare occasions, if the subject is extremely violent for example, you may need help from someone more experienced.

Study 6: Final thoughts on healing and freedom ministries

OUR PART IN THE SESSION

We have already stated that the key to helping people come into the provisions of God is all about positioning them to receive. In the case of deliverance, if nothing is happening with the person, or if there is but they are not getting free then most probably it isn't to do with your spirituality, and certainly not with the authority of Christ. Remember, we are ministering based on our faith in the name of Jesus, the will of the Father, and not because of our own Holiness or godliness.

*Acts 3: 12 When Peter saw this, he said to them: "Men of Israel, why does this surprise you? Why do you stare at us **as if by our own power or godliness (Note: also godliness can be translated holiness)** we had made this man walk? NIV (Emphasis mine)*

and

*Acts 3: 16 **By faith in the name of Jesus,** this man whom you see and know was made strong. It is Jesus' name and the faith that comes through him that has given this complete healing to him, as you can all see. NIV (Emphasis mine)*

1. Revelation
If they have not understood the nature of their problem and been able to accept the spiritual component, they may struggle to get free. Jesus taught them first. *Hosea 4:6*

2. Confession
To confess means to say the same as. It is when we say the same as God does about our problem, rather than to deny it or try to justify it. Then we are in a good place to receive freedom. If, for example, we have a demonic element to bitterness, but in our minds feel that we have every right to hold our unforgiveness and bitterness then we may struggle to receive our freedom. We are not falling out of agreement with the spirit and into agreement with the word of God or taking responsibility in our part of the activity.

3. Repentance
If we are not prepared to *change our thinking or reconsider our ways* then we may block our freedom. In the case of inner thinking, we may need the beliefs dealt with, before we can cooperate for the deliverance. For example, if we have had a fear producing episode, that has given us fear beliefs, then unwittingly we may want the spirit to remain because we have the perception that it helps to protect us in some way.

4. Forgiveness
A common reason that people don't receive freedom is because they refuse to forgive others. Again, there may need to be healing of the hurts before the spirit loses its place, and consequently the will of the person becomes to no longer participate. *Matthew 6:14-15*

5. The 'strongman's goods'
We have explained this already in detail and this is why most often deliverance is along with *Truth Encounters* where necessary, rather than the other way around. As we have said, many of these same problems can exist without having demonic power on the inside attached that needs to be evicted.

6. A mouthpiece
Once we have covered these positioning issues, all that remains is commanding the spirits to leave in the name of Jesus. You are simply God's mouthpiece; it is the Holy Spirit's work to manifest the promise of deliverance. I have seen many spirits come out of people, and I am well aware that it is the goodness of God, faith in Jesus name, and the work of the Spirit that has accomplished this, and not because I am anyone special.

SPONTANEOUS DELIVERANCE
I have experienced in different settings across the world, times when praying for people in a meeting that they manifest a spirit and it convulses them as it comes out, as they did in Jesus' bodily time on the Earth. I very often have no idea what the spirit is. It is the presence of the Holy Spirit on the person that causes the reaction as He comes in through us. Making ourselves available simply makes us a door or gate that the Spirit can work through and do whatever He wants. *Mark 9:26* At times people receive some kind of deliverance along with baptism in water or in the Spirit. This does not necessarily mean that they are free of everything.

FALLEN NATURE OR DEMONS?
Is your sin problem or bad habit demon powered or just your fallen nature and lack of self-discipline? If you press in, pray, build yourself up in the Holy Spirit and discipline yourself to study the word and avoid unhealthy exposure to the world, and;

- You take ground and improve over time, even though you might be taking two steps forward and one step back, then your problem is most likely external pressure, unresolved beliefs, or fallen nature tendencies that have not been dealt with.
- Your problem gets worse than before, then in that instance it is probably an evil spirit within you that you are dealing with. We are mainly talking habits and sin here as opposed to hurts. A spirit, if it is still armed with some unresolved possessions such as deliberate sin or emotional pain then it will immediately seek rise up, exert pressure, and bluff you that it is too strong for you, in order to get you or the minister to give up.

There is personal responsibility that the person receiving ministry must be prepared to take.

1. Man is responsible for his choices and responses. Once you realize that you are participating with another will that is operating inside of you, then you must conclude that there is no substitute for repentance.

2. It has been well said that deliverance will not give a person self-discipline,* as it must be learned, practiced and exercised. It brings order to a person's life. The devil does most of his work through disorder. *(Pastor Carroll Thompson, 1977) *Proverbs 25:28*

The best defense then, is restoring God's order to the life of the person. Remember that the demon can be cast out but the *place* or *topos* cannot be cast out. It must be brought under the authority of Christ or be healed. Unless the ground is dealt with, the deliverance may not be maintained which is why the main focus is on *Truth Encounters*. Clearly, the human will and desire is a very important factor in coming to freedom. If sin is the ground that the spirit occupies then often the strength of the enemy may depend on the amount of submission and cooperation that he has received.

FIGHTING WITH A DEMON
In the event that, as a minister, you find yourself fighting with a demon for some reason, let me suggest a couple of possibilities as to why;

1. The person has unforgiveness, unhealed belief areas, deception, lack of repentance, a failure to confess something relevant, or doubt and unbelief.

2. You may actually be wrestling with your own doubt and unbelief that the battle is over. Or, that you are worthy to have been given complete authority over all of the works of the enemy.

If you are fighting, it may be because you have been taught that the enemy is not defeated and has not been totally disarmed, or that Jesus has triumphed *(Colossians 2:15)*. In that case you believe that you have to fight which is not true. The only power that the demon actually has, is willful or deceptive cooperation from the host. Jesus never argued with demons because He knew that He was in the Father and that the Father was in Him. Now we are seated in Christ *(Ephesians 2:6)*. Jesus never told us to fight with demons He instructed us to expel them and set the captives free. *John 14:10-13*

FINALLY
Let me say that, although I have discussed the topic of demons or evil spirits at length, in ministry they are not our focus and I rarely think about them. The purpose of this section is simple awareness of their workings so that they can be discerned if present. Let me encourage you again to not make the ministry about looking for them. In practice you are working on the person's wholeness and you may simply, with the permission and cooperation of the person, cast one out here and there as you go along where applicable.

LESSON
Jesus has made us perfect to the Father through redemption. This foundation in Christ qualifies us to minister. *Hebrews 10:14*

As we step in with our mustard seed of faith looking to God and not our own abilities, we are often surprised at what happens.

> *Ephesians 2:8 [8] God saved you by his special favor when you believed. And you can't take credit for this; it is a gift from God. [9] Salvation is not a reward for the good things we have done, so none of us can boast about it.[10] For we are God's masterpiece. He has created us anew in Christ Jesus, so that we can do the good things he planned for us long ago. NLT (Emphasis mine)*

UNIT SIX

Discernment

Study 1: Rejection - Broken heartedness

As we begin to look at the subject of rejection in brief, let us first define it and put it into perspective. Rejection is *non-acceptance*. The definition of rejection includes the following:

- to refuse to acknowledge or accept
- to forsake
- to refuse to have or use
- to cast or throw away as useless, worthless, or unsatisfactory
- to refuse to love
- to discard as unwanted or not filling requirements.

Many people hold *heart beliefs* that they are not wanted, don't belong, or perhaps that they are not loved or loveable. Still others feel as though they are worthless, not cared about, will never be good enough, or don't measure up to what is wanted. They feel that they fall short of the expectations of others. These beliefs all drop into the category of rejection, or not being accepted.

In the Garden of Eden mankind submitted to Satan and rejected God as Lord. They rebelled against His commands in regards to the tree of the knowledge of good and evil. Whatever kinds of spirit that you participate with and submit to, you give authority to them over you in the area of your submission. Rejection was now a covering power that all future mankind was born under as a consequence of the fall.

I have previously pointed out that God never rejected humanity, rather we rejected Him. This was joining with Satan who had rejected God's Lordship in favor of *self-realization*. God is always redemptive and immediately He promised to repair the situation for His creation as we see in the following passage. *Genesis 3:15*

Jesus carried the rejection due to us as a result of our sin, and now we have God's acceptance. *Isaiah 53:3-4*

Not being received and accepted by another produces separation in relationships and cuts us off from love and nurture. This is true in terms of how we relate to God, but also how we receive others and even ourselves. If we don't believe that we are acceptable then we will struggle to receive love. Without the assurance of love, we are going to have anxiety problems as is well evidenced in modern society. When we have our *heart beliefs* resolved, and also understand fully at a conscious level as well, that through redemption Christ dealt with our punishment and separation from the Father completely, we can then receive His love. *1 John 4:18*

LESSON

Man rejects God. The Lord is by very nature accepting and embracing, wanting that none should perish, but rather that all would change their thinking about Him and His Kingdom. *(2 Peter 3:9)* We could say then that God loves the whole World, enough to send His son to pay for our sin, *(John 3:16)* but not everyone loves and accepts Him. As, with Adam and Eve people are deceived about His true nature and character.

THE POTENTIAL DAMAGE OF NO ACCEPTANCE

Around twenty years ago I heard a story from an English Bible teacher named Ruth Hawkey. The account that she related helped me to fully understand the potential damage to humans who do not receive nurture in the form of love and acceptance.

The setting was an overloaded institution in Eastern Europe who had in their care 97 children between 3 months and 3 years old. Now remember that mankind's most basic need is to have love and acceptance communicated to them; connection. Because of the lack of staff, there was no time available for physical or emotional nurture. Reportedly, at 3 months there were signs of abnormality with the children losing their appetites, exhibiting poor sleep patterns and their eyes were becoming vacant and looking into space. At 5 months some were exhibiting serious deterioration. They were whimpering and their faces would become twisted and distorted if anyone approached them and tried to pick them up. As the story goes 27 died the first year with no physical reason; they were considered to have shriveled up on the inside. 7 more died the second year and the survivors suffered with severe psychological disorders. There have been many such studies by people such as Rene A. Spitz that confirm the types of damage that these settings can produce.

We can testify to having seen many of these issues and manifestations present with very rejected children that we have fostered over the years. The point is that the result of not receiving love and acceptance from the parents, and subsequent lack of bonding and nurture can have pronounced effects on one's total person. These examples are of an extreme nature but they stand to illustrate that rejection has a profound impact on the human person; the only remaining question is to what degree it has touched us.

POSSIBLE BEGINNING POINTS FOR REJECTION BELIEFS

1. Prenatal:

That is, beginning before birth whilst still in the womb. Gods intention was for us to be accepted and wanted and that was to be our spiritual covering. But if we are not accepted, even in the womb then the spirit over us is rejection and we are imprinted with that on our souls, along with corresponding beliefs.

2. Adoption/ Fostering

We have previously discussed the resultant *beliefs* proceeding from the separation choices, decisions and situations leading to adoption and fostering. In the case of adoption many times the decisions are made before the birth of the child. Even though the child may find themselves in a loving and accepting family the rejection issues and beliefs will automatically be there.

In the case of fostering, there is usually a significant reason why they need to be fostered out to begin with. Children are very often egocentric and lay the reason for be moved out of the family at something that they have done, or not done. Remember these conclusions are not because of conscious deliberate mental effort, but rather a conclusion or interpretation from the experience of the situation. In any case most times they will carry rejection, having concluded that they are unacceptable in the family unit for some reason.

3. Parenting issues
Modeling
Many parents simply cannot communicate love and acceptance. This can stem from them never having had it modeled to them in terms of to how to show the worth, value, love and acceptance that a child needs. It continues then as a generational cultural omission that leaves a breeding ground for children to come to their own conclusions regarding whether or not they are acceptable.

Empty 'love tanks'
Some parents have not received love and grace themselves so they are emotionally bankrupt and have nothing to give. They are themselves rejected and many of the efforts around their lives are in trying to meet the needs of their own wounded selves. They may also be physically present but emotionally unavailable. Perhaps they are addicted to drugs, alcohol, television, digital games and media in order to escape their own pain and consequent relational problems. Sadly, rejected people are most often rejective; *rejection rejects.*

Parents have been given the responsibility to represent God in all aspects of His character. We have found that the *God picture* that most people hold is a projection off the parenting that they have received. If you never have time for them, they will expect that God is also too occupied creating universes to listen to their needs. If you are always too busy, then the expectation will be that God doesn't have time for them, or that they are a nuisance. So, if father was harsh and critical then that is how they tend to see God. If they believe that the father, (or at times mother) didn't love them, then the belief will be that God doesn't love them either.

Conditional acceptance
A number of people hold rejection beliefs learnt through only receiving acceptance if they perform and meet the standards set for them. These expectations could relate to behavior, academic or other achievements. Fundamentally what is being projected onto them spiritually and emotionally is; *If you don't measure up by doing this or that then you are not good enough, and therefore not acceptable!"*

Some parents have such high standards for their children that they create a breeding ground for anxiety about performance and depression. If a child is only ever criticized and told that they are not enough, then the consequent belief will be that no matter how hard they try, they will never be able to be what they need to be for acceptance. This is an overwhelming belief that produces hopelessness and eventually depression.

Christian parents can be as guilty as anyone of metering out conditional acceptance based on performance. A fear that our children may not be good enough for God, leads us to impose all kinds of religious standards on them. In turn they grow up seeing God as a person who is watching to make sure that you get everything right. One mistake and He will punish you. God actually doesn't expect us to be perfect. He knows that we are created beings in a hostile fallen environment, complete with our old nature which has a tendency towards sin, a world full of temptations and a spiritual enemy who is constantly trying to deceive and gain sway over us. Sometimes we need to forgive ourselves for being merely created beings formed from dust, God has! And then we can extend this grace and understanding that we have received from Him by not demanding others and our children to meet our standards.
Psalm 103:10-14

Inappropriate discipline
Excessive correction without love leaves a child to conclude that they don't matter; they are

nothing, they simply live to fulfill all your wants and needs. If they feel that this is all about conforming their lives to you being pleased, and that you do not care about them or that which they want or need, that is, them, themselves, then this will read on their hearts as injustice, which will produce rebellion.

4. Rejection through Abuse
Verbal, emotional, mental, sexual and physical abuses are all strong sources of rejection. The *language of the spirit* or the attitude behind all of these is something along the lines of; *You don't matter, you are just rubbish that has to fit into what I want, you are nothing.* At heart level, matching beliefs are now held about your self-worth and acceptability. These acts destroy how you perceive yourself, your identity, value and importance.

Study 2: Results of rejection or non-acceptance

1. A love 'vacuum'
A person who has not experienced acceptance will often be, what is sometimes termed as, needy. In other words, they always need some kind of help, support or encouragement from others. Very hurt people can have an emotional whirlpool that draws everyone and everything into it as a solution to their emptiness. This can include a propensity towards lusts, possessions, acknowledgement from achievements, possessiveness and jealousy around relationships.

These people will often crave acceptance from *parental* figures such as ministers, who now represent the authority person in the church 'family.' This person becomes the centre of their lives as a kind of replacement of the absent key figures of a father or mother.

Many times, homosexual tendencies fit in here, with psychological studies reporting a high incidence of this behavior being a response to not having received love and acceptance from a primary care giver in the critical early stages of life.

The need for acceptance and love can also be found as a strong motivator behind sex outside of marriage, adultery and even issues such as the epidemic of pornography. These illicit movies offer men the emotional stimulus of these supposedly accepting women being pleased with the efforts of the men portrayed in the pictures.

2. Narcissistic behavior
Narcissism is defined as an abnormal love and admiration for oneself. It is reasonably obvious that this is the person's solution to not being loved, regarded or treated as being important. From repeated dealings with narcissistic behavior I have concluded that the underlying beliefs are normally something such as; *I am not important and therefore not loved."*

Because self is now firmly on the throne, they are prone to the whole self-syndrome. Self-consumed, self-centered, self-indulgent, self-justified, self-gratifying, self-important, self-protective, self-righteous, self-deceived and selfish, etc. etc.

3. Hermits and extroverts
Some people respond to rejection by hiding from people in order to avoid rejection. Even in company they present as withdrawn. In a sense they have accepted that they are unacceptable and not good enough, and are therefore afraid to come out of their protective

shell. Others will gravitate to wearing a *mask* and becoming, for example, the life of the party in order to be acceptable. When they go home, they are very often emotionally exhausted from the effort to rise up and *be* what they perceive is necessary to be wanted and accepted by people. They tend to work hard at harmonizing with others in an effort to be what they believe is acceptable....and often never realize or accept their own identity.

4. Loneliness
Another result of rejection is poor bonding and the inability to make close relationships. Beliefs such as, *I am not wanted, don't belong, not worthy or worth acceptance, am not cared about'* and so on, presents a strong inner case for not receiving the affection of another, yourself, and even God. *Matthew 19:19*

5. Fear of rejection
Once a person has had the pain and negative experience of rejection, they will now be on watch to protect themselves from further rejection. Other fears such as fear of failure or fear of embarrassment, and so on, fall under this category. You must ask yourself, what will happen if you fail? In the past, most likely, you have learnt that this means you will not receive acceptance. Why did you feel embarrassed? Because you felt that something that you did or said was unacceptable!

'FRUIT' OR POSSIBLE SIGNS OF A FEAR OF REJECTION

Independence
If I am afraid that you might reject me, then an unconscious decision might be something such as, *I won't need you or your acceptance, and then I don't need to worry about you rejecting me! I will meet my own needs and be my own provision.*

Self-Pity
Feeling sorry for yourself could run closely with this kind of inner thinking. *Poor me, nobody cares about me. I feel sorry for me!* This nobody cares about me belief may at times also have an outward manifestation; *You must hear my story, how I have been wronged and then you should feel sorry for me too!'* It can lead to controlling behavior and attitudes; I must make people care about me, because nobody does! This unconscious inner thinking stems from insecurity about being accepted and loved. *Psalm 42:5*

The following symptoms of rejection were listed by the late Noel Gibson from Australia, and are used by permission: In the brackets is my expansion.

A. Refusing comfort. (This could include throwing tantrums or sulking.)

B. Rejection of others. (If you reject someone first, if they reject you back then you can justify it to yourself – you feel that if you blow their candle out, then yours will burn more brightly!)

C. Signs of emotional hardness. (Harshness, criticism, judgment, the tongue)

D. Skepticism, doubt, unbelief. (This stems from not being able to trust. Fearing people's motives towards you)

E. Aggressive attitudes. (Feeling that aggression/anger, disapproval, in a verbal or physical form is the logical way to ward off further rejection)

F. Thoughts of revenge.   (Retaliation of some kind coming from resentment to perceived hurt)

G. Argumentativeness.   (Point scoring and the need to win an argument and be right all of the time as a countermeasure to the low self-image coming from rejection - simply cannot agree or accept another's point of view).

H. Stubbornness'/defiance.   (People who feel that they have been wronged or aren't being accepted and dealt with fairly very often simply will not cooperate – feeling that their treatment is not fair, or unjust)

6. Self-rejection

This occurs when you accept rejection as being a correct assessment of your acceptability, worth and value. In a sense you continue to replay the rejection beliefs that you hold as now being your truth. In a ministry setting you will hear *self-rejection statements* overflowing from *the heart* out of the mouth. These will give you strong insights into the beliefs that people hold. It is extremely common for those who have rejection to also have fear of rejection and self-rejection issues. As they share their story or problem you may hear and note such statements as: *I'm just not good enough, I'm stupid, useless, a loser, hopeless, ugly, such an idiot, never do it right, am not as good as others, and so on.*

False humility can probably come under this banner as well. With an attitude and presentation based around; *well I am just no one and nothing, I am not worth noticing, don't worry about me!* This is not humility; this is low self-image. You can, in fact, be quite confident, but still be aware that in comparison to God you are just a created being. So, humility is actually a healthy perspective of your humanity. You have your God given strengths and weaknesses just like everyone else, you are neither greater, nor lesser, you are simply you!

SELF-ACCUSATION, SELF-CONDEMNATION AND SELF-BITTERNESS

When self-rejection is extreme, it can at times extend to self-hatred because of your perceived unacceptability and inadequacy.

Where self-rejection exists fruits such as guilt and self-condemnation will often be present. Guilt relates to believing that you have done something that you should not have done, or perhaps more likely in this situation, guilt believes that you have not done something that you should have. Hence the guilt is connected to the self-rejection via the mechanism of believing that you should do or be more and have failed.

OUTWARD SIGNS OF SELF-REJECTION

We have just discussed some potential inner workings of self-rejection; there are also some very obvious outward manifestations that may be encountered. Self-punishment for not being acceptable or not accepting yourself could present in behavior such as *cutting*, or children banging their heads against the wall or hitting themselves. This self-punishment is a sure sign that they are angry and frustrated with themselves. Adults might try to self-destruct with alcohol or drug abuse. Others try to comfort themselves with food and can at times set up a self-destructive cycle.

CANNOT, 'WILL NOT' RECEIVE ENCOURAGEMENT

We have already mentioned self-pity. Many people cannot receive affirmation, the inner rejection belief regarding their unworthiness is like a force field that cannot accept any encouragement as being true. For some self-pity is a kind of distorted *good feeling* which is a kind of demonic counterfeit for love. Often people suffering from self-rejection will present as negative, pessimistic, and are unable to receive because of unbelief regarding their acceptability. The underlying belief is something such as; *if I reject me, surely you must too!*

NEGATIVE SELF-IMAGE AND COMPARISON

Commonly, self-rejection proceeds from memories and events where a person has been compared to a sibling, or another student, and as a consequence has felt that they are inferior. If this is the case then usually you will find that they still have a problem with comparison in order to rate their acceptability today. *2 Corinthians 10:12*

There are no other versions of you in existence, found in history or planned for the future. Thank and praise God as King David did for making you, you. That is not pride; it is acceptance of yourself and who God created you to be. You are the work of His hands; you did not after all create yourself! *Psalm 139:14-17*

DISTORTED SELF-IMAGE

Self-rejection produces a distorted self-image. It can be like a belief based demonic hedge stopping people from receiving love, acceptance and belonging. It can cause people to reframe things that are said to them according to the *inner heart beliefs* that are held. Genuinely motivated suggestions for doing tasks another way or improving functionality from a friend, spouse or employer are heard, reframed by beliefs, and perceived as an attack on competency and worth.

SELF-REJECTION SYMPTOMS

A) **Low self-image:** – rejection crushes the personality
 "If they think that I am hopeless, useless etc.......then I must be!"

B) Proceeding from the depths of **low self-evaluation** comes **inadequacy and insecurity**
 "I am not enough; I don't feel safe to come out and be me!"

C) **Sadness, grief, sorrow:** These are outward signs of a wounded or crushed spirit...
 .... the evidence of deep hurt. Many people have a 'tragic look' on their faces as a result. *Proverbs 17: 22 + 18:14*

D) **Self-accusation, Self-condemnation:**
 This is where they are unable to forgive themselves and take all of the blame for the rejection. They constantly put themselves down, and cannot receive praise or encouragement.

E) **Worry, anxiety or depression:**
 "I don't know what to do to resolve this. I can't do it. What will happen if I don't fix it?"

F) **Frustration and anger:** often this is directed at not being able to achieve standards, goals or expectations, real or perceived, that relate to qualifying you to receive acceptance, love, significance, value or worth. Negativity, pessimism or hopelessness may also be present, proceeding from a belief that things cannot changed and expectations will not be met. Inner self talk could be along the lines of; "I'm too useless, it's hopeless, I just can't do it!"

G) **Inability or refusal to communicate:** This could be in the form of 'sulking' or 'packing a sad, 'or 'being in a huff' etc. The underlying idea behind the behavior is probably retaliation for how the subject is being made to feel, but it can also be a plan to cut off the source of the rejection.

SAMPLE MINISTRY TO REJECTION BELIEFS SCENARIO

A person approaches you for help.

Step 1: Explain the process to the person, and what you are looking for, namely *heart beliefs*. This process could include having them read, view or listen to material explaining the ministry.

Step 2: The person comes for the actual ministry session.
Note: They already have the problem that they are struggling with so you don't need to come up with anything. It is not your job to fix their whole life, just try to help them with whatever is presenting at the time.

Listen to their story and the issue that they are bringing to you. Make notes of the things that they *say* that may be clues to what they *believe*. Writing things down is good as it means that you don't miss things that may need to be visited, and you don't need to interrupt their story.

Step 3: Ministry Example

Fred: I felt very uneasy when I went to try out for the church choir!
Me: Why do you think that you were uncomfortable in that setting?
Fred: I think that I felt that I did not belong there, I was not a part of it.

This could indicate a possible belief such as; *I am not wanted, or I am not accepted.*

Step 4: We have them concentrate on the feeling produced by the thought that they do not belong, and are not a part of it; rejected by the group. We are looking for the earliest possibly historical place where they learnt beliefs that caused them to feel this way.

Fred: I have just remembered my first day of school. There was a group of kids playing and talking together and they ignored me!
Me: As you concentrate on the memory and feel that rejected feeling, why do you think that they ignored you?
Fred: Pauses and explores the memory. I think it is because I am not like them, I am new and so they don't want me. This must be true because they are all accepting each other, but I am on the outside!
Me: Let's ask the Lord what His truth, the real truth is. Lord what do you want Fred to understand about that time where he felt that he was not wanted because he is not like them, because he is new?
Fred: The Lord is reminding me, that these kids went to Kindergarten together and already knew each other. I couldn't get in to Kinder because they were full up.
Me: So, are you not wanted because you are different?
Fred: No, I am the same; I have just not built relationships yet. Later I did make some good friends there.
Me: How do you feel about the church choir now?
Fred: I feel excited about it now; I will be making some new friends it will just take a little time.
Me: Perhaps close in prayer thanking the Lord for His healing, or I may enquire as to whether or not there are other things which require ministry.

Clearly this example is not going to be as deeply painful as rejection often is. Some people may have very painful traumatic rejection situations from some kind of abuse or absence of love in the home. Other people may have a *profile of rejection* composed of multiple less painful beliefs.

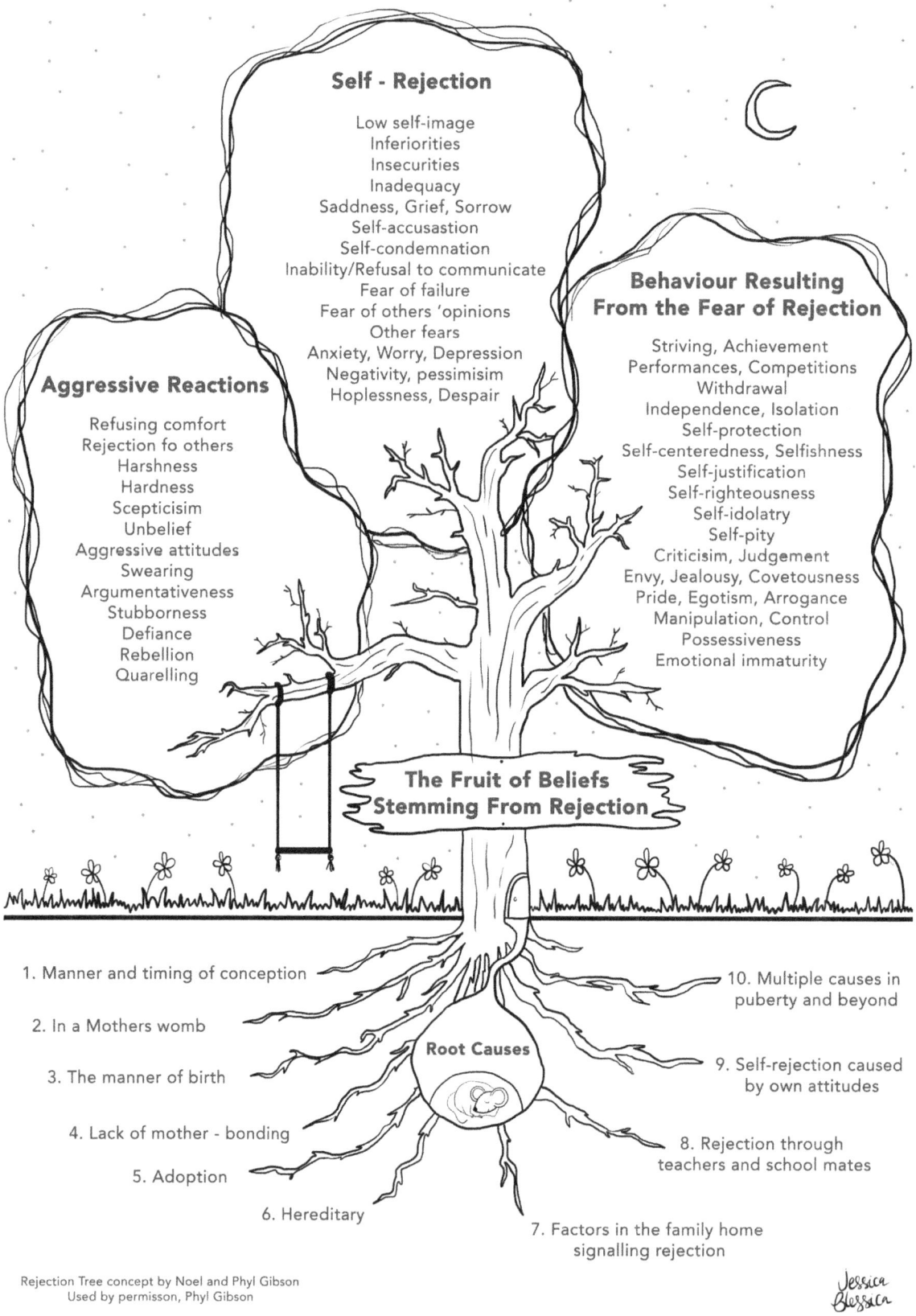

Rejection Tree concept by Noel and Phyl Gibson
Used by permisson, Phyl Gibson

UNIT SEVEN

Dealing with Fear

WE NOW CONSIDER TWO TYPES OF FEAR

Study 1: Circumstantial fear
What I term *circumstantial* fear is anxiety that is relating to a current event, such as a storm, a particular financial situation, or some other present tense happening. These do not relate to anything that you already believe from fearful times in the past.

A PRACTICAL THEOLOGY OF DEALING WITH 'CIRCUMSTANTIAL FEAR'
The Bible gives us a theology of how to deal with fear in our present circumstances where there is no historical precedent. It shows us how to practically deal with fears that are new situations, by displacing them in choosing trust and having faith in Him. This of course assumes that we are free from *fear beliefs* stemming from the past. I am told that there are 366 *fear nots* in the Bible. That is one for each day of the year and even leap year is covered. In the event that you are captive to a fear that came to you before you knew how to respond, or had God in your life, then you most probably need to be set free by a *Truth Encounter* with the Holy Spirit.

Before we examine how to be set free at heart level from historical *fear beliefs* let us first examine what our mindsets or *default position* should be in regards to submitting to *circumstantial* fear. There are some excellent pictures of this that Jesus gave us in the gospels. In Matthew 14, we see the story of an event that produced fear in the disciples that had no historical precedence. Jesus came to them walking on the water, a *circumstance* which is certainly not something that they had experienced in their past history. Their response was that they *'cried out in fear.'* Jesus described them as *'of little faith'* wondering why they doubted and chose to react in fear. *Matthew 14:22-31*

LESSON
We always have a choice. For Christians if God is for us who can be against us? *(Romans 8:31)* For believers the only real choice is faith.

Notably Peter did have enough trust and faith in Jesus to step out on His word. The principle here is that while he looked to Jesus he was doing fine, but when he heeded his circumstances, he was not fine. We could say that faith makes you float and puts you above or over your circumstances, but fear makes you sink and puts you under the power of your circumstances. Faith can make us walk over our situations because it is centered in a supernatural or *above* natural being.

 **LESSON**
Fear will make you subject to natural outcomes, as a result of being submitted to your surroundings and senses.

We call fear the *what if* spirit because it is always anxious about the possibility of negative outcomes. What if this, what if that happens? Jesus attributed their fear to their lack of faith. We will either submit to or come under one or the other. In regards to new situations, it is always a choice which we will make. Most times however, how we decide to respond is based on our previous which is interpreted through our existing history.

We could perhaps summarize our part in releasing God into our situations, and that which He wants to do through us, something such as this;

Unbelief	expects	nothing to happen.
Fear	expects	something bad to happen.
Faith	expects	something positive to happen.

Defining fear under another name
You may know fear in one of its many forms, for example, anxiety, stress, distress, worry, tension, restlessness, dread, apprehension or insecurity. Additionally, we might add in hopelessness, helplessness, doubt or unbelief. They are forms of fear because they do not include the presence, power or willingness of God to resolve whatever we are confronted with.

To summarize fear, we could define it as; *An expectation of a negative outcome.* To identify what your exact fear is you could say that your fear *is whatever you are afraid of!*
As you examine it you will know you are afraid of: not being protected, being hurt, being rejected, failing and so on.

Good fear
We use the term a *universal emotion,* as being a predictable feeling or response that can be distorted by the devil as a consequence of the fall. God gave us fear as a protective instinct. As a result, we don't normally play on highways or near cliffs. We don't as a rule, kiss snakes on the lips, this is simply not smart.

We can say that there is *good,* wise God-given fear that protects us. This includes the fear of God which helps to protect us from negative outcomes. The distorted version of fear deceives us that we need to protect ourselves, when it is in fact not necessary or beneficial. It is the fear of things that we are not meant to fear, or times when we can exercise faith to displace fear, that I am talking about.

Fear began in the garden, where man no longer believed that God had their best interests at heart, and was keeping things from him. In essence they doubted that He was good and really loved them. This was unbelief, or probably more aptly, wrong belief which is the basis of all of our anxieties. As a result, as we understand and receive God's love and acceptance both in our minds and hearts, we find ourselves being freed from our many fears. *1 John 4:18-19*

Equally we could say that the antithesis or natural enemy of fear, faith, also proceeds from believing that there is no longer any need to expect negative outcomes for us. This knowledge of His love for us, both mind and heart, receives that God has shown His love first by redeeming us and paying the penalty for our transgressions.

LESSON
God gave us fear for our protection, as with everything else that God created, the devil seeks to distort it and destroy us through it.

Fear as faith in reverse

Let us contrast Job with Daniel's friends, Shadrach, Meshach and Abednego. In the case of Job, everything was going well. He was highly regarded, wealthy, healthy, and had, by all appearances, a good family. Then everything around him began to fall apart. To what did he attribute and note as a precursor to these happenings?

> *Job 3:25 "What I feared has come upon me; what I dreaded has happened to me." NIV*

In contrast, we see Shadrach, Meshach and Abednego, and everything was not going well. However, they still refused to bow down to anyone or anything other than God. They refused to fear, and chose to put themselves under God's ability in faith regardless of the outcome. This took them out from under the potential outcome that Satan would have had for them, and put them under the supernatural power and provision of God. The outcome of their faith decision, and choosing to refuse fear in their circumstance, was finding the Lord in their trial with them, and the final result being them having favor and witness with their oppressors. Notably, they were not spared from the trial that tested them, but were triumphant in the midst of it as a result of their faith choice. *Daniel 3:17-25*

LESSON
Whatever we submit to has power over us to bring about an outcome, even if we submit through deception rather than willful choice. Truth then is our best defense.

> **Note:** The vast majority of fears that you deal with are interpreted through beliefs and conclusions which are historically rooted in earlier events which I will explain in a moment. We do however need to set a biblical 'default position' in how to respond to new circumstances that have no precedent.

LESSON
The law of sowing and reaping applies with fear. We need to be very careful what we expose ourselves to, and fill up on.

Setting the 'default position' of faith

It seems reasonably obvious that God did not give us or intend for us to be subject to a spirit of fear. We must realize that Satan is the instigator of bringing us into the bondage of fear. This invisible enemy will be seeking to bring to pass the object of our fear as we accept and submit to his plan for negative outcomes for us. Moving from fear to faith, as far as how we think in our minds is often a progressive journey as we hear from the counsel of God instructions such as; *Do NOT worry about your life, what you will eat, tomorrow,* and so on. *Do*

NOT be anxious. Cast ALL your anxiety on Him. (Matthew 6:25-34; Philippians 4:6; 1 Peter 5:7, NIV). If God says do not then I do not see another way to live other than His perfect order.

Joshua was going to be confronted with many potential opportunities to worry and fear negative outcomes. In all five times through the book of Joshua he was instructed to be strong and make the choice to be courageous. Repetition makes a deep impact on our memory. When it is reinforced with decisions to obey and make this our *default response*, it becomes a part of our thinking and being. *Joshua 1:9*

It has been well said that fear and faith are equal in that they both expect an outcome. It becomes vital as to whether we are under Satan's deception and responding to *perceived fear;* as he gives us his perspective on potentially negative events, or faith, allowing God to produce His outcomes. Remember fear exists because we have a *negative expectation* in regards to God's attitude towards us, or our worthiness to receive from Him which relates to our next area, *historical fear.* Every time that we expect or entertain a negative outcome, we are submitting to a spiritual power that is challenging God's word and nature, just as it happened in the Garden of Eden.

LESSON
Magnifying the Lord, and His power, love and abilities towards us is for our good, not His vanity. It doesn't matter how big we make Him in our lives, He is always many times greater than what we could imagine. Magnifying Him in our meditations grows our faith, and makes the choice to trust Him more obvious and eventually automatic.

In scripture, there is usually an antidote to fear along with the acknowledgement of the pressure of fear to impact us. There are examples of declarations that we can make to reinforce our decisions, and to make faith our default position and automatic response. A few examples for your consideration; *Proverbs 29:25, Isaiah 26:3, Psalm 56:3+118:6, Romans 8:31-32*

Effects of fear

Spiritually	Robs us of our faith, therefore removing our power and potential.
Mentally	Confusion, mind racing, trying to solve the problem.
Emotionally	Takes our peace, torments, feels bad.
Physically	Many negative effects on the body and health.
Fruitfulness	Makes us unfruitful, binds us and stops us walking into our promised land of abundant life and limits that which God can use us for.

The problem with us accepting fear as a reasonable response, is that in order to do so we have to downsize God and His love and power to match our beliefs. We have to believe that He is not in control, cannot protect or provide for us, or does not really love or care about us. In that instance, we have to re-define fear in our lives as doubt and unbelief.

Study 2: Historical fear

We have just spent a considerable amount of time on examining the instructions of scripture in regards to how we should deal with present tense or potential future fear *circumstances* that we may encounter. However, the vast majority of fear projects from beliefs we hold which we have already learnt in historical negative events, or fearful environments in the past. Even if we are presented with a potentially anxious situation in the present which does not have precedence, if we still hold unresolved *fear beliefs* from the past, we will automatically have expectations of a negative outcome by interpreting the possibilities of the event based on our previously existing beliefs. As a result, virtually all people who come for ministry presenting with fear and anxiety issues need to be set free from the beliefs that they have learnt from past experiences.

We have two types of fear, being circumstantial or historical in nature. We also have two kinds of fear beliefs. As we have detailed in the *Truth Encounters* section, we can hold beliefs that come from *situations* that relate to the events where we learn them, and also beliefs that relate to our *identity*. These beliefs are also marked and distinct in the area of fear.

Fear from Situational beliefs

Phobic type fear, or phobias, where people have specific fears tend to fit into this category. (*Phobos* is the Greek word from which fear is translated in the New Testament). For example, a person may present with a fear of tight spaces or elevators. As you have them focus on their fear, you are looking for a memory that holds matching feelings or circumstances as with those that they are currently experiencing. Their fear of tight spaces is not going to be to do with their identity, who they are, or whether they are good enough. We might ask them a question such as; *What is it that you are afraid of happening in the enclosed space?*

They could perhaps respond with something such as; *I will be trapped and I won't be able to get away.* I would then enquire as to what will happen if they can't get away. You may get for example a response such as; *I won't be able to breathe, and if I can't breathe, I will die.*

These beliefs can, many times, be established before going to the memory, or later in the memory examining the matching feelings. I would ask them to really embrace the feeling and ask them if there is a historical place where they felt exactly like this. That is, they are trapped, can't get away, can't breathe, and as a consequence in the memory, they believe that they will die. This is the *actual belief producing the fear*, in this case, that *they are going to die*.

At times there may be a spirit attached to the fear. If that is the case you will become aware of the probability by the intensity of the fear. Don't make casting out demons a part of *your method* in dealing with these fears. If there is a spirit there, it may simply leave when the truth sets them free. Do be aware of the possibility. I never go into ministry thinking about demons, looking for them, or expecting that deliverance from them will always be a part of the ministry. In the case of ministry, the problem is still the problem, and that is the belief producing the negative emotion. We continue to go after the belief and if there is an evil spirit involved powering up the fear response, we simply tell it to go in the name of Jesus. Think of it as shooing away a fly while you are trying to cook a barbeque. A spirit is only as big as you make it in your thinking.

Either you believe that the Bible is true and you have complete authority over them in Jesus name or not. If you believe that Jesus' is the name above all names you will have no problems.

We can summarize dealing with these kinds of fears by saying that we are simply looking for a situation where the belief/s were taken in.

> **Note:** There are times when there is a generational fear that has come through practices such as freemasonry or witchcraft curses. This comes through the sins of the ancestors who have been submitted and involved in ungodly practices further up the family line. For example, with freemasonry there could be something such as a fear of being buried alive. Usually telling the spirit behind that to go will greatly lesson the fear, although there may be beliefs involved as well. Why would you investigate if freemasonry or other possible sources are present? Because there are no memories or known prenatal events that connect with the fear.

Fear from Identity beliefs

As you understand by now, what we term *identity beliefs* relates to who you are, how you are, and what you consider to be true about your *'self.'* I will not go into a lot of detail here because we have already detailed these in the preceding studies; these are the sources of negative *self-beliefs* which we may now fear being reinforced. These project from incidences producing rejection, inferiority, injustice, insecurity, abuse and so on. I will suggest a few common beliefs that people may hold as a result of being exposed to these negative influences; *I'm weak, stupid, inferior, can't do it, not as good as others, not wanted, don't belong, am not worth caring about, am a nothing, not important etc.*

Once life has programmed these negative inner thoughts into you, you now fear that they will be proven to be true. You may fear that people will discover these *supposed* weaknesses in your person. Additionally, you may fear that people will not want you, or will think poorly of you because of these *perceived* shortcomings. The freedom from the fear regarding these beliefs about yourself comes once you no longer hold them as being true about you.

Two categories of fear

I have come to the conclusion that generally all fears seemingly fall broadly under 2 categories.

Fear of harm

This would obviously relate to being hurt or abused physically or in some other harmful way and would include anxieties projecting from accidents and traumas. It could also take in situations such as fear of no protection or no provision or even lack of finances.

Fear of rejection

Under this heading we will find such subtitles as *Fear of man, fear of failure, and fear of embarrassment etc.*

Why would you fear man?
    He may not accept you for who you are.
What will happen if you fail?
    People will reject your efforts and consequently you yourself!
Why would you be embarrassed to begin with?
    This is because some kind of weakness or supposed inferiority has been exposed with the expectation that people will reject you because of it.
In our minds:
    We know that we should not even care about the 'praises of men.'
    We know that being accepted and loved by God is not conditioned to our performance, abilities or success in man's eyes.

We know that God will be pleased by our faith, in not submitting to fear but rather trusting Him in everything, and trusting Him and stepping out in service.

However, *knowing this* in our minds and wanting to hold these attitudes and produce corresponding actions does not remove *the heart beliefs* that oppose our freedom. We really do need God to set us free to be all that we can be for His glory. I have not seen people successfully resolve *heart beliefs* with their *minds.* They are two separate and distinct areas of our beings. It is not a matter of merely changing your thinking or reading books and becoming experts on fear. I have not seen anyone set free that way. It is the truth at *heart level* that makes you free. *Romans 7:15*

Sample ministry: Situational or phobic fear

Me: "What can we help you with today?"

Fred: "Well I have a fear of flying."

Me: "So what are you afraid might happen when you get on an aircraft?"

Fred: Ponders "I feel as though I will be out of control"

Me: "I want you to focus on that thought and the feeling that goes with it and see if you remember a time in your life where you felt just like that."

Fred: "I remember being pushed down a steep hill in a little cart we had made. The big kids put me in and sent the cart racing down the hill towards the trees."

Me: "What did you believe might happen while you were afraid?"

Fred: "I guess I felt that I was going to get hurt and nobody could stop it happening. I was terrified!"

Me: "Let's hold that belief up to the Lord that 'nobody can stop what's going to happen, and I will get hurt.'" (Prayer asking the Lord to bring His truth)

Fred: "I just remembered that actually one of the big kids ran after me and eventually did stop the cart before it hit the trees."

Me: "So what does that mean to you?"

Fred: "Well it means that God will always find a way to protect me. He is always in control."

Me: "So think about flying now, are you still afraid of being out of control?"

Fred: Pauses "No. I am still a bit fearful though it is nowhere near as much!"

Me: "Alright focus on the residual fear and see if you can work out what you are afraid of."

Fred: "I have been on a plane before and it felt like there was nothing solid underneath me….it was a scary feeling."

Me: "Okay, I want you to concentrate on the anxious belief that there is nothing solid underneath you." "Lord, would you help Fred to connect with a place where he felt just like that before?"

Fred: "As soon as you said that I remembered being on a cliff edge when we were kids and it caved in underneath me. I slid down the face of it and into the river."

Me: "So you felt as if there was nothing solid under you? And what was the consequence or fear expectation about that situation?"

Fred: "I thought that I was going to die!"

Me: "Alright, I just want for you to embrace that anxiety and belief in that memory that because there is nothing solid under you, you will die."

Fred: Pauses "Do you know, that is just not true. What came to mind was the scripture that talks about the circle of the Earth. It's just hung out there in space with nothing under it just because God put it there and supports it, nothing under it, but still suspended."

Me: "So if you think about there being nothing solid under you on a plane how do you feel about it now?"

Fred: "You know it's really okay….!"

Me: "How do you feel about flying now Fred?"
Fred: "Do you know, it's weird but I think that I am a bit excited!"

Perhaps we might say a prayer thanking the Lord or certainly make a comment about how amazing our God is in setting us free and acknowledging Him as being the one who has done the freeing. Either way, God is glorified as He fulfills His promise and the session closes.

Sample ministry: Identity belief-based fear

Me: "What seems to be the problem?"
Fred: "I have been asked to do communion in church next Sunday, but I am petrified and haven't been able to sleep!"
Me: "I want you to imagine yourself up there in front of all those people. As you feel that anxiety I would like you to examine it and try to work out exactly what it is that you are afraid might happen."
Fred: Pause "I am afraid that I might not be able to do it properly."
Me: "I would like you to feel that anxiety about not doing it properly, and as you do let your mind connect you with a place that held those feelings. It will be somewhere where you actually couldn't do what was expected."
Fred: Ponders "I remember in school when I was about 7 years old. The teacher wanted me to write some cursive text on the blackboard, and I wrote it back the front. The teacher made a big fuss over it making fun of me in front of the whole class and I recall being incredibly embarrassed."
Me: "As a result of not being able to do it, and the intense embarrassing moment in front of the class, what conclusion about yourself did you come to?"
Fred: Pause, thoughtful "I'm dumb. I must be dumb because I could not do it right."
Me: "As you feel that embarrassment and the belief that you are 'dumb' because you could not do it, let us ask the Lord what the real truth is."
Prayer: "Lord Fred things that he is dumb because he could not do the cursive writing on the board. What do you want him to know about that situation?"
Fred: "Well, I didn't hear any thoughts. But I just sort of understood that none of us had actually been taught cursive yet. And the teacher liked to mock us and make fun of us. She sort of deliberately put me in that position to make sport of me."
Me: "So are you dumb because you could not do it?"
Fred: "No, the truth is that none of us could yet. I am feeling that I was alright, there is nothing wrong with me, but I think that the teacher had some issues. I forgive her."
Me: "Picture yourself doing communion on Sunday, how do you feel about messing it up now?"
Fred: "I actually feel fine about it; I will work out how to do it as best I can and really everything doesn't have to be perfect. After all, we are all family."

> **Note:** A situation such as public speaking typically may evoke a response from more than one historically learnt fear producing belief. As each one is ministered to the intensity of the anxiety normally goes down. If you just process the beliefs one by one eventually you will achieve peace. It is of course normal to be a little nervous if it is a new situation.

UNIT EIGHT

Ungodly Control and Insecurity

Study 1: Godly control versus ungodly control

Clearly God wants His Kingdom run in an orderly way, not out of control but in an organized fashion, under instituted authority. This godly control of course is meted out in the right spirit and needs to be appropriate. We could say that we are to be responsible and have authority over certain areas, beginning with our own behavior. For example, Adam was to be responsible for the garden and indeed the subduing of the Earth.

In *1 Kings chapter 21* we see King Ahab being too weak to appropriately execute his authority. The result was that his wife Jezebel presumed authority and control, and manipulated the outcome of the situation. To swing the pendulum all the way back past centre the other way, many nations have men dominated societies. Christians in these societies often use the Bible to strengthen their case of their wives being treated as second class citizens who must submit to them. This is actually often a manifestation of a controlling spirit. *Ephesians 5:25-29*

It is not the man's role to force or manipulate the woman to submit to him. His part is only, by 'his own' free will and choice, to fulfill God's intentions for him in the relationship. The woman in turn has her instructions in the Bible on how she should respond to his godly attitudes and provisions for her. When a man is insisting on 'lordship' over his wife and demands total subservience he is looking to be her 'god.' This is a tendency that was picked up in the garden where man was tempted to raise himself up in pride over others, as did the tempter, Satan. And then *be like God*, which means everyone serves you and your purposes because you have now become the central being. In order to do this, you will have to treat your wife as an inferior being that God created, which she certainly is not! *Genesis 3:5*

Although the Bible describes the woman as the weaker member, it also describes her as a helpmate comparable. If she is comparable, she is not inferior in the least. Clearly, she is weaker physically, and emotionally her hormonal state is up and down throughout her monthly cycles, whereas a mans is constant. She is the other half of God's perfect picture for us, together complementing each other with altogether different attributes and abilities. *1 Corinthians 11:10-11, Ephesians 5:31-32, Galatians 3:28*

AREAS OF GODLY CONTROL

Before we move on, let us briefly detail some areas that God wants us to be responsible for and have control over.

1. Man over his family.
This is not controlling your wife, as she is already at the age of choice, but is more in exercising fair and godly authority over children in a decreasing manner as they grow up and learn how to control themselves.

2. Pastors and leaders in Churches.
God wants His churches run decently and in order. This does not mean that a Pastor or leader can control his congregation; it means that he instigates God's order and sets the environment as loving, accepting, gracious and acknowledging free will and choice. Authority into people's lives is given by them and not taken from them. People either choose to submit to you as they learn to trust your love and motives or not.

LESSON
Evidently God gave all of His creation free will and choice, including the angels. We do not have the right to consider ourselves greater than Him, and seek to take away the free will which He has given to others.

Study 2: Ungodly control from insecurity

It was God's intention for mankind to grow up secure in identity, feeling protected, and provided for. When Adam and Eve took themselves out from under these attributes that were provided for them by God, they became insecure and fearful. To a large extent they now felt that they had to be *as God* for themselves, fulfilling these needs. It is now inherent in mankind to try to control his environment in order to feel secure. The problem is that this often involves imposing your will on others which is never God's plan for how harmony and peace should operate.

The root of ungodly control in general terms is *insecurity*. This insecurity causes us to make things happen for our own provisions. It is demonic in the sense that it is a perversion of the will area of your being, imposing your will on others, beyond intended parameters. This is driven by Satan and is not from God.

> *1 John 5:19 "We know that we are children of God and that the world around us is under **the power and control** of the evil one." NLT (Emphasis mine)*

MISUSE OF THE CAPACITY FOR CONTROL
Authority to have some measure of control is linked to responsibility. I could not, for example, walk into a church down the road and begin to tell people what to do. I am not responsible for them and consequently have no authority over them. The same goes for my family and so on. When you see people trying to get others to do things for them, they are exhibiting controlling behavior.

Often controlling people will use the *God told me or thus saith the Lord* card to manipulate a situation and have their will carried out. After all who can challenge what God Himself has said! I tend to think that often when people are making these kinds of statements that you are dealing with the *'controlly' spirit* and not the *Holy Spirit*. They are hearing what they want to hear or feel they need to hear, to get what they want or remove their insecurity and thus open themselves up to deception. This will be obvious if the outcome of the use of the Lord's name relates to something that they think should happen.

As I understand it, blasphemy is when you take the Lord's name in vain. This does not necessarily mean swearing, it can mean saying that God said, when He didn't. People need to be more careful than they realize about how they use the Lord's name.

IS GOD CONTROLLING?

We are to be 'led' by the Spirit which denotes choice. Jesus began His ministry *led* by the Spirit into the desert and finished it in the garden of Gethsemane, deciding by His own free will and choice, to lay down the easy way in preference to the Father's will. It is perhaps notable that Adam and Eve chose to follow Satan in a garden where everything was going fine, and Jesus to reverse the effects of this chose to suffer to fulfill the Father's desires.

We could state that God is not controlling at all. He instructs us in the way and encourages us and empowers us to fulfill godly choices but does not make us do anything at all. Sometimes it would probably be easier if He did, but He is looking for us to respond to the Love that He initiates and choose Him. Jesus often included words such as; *if, then*, and *but*, which denotes choice. John 6:67, 8:31, +15:7

LESSON
It is not our job to make anyone do anything. Our mission is to help them understand the ways of God so that they can make the right choices and decisions for themselves. If the ability to do this has been compromised then we have instruction from the Bible to heal them and set them free.

BRANCHES THAT COME FROM UNGODLY CONTROL

1. Manipulation
This could be in the form of kids threatening tantrums, men being physically threatening, wives withholding sex, or people saying that *God said*.

2. Domination
Violence or some kind of abuse is the typical outworking of someone misusing their authority or power.

3. Standards
"You must be how I want you to be and think you should be. You need to do what I want, how I want it or I cannot receive you! You must fit into my plans!"

4. Bitterness and unforgiveness
I will not release you or forgive you for being how you are, or who you are, and not being and doing what I want! This projects rejection because if what you want or do is not good enough then by implication you are unacceptable.

5. Self-willed; leading to intimidation
If I don't get what I want, get my own way you will pay in some way or I will explode in anger.... so look out! (Intimidation)

6. Things have to be a certain way
This could come in the form of perfectionism or obsessive-compulsive behavior which is an extreme form of insecurity and fear compelling you to control details of your life. Things have to be a certain way or there is a fear that something bad will happen. The demonic realm certainly can be working in areas of control. In order to identify heart beliefs relating to *insecurity or fear*, the best question that you can ask is; *what will happen if...?*

7. Lack of self-control
t is as if their capacity for self-control is directed outwards in getting others to do things for them, and as a consequence they have little or no self-control or authority over themselves.

8. Tendency to get others to do things for them
Controllers will always be getting others to do things for them. Remember they are insecure, so they are making sure that you care about them because underneath they believe that nobody does.

9. Blame, fault finding and criticism
They should have done it this way or that way...my way!
They are not good enough....my way is how it NEEDS to be done! (insecurity & pride)

EFFECTS OF UNGODLY CONTROL ON RELATIONSHIPS
We see many couples, even Christian couples, in conflict, wrestling backwards and forwards with each other trying to impose their will on each other. This creates instability and an insecure environment in the household which will generationally generate more insecurity down the family line. Healthy relationships can only exist in the context of free will and choice, where you lay down your right to expect or demand anything from the other.
Galatians 5:13-15

PRACTICAL OUTWORKING OF UNGODLY CONTROL

1. It pushes away the ones that you are **trying to control.** If you are trying to conform somebody else to you, then you are not accepting them for who they are ... an individual.

2. It reads as an **unfair projection**. It proposes that they are not good enough as they are and should be something else.

3. **Love must come by choice.** If you make people do things to show that they care about you it is meaningless, because even if they do your will, in this regard you know that you made it happen. It was not something that they did for you just because they wanted to.

4. **Legalistic religions.** There are religions and denominations that demand that you conform to their religious standards for acceptance. They can be very controlling in regards to who you marry, your finances, your spiritual disciplines and so on.

5. **Controlling God.** There are extremes of faith where it is taught that if you believe hard enough and long enough that you can get God to give you what you want. Essentially this can be like witchcraft, where you turn God into some kind of vending machine who does your will and becomes your Holy Spirit. We are to ask according to His will. 1 John 5:14-15

PROBABLE SOURCES OF UNGODLY CONTROL
1. *Insecurity* - as we have detailed in this chapter, the most common reason producing ungodly control are areas in which we don't feel secure.

2. *Modeling* – at times growing up seeing a controlling mother or father can cause us to replicate the behavior, believing that this is simply how you behave and act towards others. It can be inherent in some cultures, and so we see that controlling attitudes can be learnt by osmosis soaking up the environment around us.

3. **Generational issues** - there can be a spiritual element where a weakness or tendency to gravitate towards operating in this manner is present.

WHAT ARE WE LOOKING FOR IN MINISTRY?

Whilst aware of other possibilities, we are primarily looking for *historical insecurity events* matching the current need to control your surroundings. Having noted the fruit of control, you will probably have a much better response if you ask the person if they ever feel a little insecure, as opposed to *telling* them that they are controlling.

ASSOCIATED INNER BELIEFS THAT OVERFLOW FROM THE HEART

1. **Lack of attention** - *nobody cares about me*

2. **Lack of protection** - *I must look after myself*

3. **Abuse** - *I can't trust others to look after my needs, because when I do, I get hurt*

4. **Lack of provision** - *I must get things for myself, nobody really loves me or cares about what I need, so I must get people to provide for me. I must meet my own needs*

5. **Fears** - *I cannot let go of my insecurities and control, what will happen?*

MINISTRY PROTOCOL

1. **Find where the insecurity began**
   The womb; (not wanted and therefore not feeling protected or safe?). A life event or theme in the home from early life experiences, osmosis growing up, or the family line.

2. Deliverance where applicable, concurrently with healing of the associated beliefs.

3. **Sometimes teaching** as you go with how to be releasing and **hold things loosely.** Some people are not aware of what they are doing, or that it is not God's order. Once you expose the discrepancy and give perspective it leaves them free to decide on their path.

> **Note:** You do not need to remember every detail of this to minister. It is to help you understand that controlling behavior often flags *insecurity beliefs*.

Sample: Ministry to ungodly control that is presenting from insecurity.

Freda: "My husband says that I am very controlling."
Me: "Give me an example of why he would call you that."
Freda: "Sometimes he gets home later than he should from work. He complains that I am always at him to be on time. He says he feels controlled and can't even stop of at the supermarket on the way home."
Me: "What do you feel will happen if he isn't home on time?"
Freda: Ponders. "Mmmmmm I guess I feel that there will be nobody there for what I need and it's not fair."

Me:	"I want you to concentrate on those thoughts that it is not fair that nobody is there for what you need, and see if you can remember another time as early as possible in your life where you felt just like that."
Freda:	"As soon as you asked me that, the memory of my first day of school came into my mind. All of the other kids were picked up but my mum didn't arrive for ages."
Me:	"As you look at that situation what is the strongest way to describe what you believed as a result of that event?"
Freda:	"I guess I believe that I am not important and so nobody is bothering to be there for me. I feel unprotected."
Me:	"As you concentrate on that feeling let us see what truth the Lord has for you?"
Prayer;	"Lord what would you like Freda to know. She believes that she is not important enough to be there for, she feels unprotected."
Freda:	Pause. "It seems like my own thoughts but it seems as if He is saying that I am important to Him, and that He has set His affection on me, and the scripture that He will never leave me nor forsake me has come to my mind."
Me:	"Do you still believe that you are not important enough to be there for?"
Freda:	"No, I am very important. I also just remembered that my mum had a flat tire and that is why she was late. But I knew that and it didn't seem to fix the problem before."
Me:	"That is probably because you took in the belief when you were very upset and emotionally vulnerable. It is what you perceived to be true at the moment of weakness that counts. That conclusion was deeply stored in your heart and as a result it is the inner thought that remained."
	"How do you feel about your husband getting home late now?"
Freda:	"Fine. I can't believe that it mattered so much to me. It seems a bit ridiculous. He should be able to do some errands if he wants to."

UNIT NINE

Low self-image, Inferiority and Pride

In this Unit we are going to examine the normal fruit associated with the pride tree.

Matthew 12:33b "... for a tree is recognized by its fruit." NIV

Study 1: What is pride?

We could say that pride is fallen confidence. God intended for us to have good self-worth and identity within the context of being satisfied with our own *individual* self. Pride is a condition where we now see ourselves as *above* other people and not equal. It is the imprint that Satan put on mankind tempting them with; *you will be as God. This being your own god* and making your own rules is clearly seen across humanity today. It began with Satan, and we see the five *I wills* of pride represented in scripture. Isaiah 14:13-14

This propensity for self-promotion is abundantly evident in the pride profile. Pride would have us have too higher opinion of ourselves, gathering credit or glory for ourselves. It encourages us to believe that we are over or **above** others and to consider ourselves as being superior. This gives us some insight into how Satan engineers it into our lives. It is a deception, and when we believe that we are *inferior* then the solution that he offers is to build an image that we convince ourselves is superior. The deception comes as it did with the tree in the Garden of Eden as; *this is what you need, this will make you happy. James 4:6-7*

Once we have misinterpreted the situation and received this as being the solution to our inferiority, it leads us to sinful attitudes and practices towards our fellow man. It is the *fallen self-life, old nature or 'flesh'* exalting itself, as it was with Lucifer placing *self* on a self-made throne. *Luke 18:10-14*

People suffering from beliefs that hold inferiority and low self-image will either give up in self-rejection, and roll over, or gravitate to performance and achievement-based self-worth. The Bible says that the pride of life is from the world, not from the Father. *1 John 2:16*

Remember the fruit of the tree in the garden of Eden was good for making you wise; knowledge puffs up, but love builds up; knowledge can make you look superior, but love will be building up others rather than self. We have mentioned Peter failing when he denied Jesus, and as a result becoming humble, before God released power through him. It was necessary for Peter to understand his frailty and humanity for him to become humble, with a correct perspective of himself in order for him to be useable. *Acts 3:11-16*

Study 2: The fruit, or what will pride look like in behavior and attitudes

Importance
You have to be somebody; you cannot simply be. You have to be important, regarded and valued. In a Christian environment this will probably be manifested as a person who cannot serve nor do small things. It is a breeding ground for *super spirituality* where people are too great in their own eyes to receive from other people and so propose that God talks to them directly.

Religiosity also comes into the picture. This happens as people learn all of the spiritual talk and jargon, know more scriptures, listen to more preachers than others etc. to make themselves be greater or above others. We call religion the try hard spirit, trying hard to be somebody. Religion declares, *this is what you do to be good enough, this is how you look and what you say!* Religion tries to be good enough by what you do, according to what you think will make you acceptable to man, and possibly be enough to please God.

Presumption

Have you ever had those people come to visit, who sit down, put their feet up on your furniture, and proceed to change your television channel to what they want to watch? They will probably be overbearing, right about everything, full of their own opinions, arrogant and superior. The *language of the spirit* emanating from their actions and attitudes is something along the lines of; *I am and there is no other!* Have mercy on them. Although they can be annoying remember that usually underneath is a person who has been crushed or neglected, and full of low self image. In the case of King Saul, Samuel noted that he was once *small in his own eyes*. In other words, his self-promotion and subsequent presumption and rebellion were proceeding from his *low self-image. 1 Samuel 15:17-19*

Rebellion against authority often runs closely with pride. This is because authority figures have not provided the identity needed for them to feel that they are sufficient. This is perceived as unjust or unfair and the response is to bypass authority as those in authority are not to be trusted.

> *1 Samuel 15:23 "For **rebellion** is like the sin of divination, and arrogance like the evil of idolatry. NIV (Emphasis mine)*

Judgment

These people will often be graceless, harsh, critical and unforgiving towards your shortcomings, imperfections or failures. The hardness and harshness are probably because, at heart level, they have not forgiven themselves for not being up to the mark.

Comparison

We have already mentioned this under the self-rejection heading, but it is a fruit of this tree. I would like to add that when comparison is coupled with low self-image it can lead to self-pity. *Poor me, everyone else is good enough, but I will never be as good as them. I will never be important, worthy or loved. I will never be good enough for love, compliments and attention.*

Competition

Somehow, we think that if we can climb higher, run faster, gather more money or in some other way prove ourselves then we will feel better about ourselves. These people are often high achievers who will project onto you that you are not enough, don't do enough or have enough. They have arrived and you have not.

Striving

Trying hard to have the upper hand, being contentious, struggling to be right or regarded, does not promote peace or unity. Again, to not have your opinion valued strikes right at the roots of where this most likely all began. Striving may well struggle against the system and rules as well individuals. It is a part of the imprint on fallen man from the garden to want to throw off the rules and limits.

Jealousy

Again, King Saul is our example. As we have previously stated, he was once small in his own eyes, or as we would frame it, he suffered from inferiority and low self-image. When David came along, he was exalted by the people. Jealousy occurs when someone else receives what you want. Because of his low self-image, King Saul needed to be praised by men. It ministered to his inner hurt and beliefs to some degree, although clearly it did not bring healing. So, when David received more adulation than him, he burned with jealousy. 1 Samuel 18:7-11

Note: Many of the presenting symptoms relating to pride issues discussed here were first noted in an excellent study called *Possess the Land* put together by Carroll Thompson from Dallas, Texas, and Published by Carroll Thompson Ministries in 1977.

UNIT TEN

Rebellion, anger and bitterness

Rebellion or lawlessness runs very closely with pride. As we have already seen, Satan as Lucifer' no longer wanted rules. In his proud, self-elevated state he wanted to be above the laws of God and no longer wanted to submit to the authority of God and His commands. God of course would not tolerate this rebellion and Lucifer and those who cooperated with him were cast down to the Earth. He then tempted man to throw off the rules as he had and conform to, or be imprinted with, the likeness of his own behavior.

So, lawlessness or rebellion as we know it is when we won't come under authority and laws, or we set ourselves against authority. Our own will becomes our god, subject only to self, and we are no longer prepared to have rules and limits. *2 Thessalonians 2:7, 1 Samuel 15:23*

Strong's concordance cites the Hebrew word; 'meriy' as meaning bitterness, i.e. (fig.) rebellion. The reason for this may be that when someone is embittered by injustice or unfairness it will produce rebellion as a predictable response. This will normally be directed towards those who are in authority, who are perceived as not being just and fair. In the case of the Garden of Eden, Satan was saying did God *really* say do not eat from that tree? He was craftily implying that God was keeping good things from them and did not really care about them. In a sense he was saying; *did God really give you limits, surely that's not fair!*

God was painted as being unjust in keeping that tree from them and mankind doubted His love and character. It is not surprising that the way back to God for humanity is to accept His love, and the grace offered through His merciful character. God has given us the opportunity through Christ to reverse the effect of the fall and consequent separation from him. He has largely limited Himself on Earth to trusting in His nature and love and accessing all that He has for us by faith.

Study 1: Sources of rebellion

We see rebellion and lawlessness enter into mankind at the fall as mankind doubted God's justness and fairness. We decided that we could be *like god setting* our own rules, providing for ourselves, and being accountable only to our own will and wants. Rebellion then is a predictable reaction to perceived or actual unfairness and injustice. *Matthew 23:4*

REBELLION 'AS WITCHCRAFT'

As we explore this in the context of our falleness, why is rebellion as bad as, or like witchcraft? Those who practice actual witchcraft are taking control, that is not theirs, over the will and outcomes of other people. It is a perversion of the will, imposing your will on another. People in rebellion prefer their will and desires over those of another. They will struggle to submit to the position and will of instituted authority. Christian people with rebellion issues will want to bypass authority and usually consider that they have a hotline to heaven hearing directly and correctly from God. *Numbers 12:2-3 + 12:9-11+ 16:3 + 16:32-33*

SOURCES OF REBELLION

Here are some potential beginnings for *beliefs* coming from authority figures. They emanate from real or perceived unfairness and injustice when it seems to a child that they are;

- not valued   - not protected   - not noticed   - not wanted
- not loved   - not cared for   - not affirmed   - not important

These we would consider to be omissions or deficits in terms of emotional nurture that would be justly and fairly expected. The next list covers things that have been done to a person, and should not have been, such as abuses which were actually committed and are unjust;

- Physical domination or violence
- Sexual abuse
- Emotional control or manipulation
- Attitudinal: nasty, angry or disapproving looks, shrugged off, indifference
- Verbal abuse: mockery, put down, condemned
- Inappropriate discipline, expectations, or workload

Both of these lists project onto the recipient attitudes, which result in *beliefs* such as; *you are not worth the time, you are a nothing, you are not of any value, I don't care about you* etc. Being made to feel this way really is not fair and is a part of broken heartedness that needs God's healing.

Study 2: Possible struggles for those with rebellion issues

Lusts

People with rebellion issues often have trouble subjecting their flesh. They refuse godly limits and often lack self-control. Very commonly if they have grown up with injustice from authority figures they will take control of their lives as early as possible. Their inner thinking is probably something along the lines of; *If they won't look after me and care about what I need, then I will look after myself!* This is probably the hardest time in history to be a teenager. Once you have decided to care and provide for yourself you will look to the World for what is available. You are now confronted with masses of addictive material including items such as drugs, cigarettes, alcohol, porn, illicit sex, unhealthy foods, media and much more.

Protecting our children

We can protect our children from rebellion by treating them fairly, being caring and attentive to their needs, and not expecting them to be perfect in a hostile environment. It is not beneficial to try to isolate them from the world but rather teach them how to make good decisions and choices in the world. If we are to represent God to our children, we will model His fair and just nature to them. *Psalm 89:14, Ephesians 6:4*

Anger, bitterness, and resentment may also be additional responses and reactive emotions to injustice and unfairness. Self-pity could also be present. It is the *nobody cares about me* thinking that can proceed from not being dealt with properly. Lack of trust and insecurity about people's motives may also be evident, which can make it difficult for people with rebellion issues to come and submit to another for help. If you are dealing with somebody presenting with rebellion, my strong recommendation is that you reframe it around the root of the problem as injustice or unfairness issues. This is, not proposing that there is something wrong with them or their behavior, but rather that there is something wrong with how they have been treated or dealt with by others, and consequently they will be far more likely to be willing to receive help.

LESSON
We are God's representatives; He deals with us fairly and graciously in love. If we wisely replicate that nature towards others, we will avoid promoting rebellious responses in them.

Rebellion from rejection
Rejection is a source of rebellion as we see in the story of Cain and Abel. Cain felt that it was unfair that Abel's offering was accepted but his was rejected. In truth, Abel showed his heart towards God in bringing the best of what he had. People often feel that if we reject what they do or have then we have rejected them as a person. We have to learn to have sufficient grace as God did to separate what we do from who we are. In any case, Cain rebelled against the warning of God and participated with sin in murdering his brother. *Genesis 4:3-7*

Although Cain had to suffer a consequence for his actions it was evident that the Lord was fair and still accepted who he was and cared about his safety. *Genesis 4:15*

Rebellion as a 'Spirit'
Using the *Truth Encounters* principles, we are not looking for evil spirits, but at times along the way we become aware that a problem, such as rebellion, is inordinate in its proportions, *amplified* or there is a *stronghold* indicating demonic involvement. We are still primarily interested in the beliefs that are held that produce the rebellion or other issues. (See Unit 5)

We are primarily focused on the person and along the way we may tell a spirit to go as a part of the process. If we have discovered and resolved the belief and exposed the spirit, the person normally now does no longer want to engage their will in hosting the spirit.

Most, if not all of us, have had some type of rebellious thinking somewhere in our lives because it was a part of our old nature stemming from the fall. In the event of somebody having a *spirit of rebellion* I have observed some fairly easily discernible behavior. People who are captive simply cannot submit to another. At times the source of a *spirit of rebellion* is the family line where it has passed through generations. Where this is the case, there is very often concurrent evidence of mental illness which we would consider to be a curse and not a blessing.

REBELLION SUMMARY
Failure to provide love and acceptance, nurture, encouragement and security leaves a void that the child feels that they need to provide for themselves. Nearly all rebellion problems begin in childhood and you can expect them to be networked with other negative emotional reactions stemming from heart beliefs.

MINISTERING TO REBELLION

You will need to go back and look for the origins of rebellion that exists against authority figures and others, usually the parents. In the ministry session we are looking for the feelings of *injustice or unfairness*. We are also being aware of statements emanating from inner beliefs such as, for example, *that's just the way it is for me, nobody ever cares, it's not fair but it's just the way it is!* We have the person focus on the feeling or the statement which connect them to a feeling that is replicated in the past.

Having arrived at the earliest possible memory or impression, have them focus on the feeling and identify the belief, or if they are more cognitive and have the belief first as they look at the situation, have them concentrate on the belief and allow the matching feeling to emerge. Remember, your role is to ask questions to help them identify that which they believe.

Sample Rebellion Session

Me: "What seems to be bothering you Fred?"

Fred: "I've been struggling with angry feelings a bit lately when I come to church."

Me: "If you think about it, what exactly is it that is making you angry?"

Fred: Pause, reflection. "I think it is because the leaders have never shown any interest in the groups that I am starting around the church."

Me: "How does it make you feel as you think that nobody is doing that for you?"

Fred: "It's not fair; they don't care about what I am doing!"

Me: "Why don't you think they care about what you are doing?"

Fred: Reflection, some emotion. "I think it is because I am not very important...."

Me: "Fred, I want you to concentrate on that thought that you are not important. It must be a sad feeling so I want you to let yourself feel that feeling....and now I want you to let your mind connect you with other places where you have felt exactly that way."

Fred: Pause. "As soon as you said that I remembered when I was a little boy, all of the other kids getting a special meal brought home and I wasn't allowed to have any. I was probably about 4 years old."

Me: "So as you look at that situation, why do you think that you were missing out?"

Fred: "I feel a bit angry. They don't care about what I want!"

Me: "So does not caring about what you want mean that they don't care about you....?"

Fred: "Yes, I am not important, I don't matter, and they don't care about me."

Me: "Ok Fred I want you to concentrate on those feelings and see what the Lord has to say to you... His truth, which is the truth." (Then I pray inviting God to communicate truth through the Spirit of truth).

Fred: "It seemed just like my own thoughts, but it seemed like God said that I am important to Him. And I just remembered that passage from 1 Peter 5:7 that says that He cares for me. As I continue to think about it, I have also remembered that I had been sick at the time ... and what I am sensing is that even though they didn't explain it at the time they didn't give me any because I might throw up!"

Me: "So are you important? Cared about?"

Fred: "God thinks so. And apparently my parents cared enough and thought enough about me to not want to make me sick."

Me: "Fred I want you to look in your heart, not your head...is that belief that you are not important still there?"

Fred: "No, which is strange because it has always been there ... but I can't find it any more. I am important, and cared about."

Me: "How do you feel about the leaders not paying attention to your groups now?"

Fred: Ponders. "Well to be honest, I guess that I have never trusted them and let myself

>   connect with them. I wanted them to take up my ideas; I was not interested in working with theirs. I suppose I just expected them to know how I felt which was a bit unreasonable of me I suppose."

Me: "Do you feel alright about approaching them now?"
Fred: "Yes, actually I feel a bit excited about what might be ahead for me!"

Principles of Anger

In the setting of ministering *Truth Encounters* you are looking at *anger beliefs* coming from events where things were considered to not be how they should be. Perhaps this could be a father who never attended school events with their child. The child feels that *this is not how it should be,* based on what other fathers are doing. These unmet expectations or standards are probably out in front of a deeper belief such as; *I am not worth being there for, therefore I am worthless. Or I am not as worthy or valued as the other children whose dads make the effort to attend.* Usually when you resolve the hurt belief behind the fruit of anger, the anger is resolved. There can of course be multiple situations and beliefs.

ANGER AS A 'UNIVERSAL EMOTION'

The principle of anger being a predictable response to things *not being how we think that they should be* is not always sin, and not always inappropriate. At times it is the right thing to do to show disapproval of activities that *are not how they should be.* This is well illustrated when Jesus became angry at the money changers making His Father's house into something that it was not intended for. It should have been a house of prayer, but it was made into a den of thieves. *Matthew 21:12-13*

So, we see this process involved in anger:
1. 1. Things are not how you think they should be.
   (-This could be in your emotional history, for example when someone did not show you love or appear to care about you…. which can then present in how people deal with you in the present
   Or
   -It may actually be things in your present circumstances that aren't how you think that they should be, such as someone being oppressed or abused.)
2. This then proceeds to frustration about how things are….
3. And finally boils over as anger either outwardly or inwardly

SELF-ANGER

When there is anger towards others, as with other emotions, it is most often inward as well. If someone comes for ministry and their spouse is for example, reportedly making them angry, because they make them feel as though they are not good enough in some way; as well as being angry at the spouse, they are also most likely angry at themselves for not being what they need to be to be good enough. If they thought they were enough they would not be hurt by the spouse's treatment. So, you are looking for the memory and the pain that related to them 'supposedly,' not being what they are meant to be. Anger is the response and not the problem, so once the hurt relating to the expectations and standards is resolved the anger will disappear.

ANGER AND HEALTH

Whether anger is internalized or outward towards others, it is a good idea to take the loving advice of scripture and resolve why we are angry as soon as possible. There are various biological actions that cause us harm if we remain angry. Without taking the time here to go through the mechanisms involved, strong or chronic anger can reportedly lead to problems such as strokes or other physical complaints. Ephesians 4:26-27

CAN YOU RESOLVE BELIEF-BASED ANGER THROUGH HAVING KNOWLEDGE?
If you have anger that is simply because you have chosen to not forgive others for *not doing things how you think that they should be done,* then understanding this you could well help you make the decision to pull down your standards for them. If you no longer consider that things *should be a particular way,* often your way, then there are no longer grounds for frustration and anger, and the issue is resolved. However, if the reason for the anger is coming from a *heart belief* that is no longer conscious thought then ministry will be required.

SUMMARY
Whenever somebody comes to me reporting anger issues, I am immediately questioning them in regards to what may be in their lives or in their environment, and then in their history, that is *not how they think that it should be.*

Unforgiveness, resentment and bitterness

'PRESENT TENSE' FORGIVENESS
The bible gives us clear instruction to forgive others. This means that if someone does something that offends you today' then under the guidelines of scripture, we are to forgive them as many times as is necessary. This lifestyle should begin as soon as we know that this is the counsel of scripture. It is the nature of God towards us and we are to go and live likewise. If our next-door neighbor throws his empty beer bottles over the fence every night then we need to choose to forgive him daily for the offense.

Forgiveness comes before love. We cannot fully love anyone while we hold onto the things that they have committed towards us, or for that matter, the things that we think that they should have done and haven't. God had to deal with suffering a price for our offences first, before He could extend forgiveness and relationship. In much the same way when people are mistreating us, we have to take up our own crosses, absorb the hurt, and deny ourselves retaliation in order to perpetuate love and grace in the spirit of the gospel. *Matthew 18:21-22*

A 'RECORD OF WRONGS'
A record of wrongs is when you have a list of grievances against someone. Years ago, I would have considered that I had no unforgiveness towards anyone in the world. That is, I certainly had no deep pain driven hurt or resentment. However, one day I noticed that whenever a particular person came up in conversation that I could not help myself from mentioning various occasions when this person had, in my opinion, acted inappropriately towards us. As I spoke, out would tumble this list of offensive actions that I held. I realized that I had kept a record of wrongs. I made a deep decision to be like our Father in heaven and remember their sins no more. Some people say that God forgets our sins, but I believe that by a deliberate act of His will He chooses to not remember them anymore. I decided to not remember them anymore and began to pray for this person's prosperity, and that God would do for them everything that I would like Him to do in His dealings with me.

Almost immediately my *record of wrongs* list disappeared and was no longer accessed when that person came up in conversation, rather I would find myself saying only positive things.

> *1 Corinthians 13:4 "Love is patient, love is kind. It does not envy, it does not boast, it is not proud. 5 It is not rude, it is not self-seeking, it is not easily angered,* **it keeps no record of wrongs."** *NIV (Emphasis mine).*

'PAST TENSE' FORGIVENESS

We have talked about the Bible's instruction on forgiveness. So now we know how we should respond to hurts, grievances and offences. Many people come to us having been taught that they must forgive, and as a result, they have spent much of their lives endeavoring to do so but feeling guilty and condemned because they just can't seem to get there.

The problem is that the unforgiveness resides in *hurt received from historical sources*. These situations will make up the majority of times that people will come to you with unforgiveness, resentment and bitterness issues. Under these circumstances we do not initially request that the people forgive those who have offended against them. The reason that they struggle to forgive is because they do not really know what it is that they are forgiving the perpetrator of their unforgiveness for.

Let me explain it in this manner. Imagine if someone has suffered, for example, sexual abuse. Clearly, they know that the abuse is the source of their resentment. They most likely are not, however, aware of the beliefs that are causing the pain in them. Let us take a common belief that often emanates from this kind of abuse; *I am ruined, I am no longer like other people*. This belief then, is at least a part of the source of the pain, along with other inner thoughts from the event. Once it is discovered, identified and healed by the Spirit of truth, we then ask them how they regard the offender. When the healing is complete and the hurt is resolved, over and over we see that forgiveness comes easily. The abused person may now make some kind of comment such as; *Well I kind of feel sorry for them that they had that problem. Something must have happened to them to make them like that!*

This holds true of people who have been emotionally, physically, verbally or in other ways suffered abuse. It also stands fast in situations where for instance love, acceptance and encouragement have not been given as well. You may hear comments such as; *I know that mum/dad did not get much love themselves, and now that I see it, I feel sorry for them that they had nothing to give!*

UNFORGIVENESS OF SELF

As with other emotions, there is an inward version of this unforgiveness towards self. This is where we have a *record of wrongs* regarding our own failings, imperfections and shortcomings. In some instances, we can simply forgive ourselves and move on once we realize that we have held ourselves to account. Most issues that people come for ministry for in this regard may be deeply rooted in an event where a heart belief has come in such as; *I'm not as good as others, I am useless, I am not loveable* for some reason and so on. These need to be healed before you can accept your own self as a normal human being who doesn't always get things right.

PROGRESSION OF A LACK OF FORGIVENESS TOWARDS OTHERS OR SELF

For some people, if they refuse to forgive, and they stew on the matters, they will develop eventually into resentment. When resentment becomes deeply seated it can grow into bitterness towards others or self. This is the very toxic form which can end up growing into hatred and can be implicated in various diseases. The old saying; *It is eating them up like a cancer* certainly in my experience is quite accurate. I have witnessed personally as bitterness, self-bitterness and resentment have been strongly present in a number of cancer cases.

We have also seen cancer healed and know of many others healed by other ministries when the person has come for prayer and help. For some, when the bitterness progresses to hatred it often involves rebellion or retaliation against the perpetrator of the offence. This then can at times involve trying to destroy the other person in some way with the tongue which is not advisable. In the event that the person you are bitter against is yourself, there will be some kind of self-destructive, self-harming, self-punishing behavior as we witness in modern epidemics such as cutting. *Matthew 22:39*

God's perfect order is that you are loving and forgiving towards others, and also towards yourself, but often we need His healing before we can live this way. The Lord knows this very well, which is why He promised to heal the broken-hearted and set the captives free if we will come to Him. When you don't love yourself, you will probably struggle to love others as well.

The 3 LEGS of the 'Jezebelic Spirit'

Whilst there is no Jezebel spirit mentioned in the Bible there is the example of behavior that we find in the story of Jezebel that does often have a demonic element. When these spirits are in place, they may respond to any name given when the authority of Christ is exercised. In my experience the three elements that summarize Jezebelic responses are pride, rebellion and control. From these, all of the other fruit proceeds. Most of us either have or have had one or more of these expressions in some measure and they were not directly held by an evil spirit.

PRIDE	"I will make myself above"	(Comes mainly from <u>I</u>nferiority, or <u>I</u>nsignificance- aka low self-image)
REBELLION	"I will not submit to another"	(Comes mainly from <u>I</u>njustice/ unfairness)
CONTROL	"I will have my way"	(Comes mainly from <u>I</u>nsecurity)

We can of course, point the finger and describe and avoid people with this behavior and run them out of the Church. However, if we look past the fruit as God does, and see the hurt in the heart, we will have grace for them and seek to minister to the beliefs producing the **inferiority, injustice** and **insecurity** that is behind the problems.
Isaiah 58:9-11, Proverbs 19:11, 1 Peter 4:8

JEZEBEL

People with unhealed Jezebelic behavior will present doing the types of things illustrated in the Bible. In *1 Kings chapter 18* Jezebel kills off the Lord's prophets. Today Jezebelic Christians will try to assassinate Pastors, leaders and genuine ministries or authorities. This will usually be with their tongues, through attacks on the spirituality or abilities of the leaders. They often try to gather people to themselves, creating division by starting groups in or out of the church bypassing permission from those in authority. You will often hear that *God told them.* They will usually appear to be very spiritual, as was Jezebel.

Other related issues that you may encounter

GUILT AND SHAME

> *Romans 8:1 There is therefore now no condemnation to those who are in Christ Jesus, who do not walk according to the flesh, but according to the Spirit. NKJV*

Guilt is a fruit that will tie into areas such as self-rejection, inferiority and performance anxiety. By that I mean anxiety over our ability to perform to people's expectations. Usually we reject ourselves because we have learnt that we fall short in some way. As a result, we often feel as though we should have done more, been better, been able to please or do what was expected of us and so on. A consequence of these perceived failures is often low *self-image,* and *guilt or shame.*

As we have previously stated, we could summarize that guilt and shame are connected to something that we didn't do that we feel that we should have, or, something that we have done that we shouldn't have. If we have dealt with things that we should not have done from our previous years, we should have received Gods forgiveness' and also our own.

Clearly if we are still doing something that we know that we shouldn't be doing, and could stop in our own strength then guilt is probably an appropriate emotion. In that instance it is not condemnation because we can always repent, but it may well in fact be conviction. Guilt is often tied to other emotional issues and even implicated in depression. It can be one possible trail back to the initial memory for truth and healing.

DEALING WITH GRIEF

Grief is normally associated with loss of some kind. This could include loss of your identity and self-worth if, for example, you have been sexually abused. It could also relate to loss of a relationship or loved one. As with any other belief-based emotion the goal is to identify the thoughts producing the sad feelings. We take note from the following verses, that grief has an impact on both soul and body. At times, we minister to people who look constantly sad, or are continually sighing, resolved to the loss that they have suffered. It is wonderful to see the joy come into them when the Lord sets them free. *Psalm 31:9-10*

UNIT ELEVEN

Sex 'God's Idea!'

PART 1: Gods purpose and order in creating sexuality

INTRODUCTION

While we are addressing the problems that are 'common to man' it would be difficult to overlook the area of sexuality. Indeed, most of the World is reeling out of balance in this area, in one direction or another. The Bible describes all that God created as 'good' and this of course includes the sexual act. The devil has worked very hard indeed to distort all of God's creation beyond its intended order and parameters, and in the area of sex this is described as 'sexual immorality' or 'perversion.'

Personally, I feel that it is not my place to make judgments on how anyone has arrived where they are in their sexual life or related problems. As with other areas of life something has happened for us to be in the condition that we are in. Perhaps we are simply ignorant of what is right or we have been exposed to things that have caused us to be in our present situation. My purpose is to help people adjust their sexuality to the ways of the Kingdom of God in order for that area of their lives to be free. God is always redemptive, always merciful, not wanting any to perish, but wanting all come to repentance in order to be saved.
He is always ready to set us free, and if we are bound, our part in this may be seeking out people of God who are trained to help us deal with our issues.

Study 1: Beginnings

We often find ourselves visiting the events in Genesis that are described as the 'fall of man.' This was where Satan came and tempted Adam and Eve to eat from the tree of the knowledge of good and evil. Eve saw in the fruit on the tree some 'good' aspects for satisfying bodily appetites, and it also appealed to the eyes. This then became a weak area in our fallen human nature. Satan now had a right through our submission to exploit this again and again.

Genesis 3: 6 When the woman saw that the fruit of the tree was good for food and pleasing to the eye, and also desirable for gaining wisdom, she took some and ate it. She also gave some to her husband, who was with her, and he ate it. NIV

God had commanded in *Genesis 2:16-17* that man should not eat from this tree. Basically, what Satan came along proposing was that God was keeping good and beneficial things from mankind. He was suggesting that God doesn't really care about us, that He doesn't want us to have pleasure or fun, and that what He has given us already really isn't enough.

Today we have the New Testament writings to guide us, and we understand that this is not true.

> *1 Timothy 6:17b ....But their trust should be in the living God, who **richly gives** us all we **need** for our **enjoyment**. NLT (Emphasis mine)*

The Genesis account sets the scene for the basic attitudal problem that man, who does not have the revelation of the scriptures, has as a result of the sin of rebellion that was committed at the fall. Really man was unconsciously saying; "I don't want any limits; I will get for myself what is best for me." This generationally inherited perception that God does not have all we need in mind, or care about our pleasure and enjoyment is behind much sin. *1 John 2:16-17*

Immoral looking or 'lust' is the wanting to have something or someone that is not for you. So, to enjoy how beautiful things look in the Earth is a gift from God. However, desiring, coveting or looking at a thing that is forbidden for you is sin. In other words, noticing that a member of the opposite sex is attractive is natural and unavoidable. But when you look wanting them for yourselves, or even thinking about them in a sexual way, then the Bible says that it is the same as committing the act. Lust in the Bible means to desire something that is forbidden for you. *Proverbs 5:18-20, Matthew 5:28, Romans 8:1-8*

Study 2: Gods created order and purpose for sexuality

Satan is always trying to distance us from God's perfect, fulfilling and protective ways. He will do anything that he can to take what God has created and pervert and distort it. If we choose to follow the Spirit then we will need to understand Gods order and purposes so that we know how to live. So, let us have a look in overview at what the Lords intentions are for sexuality.

1. BE FRUITFUL AND MULTIPLY
God evidently planned for the Earth to be populated with mankind ruling over it and establishing authority and Gods order for it. *Genesis 1:27-28*

2. MAN AND WOMAN JOINING IN CREATION WITH GOD
What a privilege to have a part with God in producing a human being. It is very well documented that there is a bright flash of light that announces the beginning of human life as a sperm meets the egg. As Christians we would deduce that this is the moment where the human spirit and soul as life are placed in us by God, along with the union of the sperm and the egg. Scientists have captured the 'fireworks' on film when an explosion of tiny sparks erupts from the egg at the exact moment of conception. This infusion of power is considered to be the beginning point for individual life and growth in the embryo. *Psalm 139:15-16*

3. KNOWING EACH OTHER INTIMATELY, ONE FLESH
There is no other relationship that is as close as the bond that comes through sexual intimacy. In the Old Testament we find accounts of Cain and Adam 'knowing' their wives and consequently they became pregnant. This is not the same way as you 'know' other people, it is meant to be unique to marriage. This is a mental, willful, chemical, emotional, and spiritual bonding that is only meant to occur in a marriage relationship between a man and a woman. I have heard that behind the Hebrew meaning for 'one flesh' is the concept

of being so closely connected that to separate would be like pulling skin off flesh.... where some of the flesh would come away as well as the skin. In God's creation, even chemically, there is a powerful pair bonding hormone called oxytocin that is greatly stimulated when sexual intimacy occurs. *Genesis 2:24*

4. PLEASURE AND ENJOYMENT

God created and designed our bodies with various sensual nerve endings that are intended for our pleasure. For example, on the female body is the clitoris which has no other anatomical function other than her pleasure. God is not embarrassed by this; it was His idea, design, and intention all along. Any thoughts that God is against pleasure should be immediately dispelled by the amazing gift of sex. God himself considered it 'very good,' and it was both His idea and of His making and design. God is revealed as relational by nature, and in His provision, He has given us this capacity to give and receive pleasure. This is the ability to enhance and bless our relationships on every level, spiritual, emotional, the will, mind and body. In the past Christianity has proposed some kind of attitude that sex is dirty or impure. What an insult to our loving maker this is! Again, it proposes a God that is trying to keep good things from us...whereas the truth is that all of the parts of our body that give pleasure, whether used immorally or in a Holy way, were originally provided and purposed by Him. The devil takes what is intended for good and seeks to distort and pervert it. *Genesis 1:31*

5. A BIBLICAL PICTURE FOR OUR UNDERSTANDING

Many things in the scriptures that are examples of life in the World are there to help us understand spiritual concepts and realities. *Romans 1: 20*

I believe that God instituted marriage and sexual intimacy so that we could see the spiritual ramifications of our union with Christ Jesus. God of course is always multi-tasking with more than one purpose for everything. In Ephesians chapter five there is an illustration for us explaining how we should fulfill our roles in the marriage covenant. In verse 32 the Apostle Paul reveals that although he is giving instruction for the proper functioning of marital relations, basing them on how Christ Jesus deals with His bride the church.... He reveals that he is actually explaining the interaction of we, the Church, responding and relating to Christ. *Ephesians 5:21-32*

Remember that the picture in this passage is Christ as the husband and the Church (Us) as the bride or wife. So, the role that the man has in the relationship is a picture or illustration for us from the natural world to understand the Church and Jesus relationship. This is why the devil works so relentlessly to go against God's order for sexuality in society. He is trying to distort the picture. And he knows that the only way that the marriage relationship can work is in the way that God ordained and intended it. This does not mean that man is in the least bit superior to his wife, it simply means that he has a different role. The Bible says that the wife is <u>comparable</u> to the man not inferior. She is equal to him, but different, and with a different God given role and purpose. *Genesis 2:18*

6. MEN AND WOMEN ARE DIFFERENT IN EVERY WAY

I think my wife and I are a fairly typical sample of what studies report, and what we have observed. Men tend to be more task oriented, providers, protectors, problem solvers, and are looking to the future. Men tend to be more single minded, focused on one thing at a time. The ladies are normally more relationally motivated and live in the day, aware simultaneously of many present needs and items that have to be dealt with now. They are home makers and nurturers; whereas men are more suited as home builders.

Scientists considered that a brain was just a brain until recently. With modern technology they have been able to see that if given the same mathematical problem, that different parts of the female brain are activated than those of the man in working out the same answer. The truth is that there is nothing much the same about men and women mentally, emotionally, physically, hormonally or spiritually. It is not that one is better than the other, just different.

7. ROLES IN THE HOUSEHOLD

Biblically God has appointed the man to be responsible for the spiritual climate of the household. It falls to him to be responsible for the emotional wholeness of the relationship and to love his wife sacrificially, or we might say at his own expense. He is to love her first even if it is at personal cost to his own self. The old saying is: "the loved become lovely." It is the principle of sowing and reaping. Love your wife and prefer her and it will come back on your own head, pressed down, shaken together and running over. This may take time but it is a biblical principle and it cannot fail to produce an outcome.

For her part, she is to respect that he has been made responsible to initiate the dynamics in the household, and acknowledge that he will be accountable to God for what their relationship and family looks like. This includes who they serve and follow, a responsibility that Adam did not fulfill. He was given responsibility over everything before Eve was even created. *Genesis 2:15-18*

8. COVERING

Although we are discussing sexuality, let us digress for a moment onto the relational order that should exist. The following spiritual attitudes, although general, apply to sexuality as well. Jesus takes full responsibility for setting the spiritual environment that produces a 'Spirit of God' based dynamic for His church. He <u>covers</u> our imperfections and sets the attitudal standards of the kingdom of God to protect us. These spiritual dynamics are sacrificial giving, unconditional love, (which doesn't demand perfection – as I heard recently; "God's love is not based on us, it is placed on us"), grace, which makes acceptance possible, plus mercy and forgiveness for our shortcomings. He is our 'head' but He does not Lord it over us or demand compliance. He doesn't force His bride to come under the kingdom of God, it is her (our) free will choice. He simply states; "If you love me you will obey me!" It has been well said that Jesus' love language is obedience, and I add, that this obedience is being given by choice not coercion. In all of this we add to the list of spiritual attributes that He institutes over us patience.

9. FREEWILL AND CHOICE

The choice to submit is hers, she is not dealt with in some kind of dominating, authoritarian kind of manner. Some streams of the church today propose that men should be demanding submission. Actually, the true role of the man is to cover her with these spiritual attributes as Jesus does to us first. He is unbending in them and His stand on Holiness and separation to the ways of the Kingdom, regardless of the activities of His bride. If she (the church) chooses to follow another spiritual kingdom whose precepts are rebellion, control, anger, fear, rejection, resentment or bitterness, this remains her free will choice. A wife is far more likely to gravitate towards these types of responses if she is dealt with in an ungodly, disrespectful kind of way, and by demanding that she submits. This controlling type spirit is not of God. It suits man because in his mind he is 'god' to his wife. Fallen man still wants to be like God, which began in the garden with *you will be like God. Genesis 3:5*

So, before we can make judgments on the behaviors of our wives we have to see if we are in the Spirit ourselves. Do we love unconditionally, do we love sacrificially, do we have grace and mercy for things not being exactly how we would like them, and are we patient, are we accepting, are we forgiving? We cannot reasonably expect our wives to submit to Satan's kingdom of fear, control, selfishness, criticism, anger, rejection, resentment, retaliation, and unforgiveness etc. etc. if that is the 'covering' coming from us. These also are spiritual in their nature but not from Gods Kingdom or Spirit. *1 Corinthians 11:3*

10. SETTING THE SPIRITUAL CLIMATE

It falls to man to initiate these principles, as God has put him next in line after Christ to establish covering. Many godly women do take up their own biblical role and instructions even though the man is covering her with another spirit, often domination, control and self-serving or self-exaltation in the relationship.

We could summarize this by saying that if my wife is not submitting to me in working with me that it will probably be a reflection on whether or not I am dealing with her in a godly way. Therefore, if she is loved, valued and secure, sharing in her role as joint leaders of the household, then it will be obvious, and she will be my glory in the sense that I have dealt with her as God has instructed me…as next in line in terms of responsibility after Christ. For her part in the passage from Ephesians 5:21-33 that we have just been examining, the wife is instructed firstly to 'submit' to her husband and in verse 33 she is instructed to respect him. Of the verses in this passage 3 relate to how the wife should respond to the man's godly covering, whereas 10 versus are in regard to how he represents Christ and dispenses the Kingdom of God to her.

11. 'INITIATORS' AND HORMONAL REALITIES

It has been often said that hormones make the World go around. Well they make each of our own individual little Worlds in terms of physical function work anyway. Hormones are little chemical messengers that activate physical activities, emotional responses, and processes including appetite and sexual activity. Men and women are dramatically different hormonally. A man's hormones tend to go along much the same from day to day whereas pre menopause, women go through a diversity of changes throughout their monthly cycle. These will impact, amongst other things mood and sexual interest. (Post-menopausal women in general have lower and more stable hormone values)

A man reportedly can have between 10 and 38 times as much testosterone as women, with possibly on average around 20 to 25 times the amount. Testosterone is largely the hormone implicated in sexual thinking and interest. As a result, many women rarely if ever think about sex without the thought or idea being introduced to her. Men on the other hand often think about it quite a lot because of their much higher hormone levels and initial interest beginning through their eyes. So, we see from this undeniable level of hormones that man has been created to most often be the initiator of the sexual act.

This is a physical outworking of the spiritual position described in Ephesians Chapter 5 that we have just looked at. Jesus is the initiator of the spiritual relationship with His bride the Church, coming into her to make her fruitful if she will respond. The church is not always willing to respond to her husband Jesus, but when she does it is a great blessing. Women often don't feel very much like sex, but if they respond to the man and accept his overtures, it can be a source of great blessing and intimacy for both. *Song of Solomon 5*

A key is for the wife to understand that God has given her husband a relentless sex drive which simply will not go away, it remains even if he is tired. He did not ask for it, it is just there. So, it goes a long way to realize that for the girls it is at times sacrificial in the 1st instance to respond. But it's also good to know that even though it takes a bit longer to get *the 'motor running'* it will happen, if she is willing to be willing.

For the man's part he needs to realize that his wife probably doesn't think about sex as he does, and her sexuality is not visually stimulated as his is. Consequently, it is unlikely that if she sees him coming out of the shower that it would be arousing for her as it is for him. This is normal because of how the two different genders are created. So, the male needs to initiate the idea of intimacy by communicating his hopes for connecting on this level. He is far more likely to get a favorable response if he is cherishing and loving his wife, taking care of her needs, and making her feel safe, significant, cared about, and protected. This is how Christ deals with his bride, and this includes covering and having grace for imperfections. We could say that the interaction of sex is the sum of all of these things. Mental agreement, emotional wholeness and spiritual oneness concluding with the physical joining of the two. The sexual encounter improves in quality as all of these other components flourish and come to the fullness of God's order. *1 Corinthians 7:3-5, Ephesians 5:21*

SUMMARY

We could summarize then by saying that the things that need to be in Gods order for marriage to work, are the same attitudal things that we must do to be the true bride of Christ. If we can't or won't lay down what we want, and give of, or die to ourselves in our marriages, then we probably won't lay down self, and prefer what Gods wants in relationship with Him either. How we are in our married state then is often a reflection of our inner attitudes and progress in sanctification. Marriage, although perhaps the hardest relationship to work through, has the greatest potential to put us through the process of becoming Holy, perfected, and sanctified.

Study 3: Healthy sexuality

Let us put in summary what we are saying here. Healthy sexuality can only fully exist in the context of Gods intended plan for it. Everything that we are endeavoring to do here is aimed at restoring created order for the whole relationship which includes sexuality. Let us examine in brief what these precepts regarding health in sexuality are.

1. Spiritual values
If we are both looking to God to conform our spiritual attitudes to those of Christ Jesus, then we will have common spiritual ground for all aspects of our relationship. *Romans 8:29*

2. Preferring one another in love
When most of us were originally married we were probably selfishly thinking that we were engaging with someone whose whole purpose was to meet all of our needs and wants and make us happy. We didn't realize that God's model is the exact opposite of this. *Luke 6:38*

3. Sowing and reaping
This is a principle that God has instituted. If we sow love, grace, patience and acceptance you can be sure that it will come back on your own head. On the other hand, if you sow criticism, intolerance, rejection and selfishness don't be surprised if these are the attitudes coming back your way! Check your part of the relationship soberly, the condition it is in may well be a reflection on you.

4. Willing to be willing
We have already discussed *Song of Solomon chapter 5:1-6*. This is where the woman was not prepared to respond to her lovers' initiations. *1 Corinthians 7:3*

The Apostle Paul conceded in 1 Corinthians chapter 7 that because there was so much sexual immorality in the world, that being married and meeting each other's sexual needs in a godly way was the best solution. He acknowledged that because of the sexualized society that they were in, that they were going to be subjected to some level of stimulation through exposure to that environment. He concluded that it was better to deal with sexual appetites appropriately in marriage than to 'burn with lust, or passion.' *1 Corinthians 7:9*

5. The need for Godly sexuality

Without healthy sexuality every other part of the relationship lacks. Spiritual, mental, emotional, relational and physical intimacies are all activated and showcased in the act of sexual harmony. It is well worth working towards unity in every area of the relationship. The reason that we do the sexuality unit last in the training, is because for it to function as God intended, the areas that I have just mentioned usually need to be restored first.

6. Be fruitful.

I have often had ladies complain to me in the ministry room that their husbands are 'animals who just want sex all the time. *He doesn't love me; he is just an animal.* It is good to realize that behind that much stronger sex drive – that God put on him and he didn't ask for – most likely lays genuine affection and love. For his part he possibly already feels like an 'animal' too because clearly you, the female, do not have the interest for physical intimacy that he does. Indeed, he actually at times may not like himself as a result of his strong urges. If your husband has worked all day and comes in hungry, being loving and affectionate may not be on the top of his list. As with sex, the strong appetite for food is out in front of any romantic thoughts. Once it is satisfied then he is likely to show the affection that he does hold, as well as a bonding appreciation for meeting his needs.

7. Factors that affect the quality of the sexual relationship

Damage from previous experiences may require Gods healing before healthy physical relationships can occur. Let me just list a few of the potential problems and other considerations that may need to be dealt with.

A] Beginning your sex life. Many couples have very poor 1st experiences of sex, even if they are Christians. The church has largely failed to teach about healthy sexuality and adjustment because of some unbiblical prudish religious ideas.
These 1st experiences set up a basis for willingness to participate in future engagements. The absence of enjoyment, or the presence of disappointment or anxiety becomes how the sexual act is viewed in the future. It is very important that the church instructs its young people in the area of sexuality. Certainly, the impressions of the Old Testament are earthy robust activities in this area; this could be explained with the older men and women instructing the younger ones.

B] Past experiences. Probably for most people today including Christians there are previous sexual relationships in the history. These may have been exciting or romantic times, or bad experiences that left you feeling trashy and cheap. In either case they are to be 'remembered no more.' The connection made to the person or persons are still alive if you think about or replay any of those events in your mind.

C] Unrealistic expectations. Between Hollywood, the movie industry and the proliferation of porn that everyone seems to be exposed to, the devil has confused what the sexual encounter should be. If you use these scripted, acted out models of perfect romance as your guide you may indeed be disappointed. A quick glance at the number of failed marriages that actors and actresses go through should prove that it is indeed all fiction, and that these lifestyles are not working for them. In the porn industry, in reality we hear of physically and emotionally damaged people, and rampant sexually transmitted diseases.

D] Sexual abuse. The statistics that I have viewed for sexual abuse perpetrated towards females in the U.S. are startling, and I feel sure that it would be similar in other 1st world nations. Reportedly there is approximately one out of every three women who have at some time had some form of sexual abuse. This can range from full penetrative sex or rape through to being inappropriately touched by a relative, friend of the family, teacher or even a minister. We also see an increasing number of males who have also suffered various kinds of sexual abuses and improprieties.

How does this impact the sexual relationship? Virtually without exception the abuse has had some kind of affect and outworking on the sexuality of the person. For some this means that they come to the position that they believe that they are spoiled, ruined, bad, and now deduce why even try to be good. They then feel that their sexuality means nothing and is a cheap thing and so they can gravitate to becoming promiscuous. Others may come to the conclusion that sex gets them acceptance, and they may confuse this with love. The majority of those abused that we deal with go the other way. They have taken in various beliefs from the abuse which makes a normal sex life impossible without emotional healing and freedom.

The spouse many times doesn't understand why their partner does not want to engage in the sexual act as they do. Very often the spouse feels rejected, inadequate, undesirable or even not loved. Communication can be very important here so that they do not feel that the problem is with them. Normally the spouse is quite compassionate and relieved when they see that it is not their fault and understands that their partner needs help and healing. **By all means seek help. You are not stuck; we have seen God free a great many people who have been abused.

E] Relational maladjustment through unresolved emotional issues. For healthy sex to occur many times healing from low self-image, inferiority, selfishness, fear of rejection or failure, guilt, performance anxiety or other emotional problems may need to be resolved. These issues that can relate to belief-based wounds could produce the following attitudes and responses:
Selfishness, (not wanting to give- only wanting to get)
Rejection, etc (misreading the situation if a partner is not wanting to engage)

Beliefs such as;   *'I am nothing, nobody, I don't matter, I am being used.'*
                    'He/she doesn't really care about me!'
                    'I am not acceptable, attractive, good enough, etc'
……are some of the types of beliefs that suggest the need for emotional healing.

F] The Emotional element of sexuality: Sex appears on face value to be primarily a physical activity. As a result, the modern world has tried to reduce it to being just about pleasure, of no more importance than eating ice-cream. However, over the years I have come to understand that it is primarily an emotional and relational exercise that also involves the use of the body.

G] Appointments to aid in maintaining sexual health and activity. One very practical way to facilitate relational sexual maintenance is to make appointments for your physical encounters. How frequent this is may depend on your age and state of health. Let us say to illustrate, that if you are for example 40 years old, and sexual frequency of twice per week was sufficient for you both, then you may agree on Tuesdays, and Saturday nights.

The advantage in this is that for the man is, he is no longer thinking about how to make overtures or about sex in general, as he now knows that his day is coming. For the woman, the advantage is that firstly she is slower to be aroused, so if she knows that it is coming up, she can prepare herself. And secondly, she knows that any affection that she receives on other days is genuine love that doesn't have any other motive involved.

> **Note:** This may not be applicable to early marriage where romance is high and responses are more spontaneous!

Study 4: Adjusting the physical components of sex

Being instructed in what to expect in terms of how our bodies work is very important for success in sexual adjustment. Ignorance of the *'mechanics* of sex is a common cause for lack of sexual fulness and enjoyment. As we have already stated, God is not embarrassed or offended by how we are made. It was His design and purpose, not our idea, and I am sure that He is pleased and glorified when we enjoy it…having given us everything that we need for our pleasure and enjoyment. *1 Timothy 6:17*

There are physical functional elements of the sexual encounter that need to be considered and learnt. You are much more likely to want to engage with each other in this important relational exercise if it is an enjoyable and satisfying experience, and you are not left frustrated. Both men and women can experience discomfort or pain if they are aroused and do not experience the subsequent release of orgasm. In order for you to be mutually satisfied and pleasured we need to understand and implement the necessary mechanical elements. In many ways the human body is a highly sophisticated and amazing machine, and as with any machine, you need to operate it properly and understand some basic principles to get the best out of it. A good lover also needs a good working knowledge of sexual physiology; it normally must be taught and learnt before it can function properly and produce optimum results.

In the church it is our responsibility to teach Gods purposes and give help and instruction. I would make two comments before I go further on this section. One, to reiterate, God is not disgusted about any bodily function that we have. He designed them and they are perfect. Two; I am not a sex counselor or therapist. There are some excellent Christian authors who are experts on the subject of sexual adjustment, and they can be readily sourced for more detailed studies. Rather than directly quoting word for word in the following passages on sexual adjustment, I am going to indicate where I have referenced the following Christian publications. It will, unless quoted and inserted, be my words, attempting to be faithful to their information on the subject.

I am adding in this fairly graphic study for two reasons. One is that a few years ago while conducting a School in an African nation, when I glossed over the 'how to' part of the need for understanding sexual mechanics, a young Pastor about to get married complained that he wanted to know what to do. Clearly it is necessary to provide some level of instruction for fulness in relationships. Secondly, if we don't instruct our young people, they will go to the world for their information, and get the distorted version promoted through media. The devil loves to work in the dark. We, the church, need to bring sexuality out into the light.

** THE GIFT OF SEX   Clifford and Joyce Penner   Word Books
*   SEXUAL HAPPINESS IN MARRIAGE   Herbert J. Miles, Ph.D. Zondervan Books

An additional helpful Christian publication on the subject is:
INTENDED FOR PLEASURE   Ed and Gaye Wheat

UNDERSTANDING OUR BODIES

Female genitals. The predominant female sexual organs are the clitoris and the vagina.
The vagina is the opening or sheath that receives the male organ, the penis, in the sexual act. It is considered that the lower one third where the penis enters, or one and a half to two inches of the vagina is sensitive during sexual arousal. Consequently, as we discuss the male and female parts in sexual intercourse, let us also dispel some of the associated myths.

*The assumption that the larger a man's penis, the better he will be able to satisfy a woman just isn't true. First of all, most women don't gain the majority of their sexual satisfaction from the penis being in the vagina, no matter what size the penis. Women tend to be most responsive to generous sensuous body caressing and stimulation of the breasts and external genitalia. ***

The clitoris is considered to be the primary organ implicated in the female orgasm. It has no other function than the sexual pleasure of the woman and is exclusively intended for sexual sensation. It is located outside and above the vagina, at the uppermost point where the inner lips meet, on average one and a quarter inches from the vaginal passage. (32mm) The clitoris is loaded with nerve endings and its stimulation by some means is normally regarded as the primary source of the female orgasm.

*Many women report that the most pleasurable place to receive stimulation is around the clitoris, not directly on it. ***

Male genitals. The male sexual organ is called the penis, and it is inserted into the vagina in the consummation of the sexual act. Ejaculation with or without orgasm is the primary delivery system for sperm bearing semen that inseminates the woman to become pregnant. Due to the influences of modern media including pornography, many men universally have anxiety about the size and ability of their penis to satisfy their marriage partner.

Women are often concerned that their breast are too big, too small, or too whatever. A man may be concerned with the size of his penis, fearing that a smaller penis is indicative of being less of a man and less able to satisfy a woman.

The truth is that the woman has the organ of accommodation; that is, the vagina changes to accommodate any size penis. Therefore, penis size has little to do with sexual pleasure or satisfaction…. just as the length of a man's penis has little or nothing to do with his effectiveness during sexual intercourse, neither does the circumference or thickness of his penis have any importance for sexual performance.

*The woman's PC muscle can tighten so as to completely close the opening to the vagina; therefore, a thin penis can still have firm sensation from the vagina. ** (Note: this is more likely to be the case if the woman is fully aroused before the insertion of the penis. It is well worth doing the necessary preparation before penetration for the enjoyment of both husband and wife.)*

The reported size of the penis worldwide in a flaccid state may vary considerably, (flaccid means in a relaxed, unaroused condition) in its state of erection the average is 5 to 6 and a half inches in length.

Masters and Johnson have found that the unaroused (flaccid) penis size does not relate proportionately to erect penis size. A small flaccid penis, upon sexual stimulation, enlarges to a greater extent than does a larger flaccid penis. In their erect state there is not much difference in size between one penis and another, even though they may differ significantly in size when they are not aroused. **

COMMON ANXIETIES

Before we talk about the mechanics of sexual adjustment, let us preface this with the knowledge that achieving good adjustment many times is difficult because of emotional issues that need to be resolved. For example, we have just addressed a common anxiety in men regarding self-image and being equipped to please their wives.
Many women also struggle to relax and enjoy their sexuality for a variety of reasons.

How we feel about ourselves affects how we relate to another person, particularly sexually. It has been found that preorgasmic women (those who have not yet experienced orgasm) who feel unworthy and have difficulty accepting themselves as persons cannot be helped to become orgasmic until they deal with these feelings of low self-worth. **

"Nobody is automatically good at sex, it is like everything else in life, you have to learn how to do it properly if you want to be good at it. In this case it is precious to learn together."

Sexual anxiety grows out of the demand for performance. This demand may come from within one's self or from one's partner. If we enter the sexual experience with pressure to produce desirable experiences for our loved one or a response in ourselves, that demand will cause anxiety. **

Often people insecure about their self-worth and value will be compulsive in their need for sex, striving to get the bonding, acceptance and connection through the physical act, and meet the emotional fulfillment that they crave.

People with an excessive need to please their partner usually grew up in a situation where they had to work diligently for parental approval. Even with hard work they received little in the way of reward that built their self-worth. These people go through life looking for approval and reinforcement they never received as a child. **

Aside from the need to deal with general emotional issues in order to function well sexually, often anxiety comes in any area of life when we do not know what to do. Therefore, we have a responsibility to each other to study sexuality so that we can be effective in our part of the partnership.

The husband is responsible to meet his wife's sexual needs. He must regularly and lovingly arouse her to a complete sexual experience, climax (or orgasm). Likewise, the wife must meet her husband's sexual needs. She must regularly and lovingly arouse him to a sexual experience, climax (or orgasm). *

In a Christian setting, normally it's not that we do not want to do the right thing, it's usually more that we don't know what to do. Which leads us into the next section.

THE 'MECHANISMS' OF THE SEXUAL ACT

There are two major problems that tend to block good sexual adjustment in marriage. To make it easy to remember these two problems, we will call them "time" and "space" and discuss them in that order.*

The "time" problem
Remember, God created us differently from each other. In His plan for most things to work we have to be prepared to give of ourselves. In the sexual act we find that the first thing that we must deal with is the matter of timing. Men and women have different timing in arousal. A man can become excited very quickly, in part, because he is visually and mentally stimulated. A woman typically takes longer, and being emotionally based is responsive, in part in the first instance, to romance and touch. The man must learn patience if he cares for the pleasure of his partner.

Both man and woman have been given the ability to experience pleasure through orgasm. But another problem emerges. A man can be ready for orgasm in a comparatively short amount of time. His wife may need a considerable amount of stimulation to arouse her before she comes to that place.

By "time," we refer to the fact that, sexually, male and female bodies are "timed" differently. Sexually, man is timed quickly. He can become aroused through sexual stimulation with his wife and usually reach orgasm in a very short time, two minutes, one minute, or in even less time. This is normal for him. He will gradually learn to control himself, but he will always tend to be "quick on the trigger." The wife should realize that all other women's husbands are "quick on the trigger." *

Remember that success for a man sexually is very important for his self-esteem. The wife then is more likely to get the results that she wants by encouraging him, so that he can grow confident and achieve self-control, rather than deriding him if he lacks endurance, adding to his anxiety.

On the other hand, sexually, a woman is timed more slowly, sometimes very slowly, as compared with a man. We can safely say that it takes the average woman ten to fifteen minutes or longer from the time that she starts sexual arousal with her husband until she experiences an orgasm. *

Note: This time would usually include the beginnings of sexual activity, such as kissing and fondling, preparing for, and prior to the stimulation of her more sensitive sexual parts.

Sometimes she may have an orgasm in ten minutes, five minutes, or even less. A few women on special occasions have an orgasm in one or two minutes. This is the exception. *

Note: other studies have indicated typically 7 minutes as an average. But there can be many factors involved, such as tiredness, stress, age, and even anxiety from previous experiences.

Many other circumstances such as what is happening in her personal life, or where she is in her monthly cycle may play a role in this, more so than her husband. He should realize that this is the case for all men's wives, and that she is created this way. She takes longer. Perhaps in Gods economy for sexuality to work, the man must be patient and loving, caring more about her needs than his own wants. In fact, in my personal opinion, the man's attitude to sex should be all about her pleasure, and not his own. It truly is better to give than receive.

When a young couple understands the difference in their sexual timing and when they accept it and cooperate with it, it is no longer a major problem, but may actually be a blessing. By being a blessing, we mean that this period of sexual stimulation and arousal, whether it be 10 or 20 minutes, may become one of the sweetest, most meaningful and spiritual experiences in husband-wife relationships. *

The "Space" problem

The second major problem that tends to block good sexual adjustment we have called "space." "Space" refers to the distance on the body of the wife between the clitoris and the vaginal passage. The clitoris is the external arousal trigger that sets off orgasm in the woman. It is made up of many nerve endings designed by the creator to arouse a woman to an orgasm. *

As we have already noted, the clitoris is situated about 30mm or one and a quarter inches above the vagina, out in front to some degree at the upper meeting point of the inner lips. It has been described as a 'mini penis' having a shaft and being very sensitive.

When this fact is visualized and understood, it should become clear that in normal intercourse the penis does not touch or contact the clitoris. This fact is of major importance. Since the penis does not move back and forth over the clitoris in intercourse, the wife may not become fully aroused and thus will not have an orgasm. *

It has been suggested that any 'positions' which may allow the penis to contact the clitoris may not be very comfortable for either the wife or the husband. Coupled with this, most husbands cannot control themselves for 10 or 15 minutes so that the wife has sufficient stimulation to have an orgasm.

Since the clitoris is the arousal trigger of the wife, and since the penis does not contact the clitoris in normal intercourse, marriage counselors recommend what is called "direct" stimulation. That is, the husband, in the process of love-play before intercourse starts, will gently stimulate all the erotic zones of his wife's body. This includes kissing her lips and breasts and using his hands and fingers to explore her total body, including the inner thighs, her outer lips, the opening of her vagina, and finally her clitoris.*

If you have not been exposed to these concepts on good sexual mechanics before, you may be struggling in the directness of the quotations.

If you read the book of Song of Songs from the Bible you will find that it is both blatantly descriptive of erotic activity, and poetic and sensual in its illustration of sexual anatomy. It eludes to the activities that are being described in a beautiful and tasteful way.

He will continue the stimulation of the clitoris for ten or fifteen minutes, or whatever time it takes, until he is sure that she is fully aroused sexually and ready for intercourse. *

Note: each woman knows what she prefers in this preparation phase, and this may vary from encounter to encounter. Some women do not want continuous manual stimulation of the clitoris without other touching and caressing taking place. (A sexual meeting can take place beginning with the man giving the wife a back massage, which shows affection, and gives the man's arousal time to settle down before intercourse takes place.)

The important thing to remember here is that the clitoris is the external arousal trigger; that there must be stimulation of the clitoris and the area near the clitoris for a wife to have an orgasm. The method of stimulation of the clitoris is not so important. *

To summarize here. After suitable sexual arousal of both man and wife, which will invariably include direct stimulation for her, the penis is inserted and one following the other in movement they move together towards orgasm with the penis inside the vagina.

WHAT IF THIS IS NOT SUFFICIENT FOR BOTH TO ACHIEVE ORGASM AND SATISFACTION?

Let me preface answering this by citing the results of question 54 in the book; SEXUAL HAPPINESS IN MARRIAGE

54. When the wife is aroused near an orgasm, can she reach the orgasm after intromission (inserting the penis in the vagina) during the process of intercourse without further direct stimulation of the clitoris?
Yes 58.7%   No 41.3% *

The evidence is that a significant number of women cannot reach orgasm without continued direct stimulation. I have read other more recent statistics stating that this is the case with well over 60% of women.
So, how is this lovingly negotiated, caring for the needs of the wife?

1. One way is as follows. After the arousal period and immediately after intercourse is started, the husband may place the weight of his body on his left arm, put his right hand down on his wife's clitoris, and give her further direct stimulation while intercourse continues. This is somewhat awkward....

2. ......if the wife can have orgasms by direct stimulation but cannot get to an orgasm in intercourse, it is wise for the wife to have further direct stimulation of the clitoris while in the process of intercourse.
*After the arousal period as the husband shifts to start intercourse, the wife may put her finger on her own clitoris and continue giving herself the same direct stimulation that her husband has been giving her. ***

Of the two methods, it is considered that the second one is the most comfortable, and the most efficient. Remember the goal is to work as a team caring about, and meeting each other's needs.

*This pairing of clitoral manipulation with intercourse has been found to be quite effective for many couples. ****

At times as the wife nears orgasm but is taking time to climax the man may be unable to control himself and hold on until she has climaxed. To remove the pressure on each partner and diffuse potential future anxiety, the husband can continue to directly stimulate his wife after his orgasm until she is also fulfilled. The main thing is that emotionally and relationally you are accepting of each other's needs, and caring about giving the partner enjoyment and arrival at completion. Indeed, God's gift of sex is to be able to pleasure each other in this way.

Some meaningful time spent together caressing, embracing or resting together is loving way to complete the encounter.

All of this requires good communication about what is liked or disliked to get it to work well. This usually takes time and patience, but if you are dedicated to each other you will get there. Good sex then becomes a strength for your relationship protecting you from the temptations of illicit sexual expression.

PART 2: Distorted sexuality
We see judgments for sexual immorality listed 19 times in the New Testament from Mathew to Revelation. In the Old Testament it is revealed that the devil's way for sexuality brings a curse for up to 10 generations, highlighting the seriousness of this type of offense. *(Deuteronomy 23:2) Psalm 115:8, Romans 12:2*

SEX AND THE 'MEANING OF LIFE'
Living for sex and being ruled by our primal appetites is clearly wrong. It becomes idolatry of the flesh, of the creation and not the creator. Much modern media seems to make it central, and in a sense, 'the meaning of life.' Personally, I think that it should be regarded as a gift, and even at times an appetite that needs to be dealt with periodically, in order for your relationship with God to not be distracted.

Study 1: Sins of 'Omission'
As with other areas that we have discussed, with sexuality there can be times where the problem is not in things that we have done, but rather, in things that we should have done, but have omitted to do. To deny sexuality as a 'very good' God purposed part of creation is also sin. Sin means 'to offend,' or 'an offense.' To discard God's gift as not good may well be offensive to Him.

You cannot deny being a sexual being because you are going against created order. You can only express it appropriately in a biblical manner. *1 Timothy 4:1-3*

We could summarize all of this by saying that to deny ourselves or our spouses' healthy sexual expression is unhealthy. It leaves us open to temptation, potential immorality, or sinful responses such as bitterness and resentment. Remember rejection can produce rebellion, because in affect it is projecting onto the person that what they need or want means nothing to you. This will read as unfairness or injustice on the recipient as they are feeling that you do not care about them. *1 Corinthians 7:2-5*

SUMMARY
We do not want to be:
Ignoring or refusing Gods gifts in creation
Denying your partner blessing and intimacy, acceptance and value
Trying to deny the God created needs of your own body
Not be willing to accept and cooperate with Gods order

Denial of your sexuality will not make it go away. It can only be expressed how God intended.

Study 2: Sins of 'Commission'
These are sexual sins that are done, and should not be. *1 Corinthians 6:9-10*

1. Adultery
In the following passage Jesus points out that adultery is something that happens at heart level. In this context, we can say that there is mental and or emotional adultery. This is where you are desiring emotional interaction with a person other than your spouse. *Matthew 5:28-29*

Clearly, a healthy relationship at home is the best defense, where your emotional needs are met. But even if they are not being fulfilled, perhaps because healing is needed, there is no biblical basis to justify this behavior. Having said this, the most common reason that we have found for adultery is the need for acceptance. People who come for ministry who have been involved in adulterous activities invariably suffer from rejection. Often a marriage partner does not build up the person who is drawn into the offense, or even if they do, their efforts simply do not touch the unhealed area that needs acceptance.

2. Fornication

The word fornicator is translated from the Greek word 'pornos,' and along with fornicator it means a whoremonger, or a male prostitute. It carries the sense of someone who gives their body for illicit sexual activity. The dictionary meaning for fornication is consensual intercourse between two people not married to each other. Satan's intention is to reduce sex to animal urges – just fun for yourself – when in fact it is meant for deep spiritual and emotional bonding. Intended as a vehicle for deep valuing, love, affection, acceptance, security and giving. *Revelation 2:20-22*

3. Oral sex

This is a controversial issue. Many, even Christian counsellors consider this to be appropriate and acceptable, as long as both partners don't object. This does sound a bit like the humanistic mindset that we hear; *if it's right for you, it's right!* Personally, I am more concerned how God views it, than how I view it! Is it perversion?

Statistics report that research has proven that people engaged in oral sex are 58 times more likely to develop throat cancer because of the HPV 16 virus that is reportedly present on the genital area. I am pretty sure that God already knows this! Would you consider that to be a blessing or a curse? The very nature of things suggest that oral sex is not a clean activity given the proximity to, and functions of, the genitals in the process of waste disposal.

Deliverance sometimes occurs from demons who are attached to people who have been involved in these practices, which at times are producing some kind of throat or mouth problem. Perhaps the question is, would you do this if you had not heard of it and been encouraged in its normalcy and desirability through peer contact or media?

4. Homosexuality/ Sodomy.

Unrepentant sexual activity with someone of the same sex is recorded in the scriptures as behavior that will bring problems now and judgement later. We do not say this to judge people who are caught in it, because sin is sin. But if a bus was about to hit you, I imagine that you would want me to call out a warning. So, in love, without judgement we offer help if you want to be free. We respect your free will and choice, and understand that if you do not believe that there is a God, or for that matter a Satan, then you don't care what anyone says anyway. The responsibility of it being reasonable behavior then falls back on you. I personally don't deal any differently, or make a greater distinction with homosexuals than with anyone else. They are people that something happened to, just like everyone else. God doesn't want to see them perish, as He does not want anyone else to perish. *Romans 1:24-27*

A medical friend of mine said that many homosexual men who practice sodomy have problems in the anus (back passage) which was designed for one-way traffic. Women who are sodomized suffer similar problems, and there are very often unclean spirits involved. As with any area of bondage, the attitude of the church should be to help these people receive the Fathers love and grace and be set free.

SODOMY
In today's world young people are brought up to think that sex in the anus is just a normal part of sexual experimentation. Some cultures and even religions promote it as a suitable alternative to 'fornication.' Later they carry the practice into marriage.

5. Sexual abuse. We have already discussed the incredibly damage done to the identity through abuse of this kind. One statistic reports: 1 in 4 girls under the age of 10 in the U.S. and almost the same for boys. Sadly, many abusers were themselves abused which gives them a predisposition to this practice. They are infected with sexual and spiritual issues that have to be dealt with. *Matthew 18:6-7*

6. Incest
In today's world there is what is called 'incest porn' which promotes immorality within the family. Sadly, this is often directed towards children. Regardless, the Bible clearly states that this kind of behavior without repentance and a probable need for deliverance will bring a curse. We often minister to people who have a 'tragic' look on their faces as a result of the long-term damage from these types of events. *Deuteronomy 27:20-23, 2 Samuel 13:12-20*

7. Bestiality
Bestiality is primarily having sexual with an animal. It can also relate to savage and depraved behavior. *Deuteronomy 27:21*

8. Pornography
Porn is such a pervasive sin epidemic, that Part 3 is devoted to how to help those bound to be extracted from this destructive bondage.

Part 2: Conclusion and summary
The best way to deal with God given appetites and avoid immorality is to:

1. Eat well- in much the same way as healthy food is good for us, and balance is important, so it is with sexuality. Healthy sexual activity is good for our entire being and relationships.

2. Eat enough – the best way to not crave something that is not good for you is to be satisfied. If your sexuality is fulfilling enough, temptations such as pornography are easily resisted.

3. God is the Creator, and everything that He designed is good – to deny His gift could be disrespectful. We are made in His image. He is creative, and so we can be as well in our sexual expression, within the bounds of propriety and morality.

UNIT TWELVE

Freedom from Pornography

LIKE A FLOOD
ISAIAH 59: 19

Over many years of ministry, I have had a significant number of men come to me with the problem of being bound to pornography. Most get free if they are really committed to walking away from it. It IS doable! Some others seem to justify it as 'under grace' and others simply prefer to follow their fleshly desires. Those that take this approach usually lose their families if they are married, and almost all struggle in the area of self-respect. Guilt and not liking yourself can have a devastating effect on your health. Sin and serving the kingdom of this World will always produce some sort of consequence. The good news is that God sets the captives free! He will show you a way out and what to do so that you do not need to give in to it again. *1 Corinthians 10:13-14*

Pornography has been described as a mental illness, possibly because it produces a kind of torment of the mind. Many men, and possibly women, cannot stop thinking about sex as a result of their exposure. Media has always had its role in propagating these excesses, with the earliest movies, and even the beginnings of the internet being used almost immediately for explicit pictures. The devil is very much using this in our time to flood the World with sin, and have peoples bound under his power. But we can be free! We know the World will be under this influence, but the church needs to make its stand. As someone has said, "It is ok to have the ship in the sea, but it is not ok to have the sea in the ship. It is ok to have the church in the World, but it is not ok to have the World in the church."

Study 1: The scale of the problem

Some of the statistics that are being thrown around are alarming, with some people citing figures such as 96% of 16-year-old boys being addicted to porn in the western world. This is addiction that is quoted, not just occasional viewing. This has many times begun at school, where, I have heard a report that as many as 93% of boys have seen porn on a smart phone by the time that they are 13 years old. The same statistic is reported to be true of girls by 15 years of age. One man that I met who is working in the computer industry suggested to me that there are at least as many teenage girl users if not more. They often initially watch porn to see what they need to do to please the boys. Other viewings may be attributed to peer group pressure and an effort to conform to, and be accepted by the world system.

In the early 2000's I heard a figure of 30 million Americans being addicted to porn, consisting of 72% men and 28% women. This is now many years ago and I shudder to think what the situation would like today.

A Current affairs program in Australia stated that the porn industry there has an estimated turnover of 2 Billion dollars per year...considerably more than the yearly GDP of some nations. The show also said that pornography accounts for 12% of all websites worldwide with 33% of the web being devoted to porn, 25% of all search engine requests, 8% of email requests and 35% of all peer to peer downloads. (2010)
Considering that much of the secular world accepts the viewing of pornography as normal, and even desirable, I would say that we have a problem.

How is the church doing?
In the church I have found that many if not most young people do not even know that sleeping together before marriage is a sin, let alone that porn is immoral. Porn is rife, and so consequently is the type of distorted sexuality portrayed on the screens visited by young Christians. The church has failed to teach healthy sexuality, so as a result our young people are taking their lessons from a sin sick world.

The percentages of <u>addiction</u> to porn from a study of evangelical churches in the U.S. are quite alarming. Reportedly 65% of Christian men, (another study said 68%), 25% of Christian women and 54% of Pastors are <u>addicted</u> to this problem.
In Australia the claims are 33% of clergy visit sexually explicit websites.

A BIBLICAL PERSPECTIVE
The Greek word used in the New Testament for prostitute is 'porne.'
And the word from the Greek used for write or inscribe is 'grapho.' So, when we put the two words together, we get a picture of people selling their bodies in a viewable, repeatable scribing for other people's illicit sexual pleasure. This means that when a man or woman views pornography they are actually joining with prostitutes for their sexual gratification.
If you are not married fornication is by relating with another person in a sexual act. If you are married, we would consider this to be adultery, because you are meeting your sexual and emotional needs by connecting with someone other than your wives or husbands.

At times I have had wives ask me if they are Biblically able to leave their husbands because of their partners' porn addiction. Sadly, it would be difficult to say with any conviction, that the husband or wife who has gone to porn for their sexual release, is not been unfaithful to their spouses. However, to qualify that, God is always redemptive and always willing to have grace for sin that is confessed and genuinely repented of. If we are to become Christ like then I think that our first position should be forgiveness' and working with the victim if they are willing, before we give up on them. Having grace, love and compassion for them, and realizing that most often they did not want to find themselves in this trap will go a long way towards a wonderful relationship in the future. Of course, this is dependent on them being genuinely repentant. If they are not then you still need to forgive them even if you choose to separate.

What does scripture say? Let's take a look at *1 Corinthians 6:9-10* to settle the matter. This passage lists behaviors that will NOT inherit the kingdom of God. The word translated fornicator here is from the Greek word 'pornos.' One commentator that I heard stated that this includes viewing or watching, as well as various other kinds of perversion. This is serious business and not to be treated lightly. The good news in this passage is that the Apostle Paul states that these people were in these practices and are now free. Evidently the fear of God elicited genuine repentance in those times, and the church clearly was well equipped to help set the captives free! *1 Corinthians 9-11*

Study 2: Steps to Freedom
There are 8 areas that may need to be considered and addressed
I usually use the analogy of cutting off the 8 legs of a spider that has you entrapped in its web. Recently someone who I was helping pointed out that spiders have the ability to grow back their legs. I didn't know that, but after some consideration I concluded that it is still a reasonable example. Once you cripple the beast, as with any addiction you need to be on guard to not reopen pathways. So, I present these 8 areas as places that may need to be dealt with in order to come to freedom, and then maintain the ground that you have repossessed.

Any area out of God's perfect order can give a place to the devil. *Ephesians 4:27*

Leg 1. The 'Will'
Conforming to the World
Romans 12:2, Ephesians 2:1-3
For non-Christians there are only the standards of the world to base their decisions and actions on. Consequently, many of them watch porn simply because they want to. So, the battle for their choices and the activity of their will is all but nonexistent. The world tells them that it is perfectly acceptable and even desirable to watch explicit material.

Conforming to Christ
Romans 8:29
For real Christians however it is not so simple. The scriptures make it clear that we are being tested. Temptation is translated from the Greek word 'peirazo' which literally means testing. The desires of our soul and the lusts of our bodies do not simply disappear at conversion.

What has happened now is that we have been indwelt by the Holy Spirit who brings to us a new nature, a nature which desires to follow and please God. Now there is conflict in our will. *Romans 7:14-25, + 8:29*

Wooing the will
I find it vital to study passages that instill in me the fear of God and strongly influence my decisions and choices. God is no respecter of persons and we know that we will all be judged by the Word of God. I suggest careful study and meditation on the following passages. We have to 'lean on' our thought life in order to discipline it to move our <u>will</u> in the direction of the 'narrow path of God.'

Further reading: Romans 8:1-14, Galatians 5:16-25 + 6:7-8

> *Romans 8: 13 For if you live according to the sinful nature, you will die; but if by the Spirit you put to death the misdeeds of the body, you will live,*
> *14 because those who are led by the Spirit of God are sons of God. NKJV*

Dealing with recorded images and the 'screen' of your conscious mind
To deal with this we must understand that our conscious mind or the viewing place of immediate thought, memory, or imagination is extremely limited. If we liken it to a computer screen, and use it as an example, we might get a glimpse of what we are dealing with. The point is that I choose which program that I open and view on my computer screen. Indeed, I could open the internet program, or access stored files and have porn on my screen.

It is MY screen! I choose and decide what I will allow to be viewed on it. In the same way it is YOUR mind, and you totally ALWAYS choose what you are going to allow to be viewed in your consciousness.

We know from scripture that God remembers our sins no more. The Bible doesn't say that He has forgotten them. He could access them and view them if He wanted to, but He has chosen not to remember them. We, created in His image, have the same capacity to have images on file but not view them. We too choose to remember them no more. But how do we do it?

Subjecting our thought life
One of the most powerful verses in the Bible pertaining to overcoming this area is found in second Corinthians. It actually tells us that it is necessary to subdue every thought that was initiated from a source outside the Kingdom of God.

> *2 COR 10: 5 We demolish arguments and every pretension that sets itself up against the knowledge of God, and we take captive every thought to make it obedient to Christ. NIV*

Once we entertain a thought or imagining for even a second on the screen of our conscious mind we are in trouble. There is only one way to deal with it! *"That doesn't belong in my mind and I absolutely refuse to let it be there for even a millisecond!"* This IS the <u>KEY</u>. If you give it any time at all in your mind it will take hold.

I have known of people who literally shake their heads as if shaking the thoughts out as they willfully refuse to let their minds be used. Many are amazed at how quickly they get the victory when they take authority over the screen of their minds! *James 4:7-8*

Thought Displacement
Another powerful tool in defeating the images that are looking to access the screen of your conscious mind is displacement. This is basically like filling your bath tub right to the top. When you hop in the waters are displaced and go all over the floor. Or if you put compressed air into the ballast tank on a submarine it pushes out all of the water and the vessel rises.

In much the same way we can take control of our minds by pushing out the sinful thought with a Holy one. You can't stop thinking, so you need to train yourselves to replace the unhealthy thoughts with beneficial thinking. *Philippians 4:8*

Conclusion
What a terrible state it is to be in where most of your thought life is consumed with sexual materials. I have heard reports of some men thinking about sex every few minutes all day long. What an empty life this is. The enemy comes to rob you of life. The area of the will needs to be forcefully taken hold of with the mind being brought into subjection.

'Leg' 2. Trigger patterns and associations
The connection between association and addiction

Imagine that you are going through a period of time where you are stressed and under load. As a result, you are feeling a bit tired and run down. One day you happen to have a drink of a caffeinated soda drink. The caffeine and sugar give you a bit of a boost and you feel a bit happier and a little more energized. Your brain stores this information in a file titled; 'feeling flat and what to do about it,' in the limbic system area of your chemical mind. The next time you feel flat your brain does a data search on information relating to this problem.

Right on top of the list is a record that drinking caffeinated soda gave you a boost and made you feel a little better in the past. So, your brain has kept a record and created an association between tiredness and the boost received from the drink.

Clearly if you continue to be tired you will continue to access that file titled 'feeling flat and what to do about it.' Before long, you have developed a habit. If you serve the habit long enough over time it becomes an addiction. *1 Corinthians 6:12-13*

Porn, in the short term may appear exciting, even as with the Garden of Eden, seemingly 'what you need to make you happy.' But in the long run it is a terrible mind destroying bondage. *Proverbs 6:25-26*

Porn has usually begun with exposure to material that produces intense emotional excitement and response. It also has a chemical element which we will discuss in the next 'Leg.' In order to be free, it is necessary to break down the 'associations' that trigger the behavior. For many men this could be sexual rejection from the wife who is tired, uninterested, or perhaps unable to engage because of her own historical issues relating to previous sexual experiences. This could even include beliefs stemming from a religious background or setting where she (or he) has been taught that sex is dirty or bad.

As with other addictions a part of the power of the bondage to porn is association. For example, imagine a young man goes to his laptop computer to check his emails. Before he gets to his mail box he is confronted with advertisements featuring girls in skimpy clothing on the home page of his internet service supplier. Understanding how association works is the best defense. If you let curiosity get the better of you, and you go to the site and are visually stimulated by whatever is on those pages, you would have created an association. Your mind will now remind you that this is not now merely a laptop computer, but is now an instrument of potential sexual gratification and arousal when you go to use it.

Breaking the media link

Many men have an association between their laptop or now smart phone and their sexuality. My advice to them in regards to this media link is to deal with it harshly and with finality. Jesus said that if your eye is the problem that is causing you to sin, get rid of it! If it is your hand. Get rid of it! If it is your laptop or smart phone, get rid of it! Throw it over the fence. If you have a job that needs a laptop and you can't get control, get yourself a job digging ditches! *Matthew 5:29-30, Hebrews 10:26-27*

I have found that the men who make the necessary decision to break the links and associations by radically dealing with their media get free. This often means saving your marriage and keeping your family. Those who try to justify or rationalize it will most likely remain bound permanently or until they are prepared to bear fruit in keeping with repentance. *(Mt 3:8)* These men often lose their families and even if single never overcome the guilt and find peace and joy.

I used to have a bag of smart phones in my office from those who were repentant. It was great to observe the blossoming relationships as a result of this commitment to freedom. Phones without internet connecting capabilities are still readily available, and wives are more than willing to share their computers with husbands who are walking away from this illness.

Other ways that association is relevant to porn

For some men a 'trigger' comes when an association is made between an empty house and watching pornography. So now the wife says that she is going to do the shopping. His mind connects him with the 'what do I do when I have the house to myself' memory file. At the top of the list is an opportunity for going to the internet to watch porn.

'Leg' 3. Addictive cycles and chemical programming

Chemical hormonal considerations

Hormones are chemical messengers that help in part to elaborate our thought life into feelings in our bodies. Many of these travel through our bodily systems and attach to receptors, which in turn produce feelings, emotions and various responses.
If we think about sex our body begins to prepare for the act by releasing hormones to stimulate our sexual parts. But remember this arousal was a thought before it became anything else. The problem is once the thinking has happened, even if briefly, the thought has produced a chemical response. This of course includes memories of explicit images. If

the devil has your mind, he has you! This is why the section on the 'will' and the 'mind' is so vital in getting free and staying free.

Male sexuality and wiring

I heard some time ago that a male's sexuality, even at its peak is quite manageable without outside stimulus. In other words when a man is exposed to sexual materials it 'hypes' up his system because of the chemical release. We live in a much-sexualized society with media such as television absolutely full of programming based around sexual themes. Even how women dress in the Western World is testing for modern man. I believe that for the most part girls are simply trying to keep up with fashion, not realizing the sexual nature of their appearance. However, if women understood that men do not view them in the same way as women view men, I think many of their habits would change.

The Bible does not dispute either the beauty of women or for that matter the physical attractiveness of men to women. The counsel of scripture is to fill up visually on the wife that you have been given, and for her to be enough for you. God sets His affection on us by choice. We are blessed if we have chosen to set our affection on our wives. *Proverbs 5:18*

Media based brain stimulus

Another chemical factor with viewing this type of material is its effect on the pleasure centre in the brain. When this is stimulated there are hormones implicated which produce pleasure feelings. Commentators tell us that masturbation is often involved, or other sexual activities. So, you are also connecting and relating the whole viewing event by associating it to the dopamine release and consequent pleasure in orgasm. Other complex hormones are secreted in the excitement phase which can also be addictive.

The bottom line is that it still all begins with a thought. It could be thinking of memories from past viewing. Or perhaps it could be the thought to look for something of a sexually explicit nature now or in the future. It is your mind, and you are responsible for what goes through it!

'Leg' 4. Dysfunctional sexual relationships

Let me begin this area by saying that sexual issues often appear in people's lives because of broken relationships. When I am proposing that God's order is to meet each other's sexual needs to the point of not needing stimulus from outside areas, I realize that I am suggesting an ideal, and that other ministry may need to take place before this can become achievable. However, a healthy sex life is Gods perfect order for protecting each other from the temptations of perversion and sexual sin.

As noted, this may well be unrealizable and unrealistic before emotional healing has taken place for the partner who has been abused. They may be unable to be fully engaged before they have received ministry for this problem, and for that matter any related emotional issues, for example fear of failure. Fear of failure could drive a man towards porn because there is no expectation on him to perform or to meet some perceived standard of sexual success.
It is necessary to be able to fulfill each other's needs. It is a form of spiritual covering and protecting each other. *1 Corinthians 7:3+5+9*

Sex is to some degree an 'appetite' and a part of the natural life. Just like eating it is meant to be expressed and satisfied within proper limits. A healthy 'meal' so to speak, and then no need to think about it again until mealtime comes around again. This desire to seek sex is the very thing that the devil plays on in his attack on man in particular. Often the men then lead their partners into viewing pornographic materials. So, an understanding wife who is prepared and able to cover a man's sexual needs is an enormous asset in helping him get free and him staying free.

*Footnote. Some sexual issues come to people through the generational influences of sexual sin in the family line. It can also come through an ungodly sexual bond to someone who has the problem. This increasingly includes a drawing towards porn.

'Leg' 5. Emotional stressors, real or perceived

Right at the top of the list I would place rejection. Remember we have discussed associations and memory-based brain 'files.' One of the coping mechanisms for rejection is independence. Basically, somebody rejects you, and a way that you choose to deal with it is by cutting them off. It may not be a conscious thought but in your heart, you are 'saying' "well if you don't want me, then I am going to live a life where I don't need you." Then I don't have to worry about you rejecting me, my needs, or my attempt at having a relationship with you again. So, this is a general response to rejection probably learnt in some environment of hurt in the past. It surfaces when some kind of rejection comes. Then out of the memory bank comes the 'what do I do if people don't receive me or accept my trying to be in relationship.'

A common emotional situation or stressor would be when the person makes overtures for sexual intimacy, and the response is something like; 'in your dreams honey, I am not doing anything tonight, I am tired!' For the rejected person, invariably they will feel not wanted or not good enough, or perhaps not attractive enough. This can be a common stressor for a sense of rejection in men in particular. They already feel that their wives aren't as turned on by their appearance as they are by looking at their wives. And their wives never seem to want sex like they do. Therefore, they reason that they are not attractive! The truth is however that the women do not have their sexuality wired into their eyes as do men, or the strong sex hormones to initiate that a man carries.

If the man perceives rejection, he may go to his default position of independence. This means that now he will take care of his own sexuality, and choose to not need the response and involvement of his wife. The options for him nowadays are a multiplicity of readily available sexual materials. These are full of women who are portrayed as accepting of men's advances. They are seemingly much more than willing to engage in sexual activities, and apparently want sex as much as the men. Part of the list of solutions stored in the mind for sexual rejection now becomes pornography and masturbation.

Possible general emotional triggers

> *Proverbs 4: 23 Above all else, guard your heart, for it affects everything you do. NLT*

Other 'triggers' could be work pressures, an unhappy home life, even a general dissatisfaction with life. If porn is used as entertainment or escape from these or other emotionally driven situations, then your mind will make the connection. From then on whenever any of these situations present you will gravitate towards the solution that you have encoded in your 'heart.'

This is why the scripture tells us to guard our hearts...be careful what conclusions and solutions that we decide on and establish. This is very important because it affects everything. Relationships with God, others, and even how we consider ourselves. If you have historical rejection and fear of rejection issues, I would recommend that you seek out emotional healing for this problem. If you don't the anxiety proceeding from the brokenness will continue to cause you problems and leave you potentially vulnerable in the sexual area.

'Leg' 6. Sexual 'trauma' (embedded memories from the initial impact)

We have already noted many men struggle with the images already imprinted on their minds from previous exposure. An expert that I was listening to on the subject stated that the images are permanently burned into your mind in 3 tenths of a second. I would liken this to a trauma because of the explicit and impacting nature of the materials. This happens through an electro-chemical process known as protein synthesis. I believe that God could erase these memories and I am sure at times He does. As we have pointed out the vast majorities have these pictures indelibly etched into the brain, and push they themselves relentlessly into the mind at every opportunity.

Our minds do have the capacity to suppress or repress memories and thoughts. The neuroscientists tell us that we have neurological pathways which become stronger the more we use and activate them. But the good news is that the less we use them the less the brain does to maintain them and they breakdown and weaken.

'Leg' 7. Natural desires amplified by 'exogenous' [outside] stimulation –

Drag racing cars and indeed some street cars use a product known as 'nitrous oxide.' The effect of adding this to the fuel changes the oxygen mix which in turn allows the fuel to be burned faster. The result of this additive is a massive burst of power supercharging the machines system.

It is considered that a male's sexuality, even at its hormonal peak is quite manageable without outside stimulus. However, when a man is exposed to imagery or literature of a sexual nature, it 'hypes' up and supercharges his hormonal system, increasing the chemical release.

Our society has seemingly made sex 'the meaning of life.' Whilst we continue to thank God for His wonderful gift, if we keep it in perspective it is actually a relatively small part of our existence.

There are times when it is beyond your control to be exposed to women dressed in a sexually provocative manner. There are other times when it is a matter of your personal choice what you see, hear or read. Even T.V. today is full of sexual images, nudity and suggestive or explicit comments. We need to take some control and responsibility for the stimulus that is around our lives. Once the exposure has taken place it will likely have some kind of hormonal outworking that perhaps you could have done without. If you are planning to be free from the bondage of pornography it is probably wise to minimize even seemingly harmless sexual exposure.

'Leg' 8. Spiritual powers behind pornography

Dealing with the spiritual factor
We live in a World that is spiritual before it is anything else. Both God's kingdom and the kingdom of darkness are present influencing the natural sense world. We serve, follow and submit to either one of these kingdoms or the other. Whomever we serve becomes lord of that particular area.

If you serve porn then the ruling spirit over your sexuality is not God it is the opposer, Satan. Clearly, he is the instigator and motivator behind this perverted industry. So, when you are serving sin in this area you are submitting to significant 'spiritual forces of evil in the heavenly realms.'

Interestingly the pornography industry has had its greatest and most prolific acceleration and influence through the internet. This along with other misused media comes to us through the 'air.' It is indeed a power of the air in our times. *Ephesians 2:1-2 + 6:12*

When you offer your sexuality to the devil in this area, he will very happily keep you in bondage and make you miserable. It is vital that we realize that submission, cooperation and participation put you under the authority of the one that you serve and receive from. Jesus' came to free us from the power of sin and forgive us, not to leave us captive to its power. His purpose is always to destroy the works of the devil in our lives. *(1 John 3:8)* But in order to achieve this, He also requires cooperation and participation. We call this repentance, and it is our most powerful spiritual tool, because it moves us from submitting to an evil spiritual kingdom to serving the kingdom of God. *Acts 28:18, Romans 6:16 + 12-13, 2 Peter 2:19b*

The Generational component

I often ask people who are struggling in this area if anyone in their family line such as a father or grandfather had a problem with this addiction. Very often this is the case and so there is already a spiritual power drawing the victim towards this particular sin. In scripture we understand this power and its limitations if somebody repents and has prayer for freedom. Until we know that it may be a spiritual power that is involved then we probably won't be looking to claim the freedom that is referred to in the New Testament. *Galatians 3: 13-14*

We need to appropriate and receive the finished work of Christ by faith. It is good to find someone who has faith to pray for us for our freedom. *Exodus 20:5, Psalm 51:5*

Transference

Any sin that is served can lead to the inhabitation of an evil spirit. If you are serving lust then there is every possibility that the spirit promoting lust that is pressuring you from outside of your body will enter into your body where it will have greater influence. This spirit that is holding the sin of lust could gain entry through the trauma of the initial viewing of porn. This would be an emotional opening through the shock of what is being seen...temporarily your normal emotional composure is gone and a door to your personality is open.

It most often will come in through regular deliberate exposure; thereby you are voluntarily participating with an evil spirit. It could also enter through an illicit sexual relationship with somebody who already has a spirit that promotes porn.

Demonization

As I have pointed out people often struggle to get free because they do not understand that one part of their problem is demonic power with a stronghold on that area of their personality. Once the evil spirit has gained access it has strong influences on the soul. It will move the will towards more and more sinful activity. Whether you have deliberately or unwittingly joined with it, it now has partial use of the members or parts of your person that you have yielded to it as we have already cited in *Romans 6:12-13*. In this case it is your eyes, the chemistry in your brain relating to the visuals, your emotions, and your thought life in regard to sexuality.

This is why we see people unable to have normal sexual relationships without perverse acts, and they are subsequently unable to be excited by normal sexuality.

Separation
Before we pray for a person to be set free from the evil spirit or spirits, they must first have a realization of the demonic activity. They must understand that when they have thoughts urging them to go and view something that in all probability it is not merely their own minds. They readily follow the prompting because they think it is just their own idea, or what they want. You think it is you that wants to look at the material or fantasize about things you have viewed. In fact, it is actually a someone; a spirit being that is in you that wants you to do it.

The reality is that it is something else that is doing the initiating, and wants to be fed and have greater power over you; it does this by drawing you into more and more exposure. Most people desire separation from the evil spirit once they have realized what is really going on. They have been had…. deceived into thinking that they are merely following their own desires.

What do we do, and how do we pray?
Assuming that the person can discern the spiritual element of their problem, then you can pray a simple prayer commanding the spirit to go in the name of Jesus Christ. The results are more dependent on the person being prayed for wanting to separate from the spirit than your spirituality. Also, they have to be truly repentant and determined to take back control of their minds. You may or may not see something that indicates that the spirit has left. If the person really means it then God <u>will</u> set them free, but God will not be mocked, and if they secretly want to continue at a later date, they may not be delivered. *(See Galatians 6:7-8)*

If they truly have set their hearts on freedom, then after the spirit is gone it does not mean that there will be no temptation. What they will find is that it will be much easier to resist, as the spirit is now outside of their person. They then need to respect the potential for re-infestation if they return to their sin.

Be aware!
If you have a spirit of lust as a result of viewing pornography, the same spirit will probably be finding reasons why you shouldn't get ministry. Or it may justify to you why it is ok. Or perhaps you may feel very anxious about getting prayer. In reality many of these thoughts and feelings which seem to be your own, are the work of the spirit that you have joined with in sin. It does not want to be evicted and will most probably pressure you away from help. The same is true with many other areas that we might need help with.

CONCLUSION
I think that we have proven that it is not optional as to whether or not you should be working towards complete freedom in this area. The Good News is that Jesus is the anointed Christ who announced that His purpose and intent is specifically to set the captives free. *(Luke 4:18)* So you have all of the power of heaven behind you if you decide that you genuinely want to be released.

The only thing that can stop you breaking loose is your own desires and decisions, and perhaps the lack of ministry help that you may need for support. Because Earth is presented to be a testing ground for humanity, God for the most part seems to leave us with free will and choice. God will not override what we choose. It seems that testing and sanctification is

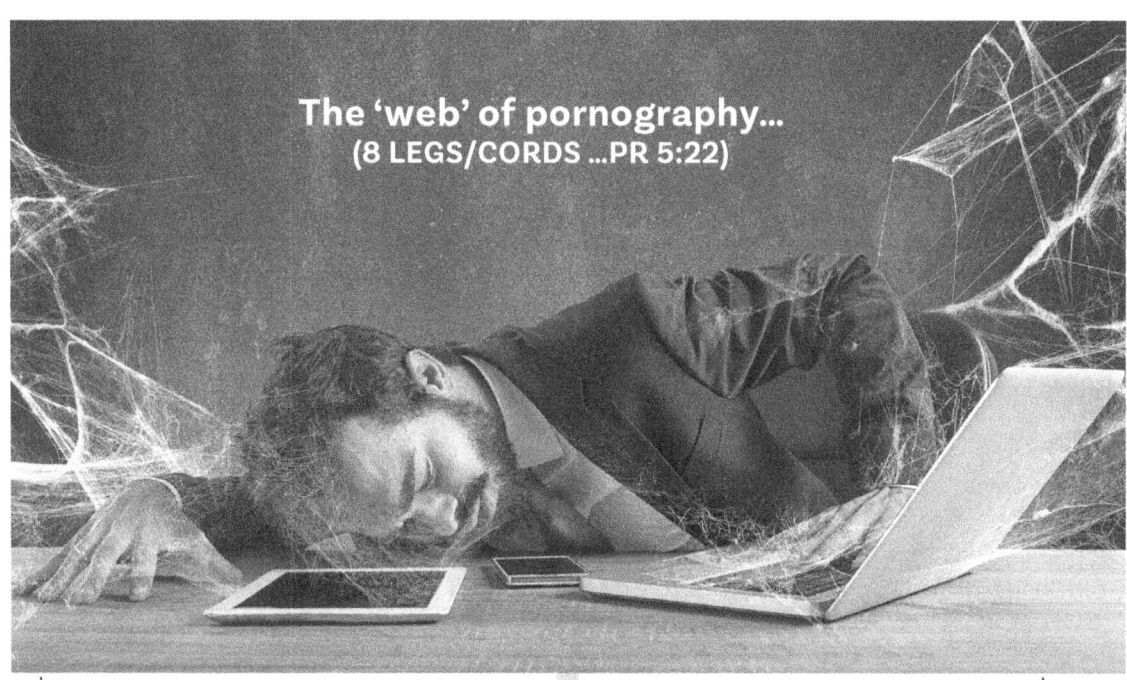

The 'web' of pornography...
(8 LEGS/CORDS ...PR 5:22)

 Natural desires amplified...
(environmental visual stimulation = 'nitrous oxide' (fuel) for the sexual machine)

Emotional stressors
(real or perceived) Rejection, fear of rejection, loneliness, anxiety:
(Note: fear increases visual arousal)

 Dysfunctional sexual relationship
(in marriage) [appetites not fulfilled]

Sexual 'trauma'
(Initial visual shock) (strong embedded neural memory pathways from first impact..) [protein synthesis]

 The 'Will' = you just want to!
(given willingly to strong desires, FLESH, No conviction/the deception that 'it's o.k.' ECC 1/8

Trigger patterns
(Memory associations with previous times of opportunity and enactment situations) i.e. At work, alone, night contact with girls etc

 Spiritual powers
behind porn: 'demonization' *(perhaps through SIN, the Generations, or spiritual ties from ungodly sexual relationships)*

Addiction / Distorted chemical stimulus 'programming patterns'..

Note: for further information on Spiritual freedom see the unit on the subject.

for this life, and judgment and punishment for the unrepentant is for the next.
It can be helpful to pray for the gift of repentance and a change of heart.

> *2 Timothy 2: 25 In meekness instructing those that oppose themselves; if God peradventure will give them repentance to the acknowledging of the truth;*
> *26 And that they may recover themselves out of the snare of the devil, who are taken captive by him at his will. KJV (Emphasis mine)*

Self-deception and self-justification will need to be negotiated, most times with some genuine soul searching done before the Lord. *Psalm 139:23-24, Jeremiah 17:9-10*

FINALLY

I compile this manual in the hope that the body of Christ will be further equipped to not only speak of the good news but to be the good news. There are many who need to be touched by God through believers walking in the Spirit who know how to help. In this, we, as did Jesus, prove God and His word to be true and uphold His integrity. *Psalm 23:1-6, John 15:7-9*

APPENDIX ONE

Sample Sessions

SAMPLE MINISTRY TO REJECTION BELIEFS SCENARIO

A person approaches you for help.

Step 1: Explain the process to the person, and what you are looking for, namely *heart beliefs*. This process could include having them read, view or listen to material such as this explaining the ministry.

Step 2: The person comes for the actual ministry session.

> **Note:** They already have the problem that they are struggling with so you don't need to come up with anything. It is not your job to fix their whole life, just try to help them with whatever is presenting at the time.

Listen to their story and the issue that they are bringing to you. Make notes of the things that they **say** that may be clues to what they **believe**. Writing things down is good as it means that you don't miss things that may need to later be visited, and you don't need to interrupt their story.

Step 3: Ministry Example

Fred: I felt very uneasy when I went to try out for the church choir!
Me: Why do you think that you were uncomfortable in that setting?
Fred: I think that I felt that I did not belong there, I was not a part of it.

This could indicate a possible belief such as; ***I am not wanted, or I am not accepted.***

Step 4: We have them concentrate on the feeling produced by the thought that they do not belong, and are not a part of it; rejected by the group. We are looking for the earliest possibly historical place where they learnt beliefs that caused them to feel this way.

Fred: I have just remembered my first day of school. There was a group of kids playing and talking together and they ignored me!
Me: As you concentrate on the memory and feel that rejected feeling, why do you think that they ignored you?
Fred: ***Pauses and explores the memory.*** I think it is because I am not like them, I am new and so they don't want me. This must be true because they are all accepting each other, but I am on the outside!

Me:	Let's ask the Lord what His truth, the real truth is. Lord what do you want Fred to understand about that time where he felt that he was not wanted because he is not like them, because he is new?
Fred:	The Lord is reminding me, that these kids went to Kindergarten together and already knew each other. I couldn't get in to Kinder because they were full up.
Me:	So, are you not wanted because you are different?
Fred:	No, I am the same; I have just not built relationships yet. Later I did make some good friends there.
Me:	How do you feel about the church choir now?
Fred:	I feel excited about it now; I will be making some new friends it will just take a little time.
Me:	Perhaps close in prayer thanking the Lord for His healing, or I may enquire as to whether or not there are other things which require ministry.

Clearly this example is not going to be as deeply painful as rejection often is. Some people may have very painful traumatic rejection situations from some kind of abuse or absence of love in the home. Other people may have a ***profile of rejection*** composed of multiple less painful beliefs.

SAMPLE MINISTRY: SITUATIONAL OR PHOBIC FEAR

Me:	"What can we help you with today?"
Fred:	"Well I have a fear of flying."
Me:	"So what are you afraid might happen when you get on an aircraft?"
Fred:	Ponders "I feel as though I will be out of control"
Me:	"I want you to focus on that thought and the feeling that goes with it and see if you remember a time in your life where you felt just like that."
Fred:	"I remember being pushed down a steep hill in a little cart we had made. The big kids put me in and sent the cart racing down the hill towards the trees."
Me:	"What did you believe might happen while you were afraid?"
Fred:	"I guess I felt that I was going to get hurt and nobody could stop it happening. I was terrified!"
Me:	"Let's hold that belief up to the Lord that 'nobody can stop what's going to happen, and I will get hurt.'" (Prayer asking the Lord to bring His truth)
Fred:	"I just remembered that actually one of the big kids ran after me and eventually did stop the cart before it hit the trees."
Me:	"So what does that mean to you?"
Fred:	"Well it means that God will always find a way to protect me. He is always in control."
Me:	"So think about flying now, are you still afraid of being out of control?"
Fred:	Pauses "No. I am still a bit fearful though it is nowhere near as much!"
Me:	"Alright focus on the residual fear and see if you can work out what you are afraid of."
Fred:	"I have been on a plane before and it felt like there was nothing solid underneath me….it was a scary feeling."
Me:	"Okay, I want you to concentrate on the anxious belief that there is nothing solid underneath you." "Lord, would you help Fred to connect with a place where he felt just like that before?"
Fred:	"As soon as you said that I remembered being on a cliff edge when we were kids and it caved in underneath me. I slid down the face of it and into the river."
Me:	"So you felt as if there was nothing solid under you? And what was the consequence or fear expectation about that situation?"
Fred:	"I thought that I was going to die!"

Me: "Alright, I just want for you to embrace that anxiety and belief in that memory that because there is nothing solid under you, you will die."

Fred: Pauses "Do you know, that is just not true. What came to mind was the scripture that talks about the circle of the Earth. It's just hung out there in space with nothing under it just because God put it there and supports it, nothing under it, but still suspended."

Me: "So if you think about there being nothing solid under you on a plane how do you feel about it now?"

Fred: "You know it's really okay….!"

Me: "How do you feel about flying now Fred?"

Fred: "Do you know, it's weird but I think that I am a bit excited!"

Perhaps we might say a prayer thanking the Lord, or certainly make a comment about how amazing our God is in setting us free, and acknowledging Him as being the one who has done the freeing. Either way, God is glorified as He fulfills His promise and the session closes.

SAMPLE MINISTRY: IDENTITY BELIEF-BASED FEAR

Me: "What seems to be the problem?"

Fred: "I have been asked to do communion in church next Sunday, but I am petrified and haven't been able to sleep!"

Me: "I want you to imagine yourself up there in front of all those people. As you feel that anxiety, I would like you to examine it and try to work out exactly what it is that you are afraid might happen."

Fred: Pause "I am afraid that I might not be able to do it properly."

Me: "I would like you to feel that anxiety about not doing it properly, and as you do let your mind connect you with a place that held those same feelings. It will be somewhere where you actually couldn't do what was expected."

Fred: Ponders "I remember in school when I was about 7 years old. The teacher wanted me to write some cursive text on the blackboard, and I wrote it back the front. The teacher made a big fuss over it making fun of me in front of the whole class, and I recall being incredibly embarrassed."

Me: "As a result of not being able to do it, and the intense embarrassing moment in front of the class, what conclusion about yourself did you come to?"

Fred: Pause, thoughtful "I'm dumb. I must be dumb because I could not do it right."

Me: "As you feel that embarrassment and the belief that you are 'dumb' because you could not do it, let us ask the Lord what the real truth is."

Prayer: "Lord Fred thinks that he is dumb because he could not do the cursive writing on the board. What do you want him to know about that situation?"

Fred: "Well, I didn't hear any thoughts. But I just sort of understood that none of us had actually been taught cursive yet. And the teacher liked to mock us and make fun of us. She sort of deliberately put me in that position to make sport of me."

Me: "So are you dumb because you could not do it?"

Fred: "No, the truth is that none of us could yet. I am feeling that I was alright, there is nothing wrong with me, but I think that the teacher had some issues. I forgive her."

Me: "Picture yourself doing communion on Sunday, how do you feel about messing it up now?"

Fred: "I actually feel fine about it; I will work out how to do it as best I can and really everything doesn't have to be perfect. After all, we are all family."

> **Note:** A situation such as public speaking typically may evoke a response from more than one historically learnt fear producing belief. As each one is ministered to the intensity of the anxiety normally goes down. If you just process the beliefs one by one eventually you will achieve peace. It is of course normal to be a little nervous if it is a new situation.

FLOW CHART

The ministry process:
A person comes to you with a problem. This could be a mental, emotional, relational, addictive, spiritual, sexual or physical issue.
↓
They may have been *set off* or *triggered* by a life situation producing for example: anxiety, anger, sadness, bitterness, resentment, guilt, inferiority, rejection and so on.
↓
Your role is to help them focus on these feelings and reactions and to identify the beliefs which they believe at *heart* level, and which they may no longer immediately consciously access.
↓
The key components that you are trying to connect here are: The emotions, the beliefs producing the emotions, and the matching memory pictures. (No pictures could mean it's imbibed prenatal, perhaps connect with a feeling or a sense of something)
↓
You have them focus on the presenting feelings and using questions help them to discover the beliefs producing the emotion, OR
↓
If they have a belief, such as, *I just never think that I am good enough*, have them connect with the feeling that should be associated with such a thought. (The emotion often comes up as the story is related or the memory is accessed and described.)

In the instance of such beliefs as; "I am not good enough, not loveable, not important…" and so on a qualifying phrase can be helpful. For example, ask the question; "why are you not good enough?" You can then offer the belief with the qualifying phrase, such as: "Lord Fred believes that he is not good enough and is dumb **because** he cannot do what others can do."

The conclusion is that he is 'dumb,' but there can be many reasons why he may believe this. So when we offer it to the Lord for truth we make it specific by adding in the phrase that 'he believes that he is dumb, **because** he cannot do what others can do.'
↓
Request that they let memories come to them or wilfully look for the memory picture, if they don't already have it, which contains the beginnings or original source of the thoughts and feelings. (With some pictures that are remembered, it is not always immediately obvious as to why the beliefs have been interpreted here.)
↓
Having refined and identified the belief that was learnt, invite God to bring Truth. (You can be creative in how you request this to avoid being repetitive, but using phrases such as, **Lord, would you like to show Fred how you see this situation? Lord, would you touch Fred by revealing your Truth to replace what he perceives as the truth here? Lord, what would you like Fred to know about the belief that he holds?** and so on.)

APPENDIX TWO
Popular Redemption Scriptures

SCRIPTURES QUALIFYING US FOR HEALING AND FREEDOM

All of the following passages are taken from the New Living Translation of the Bible and the emphasis is mine.

> PSALM 103:2-4, 10-12
> ² Praise the LORD, I tell myself, and never forget the good things he does for me. ³ He forgives **all** my sins and heals **all** my diseases. ⁴ He ransoms me from death and surrounds me with love and tender mercies.

……..And………

> ¹⁰ **He has not punished us for all our sins**, nor does he deal with us as we deserve. ¹¹ For his unfailing love toward those who fear him is as great as the height of the heavens above the earth. ¹² **He has removed our rebellious acts as far away from us as the east is from the west**.

> ISAIAH 44:22
> "I have swept away your sins like the morning mists. I have scattered your offenses like the clouds. Oh, return to me, for I have paid the price to set you free."

> ISAIAH 53:5-6, 11
> ⁵ But he was wounded and crushed for our sins. He was beaten that we might have peace. He was whipped, and we were healed! ⁶ **All of us** have strayed away like sheep. We have left God's paths to follow our own. Yet the LORD laid on him the guilt and sins **of us all**.

……..And………

> ¹¹ When he sees all that is accomplished by his anguish, he will be satisfied. And because of what he has experienced, my righteous servant will make it possible for many to be counted righteous, for he will bear all their sins.

> ROMANS 3:22-25
> ²² **We are made right in God's sight when we trust in Jesus Christ to take away our sins**. And we all can be saved in this same way, no matter who we are or what we have done. ²³ For all have sinned; all fall short of God's glorious standard. ²⁴ Yet now God in his gracious kindness declares us not guilty. **He has done this through Christ Jesus, who has freed us by taking away our sins**. ²⁵ For God sent Jesus to take the punishment for our sins and to satisfy God's anger against us. **We are made right with God when we believe that Jesus shed his blood, sacrificing his life for us**.

1 CORINTHIANS 1:30-31
³⁰ God alone made it possible for you to be in Christ Jesus. For our benefit God made Christ to be wisdom itself. **He is the one who made us acceptable to God. He made us pure and holy, and he gave himself to purchase our freedom.** ³¹ As the Scriptures say, **"The person who wishes to boast should boast only of what the Lord has done."**

2 CORINTHIANS 5:21
For God made Christ, who never sinned, to be the offering for our sin, **so that we could be made right with God through Christ.**

EPHESIANS 1:4-7
⁴ Long ago, even before he made the world, **God loved us and chose us in Christ to be holy and without fault in his eyes.** ⁵ His unchanging plan has always been to adopt us into his own family by bringing us to himself through Jesus Christ. **And this gave him great pleasure.** ⁶ So we praise God for the wonderful kindness he has poured out on us because we belong to his dearly loved Son. ⁷ He is so rich in kindness that he purchased our freedom through the blood of his Son, **and our sins are forgiven.**

EPHESIANS 2:7-9
⁷ And so God can always point to us as examples of the incredible wealth of his favor and kindness toward us, as shown in all he has done for us through Christ Jesus. ⁸ God saved you by his special favor when you believed. And **you can't take credit for this; it is a gift from God.**
⁹ **Salvation is not a reward for the good things we have done**, so none of us can boast about it.

COLOSSIANS 1:22
"yet now he has brought you back as his friends. He has done this through his death on the cross in his own human body. **As a result**, he has brought you into the very presence of God, and **you are holy and blameless as you stand before him without a single fault."**

HEBREWS 10:14, 17-18
¹⁴ For by that one offering **he perfected forever** all those whom he is making holy

......and....

¹⁷ Then he adds, **"I will never again remember their sins and lawless deeds."**
¹⁸ Now when sins have been forgiven, there is no need to offer any more sacrifices.

APPENDIX THREE

Other Resources from 418Centre

BY STEVE PIDD

SOHAF (SCHOOL OF HEALING AND FREEDOM) COMPREHENSIVE TRAINING MANUAL
This manual contains all of the materials contained in the books in a study format, as well as other Units relating to bringing freedom, healing and wholeness.

HEALING AND FREEDOM THROUGH TRUTH ENCOUNTERS
This popular book is a complete resource in itself. It contains much of the material found in the SOHAF Comprehensive manual. It is presented in a different order with the focus on explaining the 'Truth Encounters' ministry. It includes explanations on the demonic realm, roots of common issues, and how to work with the Holy Spirit in ministry.

YOU SHALL INDEED BE SET FREE
This publication is an excerpt comprising of the first two Sections from the book 'Healing And Freedom Through Truth Encounters.' It is a much shorter version specifically dealing with the 'Truth Encounters' ministry in isolation.

RECEIVING TRUTH THAT WILL SET YOU FREE
This booklet is designed as a basic introduction to help position those coming for a 'Truth Encounters' ministry session to understand what is involved in receiving their breakthrough.

TAKING DOWN GOLIATH
This book is directed to help guide effective ministry of the Holy Spirit to those suffering from mental disorders.

NOTES:

NOTES:

NOTES:

www.ingramcontent.com/pod-product-compliance
Lightning Source LLC
Chambersburg PA
CBHW080855010526
44107CB00057B/2585